THE
EVERYTHING®
GUIDE TO
STEPPARENTING

Dear Reader,

I was clueless when I first became a stepparent. I didn't even know what to do when I started dating a parent! I didn't think it would be any different than dating someone without a child. I was in for a surprise—a pleasant surprise! My future stepson was relatively shy, so any undesirable comments he may have had for me were left in his head, or announced out of my company. When we first met, I had no idea how to act, or how to converse with him. As a child and adolescent therapist, I thought I would breeze through our meeting, but all of my training went out the window when I was on the spot. Eventually we figured it out, and now have a great time together. I had no idea I could fall in love with someone in such a genuine and caring way. I hope that you also have a positive experience. Don't try to make everything perfect—it never will be and your stepchild probably doesn't expect it to be. Have fun, be honest and considerate, and you are on your way to having a great steprelationship.

Erin A. Munroe

Welcome to the EVERYTHING Series!

These handy, accessible books give you all you need to tackle a difficult project, gain a new hobby, comprehend a fascinating topic, prepare for an exam, or even brush up on something you learned back in school but have since forgotten.

You can choose to read an *Everything*® book from cover to cover or just pick out the information you want from our four useful boxes: e-questions, e-facts, e-alerts, and e-ssentials.

We give you everything you need to know on the subject, but throw in a lot of fun stuff along the way, too.

We now have more than 400 *Everything*® books in print, spanning such wide-ranging categories as weddings, pregnancy, cooking, music instruction, foreign language, crafts, pets, New Age, and so much more. When you're done reading them all, you can finally say you know *Everything*®!

E-QUESTION
Answers to common questions

FACTS
Important snippets of information

ALERTS!
Urgent warnings

ESSENTIALS
Quick handy tips

PUBLISHER Karen Cooper

DIRECTOR OF ACQUISITIONS AND INNOVATION Paula Munier

MANAGING EDITOR, EVERYTHING SERIES Lisa Laing

COPY CHIEF Casey Ebert

ACQUISITIONS EDITOR Katie McDonough

SENIOR DEVELOPMENT EDITOR Brett Palana-Shanahan

EDITORIAL ASSISTANT Hillary Thompson

Visit the entire Everything® series at *www.everything.com*

THE
EVERYTHING®
GUIDE TO STEPPARENTING

Practical, reassuring advice for creating
healthy, long-lasting relationships

Erin A. Munroe, LMHC
with Irene S. Levine, PhD

Avon, Massachusetts

*I am dedicating this book to my fabulous stepson, Jim. Without him,
I would not be a stepmom. He allowed me to test out all my
parenting theories on him—some successful, some not so successful.
Thank you, Jim, for being my tolerant and patient guinea pig.*

An Everything® Series Book.
Everything® and everything.com® are registered trademarks of F+W Media, Inc.

Published by Adams Media, a division of F+W Media, Inc.
57 Littlefield Street, Avon, MA 02322 U.S.A.
www.adamsmedia.com

ISBN 10: 1-60550-055-0
ISBN 13: 978-1-60550-055-3

Printed in the United States of America.

J   I   H   G   F   E   D   C   B   A

Library of Congress Cataloging-in-Publication Data
is available from the publisher.

This publication is designed to provide accurate and authoritative information with regard to the subject matter covered. It is sold with the understanding that the publisher is not engaged in rendering legal, accounting, or other professional advice. If legal advice or other expert assistance is required, the services of a competent professional person should be sought.

—From a *Declaration of Principles* jointly adopted by a Committee of the American Bar Association and a Committee of Publishers and Associations

Many of the designations used by manufacturers and sellers to distinguish their products are claimed as trademarks. Where those designations appear in this book and Adams Media was aware of a trademark claim, the designations have been printed with initial capital letters.

*This book is available at quantity discounts for bulk purchases.
For information, please call 1-800-289-0963.*

Contents

Acknowledgments

I would like to thank so many people: my husband, who hid my cell phone and screened phone calls so I could write and not procrastinate. My stepson, who is the reason I know all about stepparenting—and enjoyed it! My parents, who have always supported whatever I did. Family and friends who supported me and sometimes helped me procrastinate. My agent and mentor, Janice, who believes in me and laughs at my escapades. My high school guidance counselor, Mr. King, who got me out of high school successfully. Professor Helen Whall at Holy Cross, who was determined to make me believe in myself while teaching me better than any other. Dan Shaughnessy and Clark Booth, for entertaining my dreams and reminding me that you will never be a successful writer if you don't share your work with others. My dog Simon, who rocks.

Each one of them has encouraged, supported, and inspired me. Without them I simply could not have accomplished this and most likely would not have even attempted to share my writing with anyone. I also don't know that I could have been a successful stepparent without their support and guidance. It does take a village to raise a child, and my fellow villagers gave me the tools I needed to figure out how to be a stepparent.

Top Ten Things
Every Stepparent Should Know

1. You are not going to be the perfect stepparent; there is no such thing.

2. Kids come with all sorts of ideas of who you are and what you will be to them, but mostly they need someone who is consistent and trustworthy.

3. Kids and adults are not predictable. You cannot plan for everything, no matter how hard you try.

4. Stepparenting can be fun and rewarding. It can also be stressful and scary. That is why the rewards are so great!

5. Marrying someone with a child does not mean your stepchild will instantly love you. Your stepchild doesn't have to love you, and it might take her longer than you expected to warm up to you.

7. Your stepchild is probably as nervous, if not more so, than you are about developing a relationship with you.

8. You will never replace her biological parent, but the bond you build can be valuable and irreplaceable.

9. You will have to share your partner with your stepchild, and your stepchild will be the priority—as she should be.

10. You are bound to have rocky times, but you will get through them if you continue to respect and communicate effectively with your partner and stepchild.

Introduction

▶ *The Everything® Guide to Stepparenting* is a book to help you navigate the world as a stepparent. You will find that you have someone else to think about with every decision you make. This can feel rather overwhelming. This book is designed to help you feel less overwhelmed, teach you some tricks of the trade, educate you about your role as a stepparent, and provide a go-to resource for tough situations.

With over 50 percent of all marriages ending in divorce, stepparents are becoming the norm. Of this 50 percent, 75 percent will remarry, and often, someone in that remarriage becomes a stepparent. It is increasingly rare to see an intact original family. Most families have a stepsomeone, a half someone, or even multiples of both. Our families are ever changing, no longer the stable nuclear family of the past. Instead of grieving this, however, we need to celebrate the families we have created, and make the best out of any step situation.

Stepparents and stepchildren come in all shapes and sizes and bring many different attitudes, strengths, emotional traumas, and experiences to the table. Some stepparents may have no experience at all as parents, while some may be parents to their own biological children. So many people are taking on this role that it is becoming a huge part of our family culture. Wherever you fall in this stepparent spectrum, you will still be able to use this book to help you overcome certain obstacles and develop a positive relationship with your stepchild. This book addresses the stepparenting joys and difficulties of people who are taking on a spouse or significant other's child or children. You will learn how to face challenges that actually may become rewarding experiences with a little extra patience and self-reflection.

The role of a stepparent skates a fine line between parenting and mentoring. It is a role that needs to be taken on with extra care. As a stepparent, you are not taking the place of a parent, but you will share a part in parenting tasks such as general care for the child, discipline decisions, rule setting, and most likely monetary contributions. As a mentor, you must be prepared to role model appropriate adult behavior for the child (no matter how much you might dislike the other biological parent), be like Switzerland and not get involved in any drama that may erupt between biological parents, help the child find a way to get along with his parents, and be the adult that the child feels comfortable coming to with topics he is too nervous to talk about with his biological parents. It's quite a tricky role. This book will discuss the role and how to balance it while respecting the relationship your stepchild has with his biological parents.

Stepparenting involves a great deal of rewarding moments, but just as many stressful and uncomfortable ones. Dealing with the first meeting of your potential stepchild, getting along with the other biological parent, and living through the horrors of puberty with a child who isn't yours are all challenging. You will learn all the factors stepparenting entails and how to determine if you are ready to become a stepparent. You will learn how to look at situations from a variety of perspectives, which will make you not only a better stepparent, but also a better spouse and a trusted adult in the eyes of the other biological parent. Most importantly, this book aims to ease your fears about your new role and help you become a stepparent that your stepchild can trust and respect.

CHAPTER 1

What Is a Stepparent?

The definition of a stepparent is becoming more and more inclusive, perhaps because stepparents are becoming more common. A stepparent can be someone who took on the role of a parent because of the death of a parent, the remarriage of a parent, or an adoption; a stepparent also can be a neighbor a child feels serves the role of a mother or father. The definition has grown to include more folks than ever before, which makes defining and researching the stepparent difficult.

Different Definitions

The word "stepparent" is believed to have come from the old English word *stoep*, which means "to deprive or bereave." Adding the word "stoep," and later "step," to the word "parent" implied that a stepparent was one who cared for a child who had lost a parent due to death, and was thus a deprived or bereft child. The current dictionary definition of stepparent (according to the Merriam–Webster dictionary) is: "related by virtue of a remarriage (as of a parent) and not by blood."

The word "stepparent" no longer implies any sort of bereavement, but instead a relationship created by the marriage of one biological parent to someone else. Stepgrandparents, stepsisters, stepbrothers, stepnieces, stepuncles, and more now join stepparents in the list of "steps." Definitions of family have changed, and with this change came a broader definition of the stepparent. The idea of a stepmother or stepfather is so common that the terms are often used for a biological parent's longtime girlfriend or boyfriend, an adoptive parent, a foster parent, a grandparent who took in their child's child, or even an adult with whom a child is exceptionally close.

FACT

The U.S. Census does not define a stepparent, stepfather, or stepmother; instead, they provide only the following definition for a stepfamily: "a 'married couple' family in which there is at least one stepchild of the householder present. If the child has been adopted by the householder, that child is classified as an adopted child and the family is not classified as a stepfamily, unless another non-adopted stepchild is present."

Data on Stepparents

Over 50 percent of all marriages end in divorce, and over 75 percent of these folks will remarry, creating many potential stepfamilies. In fact, the website *www.stepfamily.org* claims that 1,300 new stepfamilies form every day.

The U.S. Census reported prior to 2000 that "50 percent of all children under the age of thirteen are living with one biological parent and that parent's partner" and that there would be more stepfamilies than original families by the year 2000. Unfortunately, the predictions made by the U.S. Census for the year 2000, and any year following, cannot be verified, as the U.S. Census stopped collecting stepfamily specific data. The reports they did make on their website, *www.census.gov/prod/2003pubs/censr-6.pdf*, such as identifying over 4 million stepchildren in the United States in 2000, were followed by the disclaimer: "[the Census] may have identified only about two-thirds of all stepchildren living with at least one stepparent because of the manner in which the data were collected." Since the definitions of stepparents and stepchildren have become so broad and ever changing, the validity of recent data is definitely in question.

The National Stepfamily Resource Center estimates that approximately 65 percent of remarriages include children from at least one of the prior families, and in turn form a stepfamily. Unfortunately, of these second marriages, 60 percent will end in divorce. Do not use these statistics as a reason not to consider creating a stepfamily; instead, use them to help you talk with your partner about how you as a couple and as a stepfamily can succeed.

Your Role as a Parent/Mentor

The role of a stepparent is a great combination of parent and mentor. With the difficulties of discipline come the rewards of connecting with another human being. A large amount of how you connect with your stepchild will depend on how old the child is and how much time you spend with him.

Interacting by Age

Stepchildren under the age of eighteen are going to view you as more of a parental figure, since your role will include more parenting activities than if your stepchild is thirty-five years old. If you do have older stepchildren, you may find your relationship is more of a sounding board than a parent. You may not have to do much discipline or rule setting with an older stepchild; however, you can still act as a mentor, which can be quite rewarding.

No matter what age your stepchild may be, you will never replace his mother or father. If the other biological parent is out of the picture, passed away, or lives far away, it may seem as though you should step into this role. Resist the urge and create your own role, that of stepmother or stepfather. In creating this role, there are no written rules for how to play it, but there are some guidelines.

As a Parental Figure

You aren't the parent. So what does this mean? You will still be required to take on parenting tasks such as picking your stepchild up at school, assisting in toilet training, disciplining a teenager who likes to test the limits, and attending parent meetings at school. How do you fill a kind of parental position without seeming like you are trying to step into the actual parental role? Try to imagine yourself as an advocate for the child. This does not mean that you will always agree with your stepchild, but instead will advocate for the well-being of the child. For example, if the child is living with you in the midst of toilet training, you will have to become a big part of this milestone. If your stepchild only visits you and your partner, you will be less involved, but can still take on a supportive role and even pleasantly remind your partner to ask if his child needs to use the bathroom if he sometimes forgets.

Disciplining a stepchild comes with many obstacles, and all the adults in the situation need to find themselves at least on similar pages; the same is true for your role in educational decisions (more on these topics in detail further in the book). For now, however, follow the biological parents' lead and stick to any punishment they have given. Do not let things slide simply to put yourself in the good graces of your stepchild. In terms of education, also follow and support the biological parents' decisions.

Your parental role is to be consistent, safe, and available. You may need to stay home with a sick stepchild, forgo the extra glass of wine at a party, and cook family meals when you have no clue at all how to cook. Consistency is key in any child's life, and being consistent in your actions as a parental figure and staying as consistent as possible with the biological parents' decisions will be in the best interest of your stepchild.

The parenting role is not as clear when you are a younger stepmother to older stepchildren. If your stepchildren are adults and you are close in age or younger, you may find you do not do much typical parenting. Where you can be helpful, however, is in the parenting your partner is doing with his children. If you notice, for instance, that he is always picking at his son's taste in women, you could mention this to your husband in a way that is in the best interest of your stepson. For example, you could say something like, "Gee Bob, whenever Joey comes over, you are all over him about his girlfriends. That would drive me crazy if I were him." Here, you are simply pointing out his behavior and how it would make you feel. You are not telling him that he does drive Joey crazy or even that Joey has said something to you—which he may or may not have done. Here, you are advocating for your stepchild by taking on your stepchild's perspective and sharing it with your husband.

E-QUESTION

Do I need to be perfect at all times now that I have this child to worry about?
No! Don't stress out about this; you are not perfect and are not expected to be. If you do make a mistake, however, come clean about it and learn from it. Don't lie and be embarrassed by making a mistake. Chances are you will make more.

Any parent can use an outside perspective, and this perspective can usually help the way the parent is parenting. It is tough to self-assess as a parent because there are so many emotions involved. As the parental figure most emotionally removed, you are in a great position to share your perspective with your spouse and encourage him to think about his parenting in another way.

The Mentor Role

This is the more fun role, and is easier to take on if you haven't been a parent before and are unfamiliar with the parenting role. Whether you realize it or not, you have probably been a mentor to someone in the past. Anyone can benefit from a mentor, regardless of age. The mentor piece of your relationship with your stepchild is what makes the relationship between the two of you so special and different from the relationship between a child and biological parent. Since you are removed from the child in a way his biological parents will never be, it will be easier for you to look at certain situations from a different perspective. When your stepson asks a girl out on a date and the biological parents are embarrassed by the situation or uncomfortable talking about it, you can remind everyone that this is also an exciting time for him. You may also be the least embarrassing adult for your stepson to talk to about the date.

Children will seek out advice on many topics, which will put you in the limelight. Since you are not mom or dad, but you happen to be an adult, you may be the least intimidating adult to approach. Enjoy and treasure this role. Use this role not as a way to get your stepson on "your side," but as a way to help guide him in the right direction. There may be times when your stepson wants you to lie for him, or keep a secret that is not a safe secret. Don't do these things, as they will make you an unhealthy role model. Remember to act in a way you would hope your stepson would act, or how you would like another adult in his life to act. Even if your stepchild cannot stand you, you are still an influential person in his life. It is imperative that you remember this with every action.

FACT

Data taken from the National Longitudinal Study of Adolescent Health indicates that adolescents with "natural mentors" are more likely to finish high school, attend college, exhibit fewer risk-taking behaviors, have higher levels of self-esteem and life satisfaction, and participate in more physical activity. Information from this study can be found at: *www .mentoring.org/access_research/natural*.

With older stepchildren, you still have an opportunity to play the mentor role; however, it is different in that they may not look up to you as a role model, but instead may look at how you are treating their father. If you are treating your husband with respect and also respecting his relationship with his children, you are giving them a good template for their future relationships. Although his children may not recognize your influence upon them at first, they may find they are using the model of how you act with their father in their own relationships.

Portrayals of Stepparents in the Media

It is rare to see a movie or read a fairytale that has a kind stepmother. The legend of the wicked stepmother dates back to Greek mythology, but is perhaps more readily recognizable in older fairytales such as *Cinderella* and *Snow White*. In many fairytales, it is the stepmother who replaces the father in the child's life. The stepmother then becomes the central figure in the child's life as far as caretaking and discipline are concerned. In most of these stories, the stepmother has more of a presence than the biological father, and the story becomes one about jealousy between two women. They are pitted against one another, and the father is rarely a figure who steps in to remedy the situation.

Stepfathers are seldom used as major characters in movies or stories. A recent use in a fairytale is in the film *Pan's Labyrinth*, which portrays an evil stepfather and his stepdaughter, who is desperately trying to protect her mother. In the news, stepfathers are unpleasantly portrayed as verbally or sexually abusive. The constant negative press is detrimental to all the stepparents who are wonderful and healthy influences in a child's life.

FACT

Coach Bobby Knight was once referred to as college basketball's "wicked stepfather" due to his outrageous behavior. But, it seems that even he is turning around the myth of the wicked stepfather. Bobby Knight has stopped his assaultive and unsportsmanlike behavior and become, "Cinderella, the unexpectedly fetching belle of the ball."

Positive Media

There does seem to be a push by screenwriters and authors to illustrate positive stepparents. The movie *Stepmom* with Julia Roberts and Susan

Sarandon is a great movie that deals with many issues of becoming a step-mother. Julia Roberts falls into the role of wicked stepmother, but manages to work her way out of it despite her angry stepchildren and their emotions about their dying biological mother. Liam Neeson portrays one of the sweetest stepfathers in the film *Love Actually*. His character is the stepfather to and primary caretaker of a young boy. His joy and care for his stepson is incredible, and stepfathers everywhere would benefit from watching this film.

Waiting for Normal, a novel by Jennifer Shulz, incorporates a relationship between a stepfather and his stepdaughter. It is a positive relationship that lasts despite a divorce between the stepfather and biological mother of the main character. True, positive stories of stepparents are making headway as well. Rusty Hancock has written *Dedicated Dads: Stepfathers of Famous People*, a kind book with pleasant stories about stepfathers. Sherry A. Wells has written the partner to the stepfather book, *Warm and Wonderful Stepmothers of Famous People*, which focuses on positive stepmothers. The more successful stepparents become in creating positive lasting relationships with their stepchildren, the more positive media is likely to follow.

How to Avoid Becoming the Wicked Stepparent

When your new stepchild hates you, it takes strength to avoid falling into the preconceived notions your stepchild has of you. It is actually quite understandable to see how many well-intentioned stepparents turn into wicked stepmothers and stepfathers.

Don't Give Up

If you are trying your hardest to get along with your soon-to-be or current stepchild and all he does is hate you more with every nice gesture you make, it is easy to throw up your hands and say, "Fine, then I won't waste my time trying to be nice to you. I will ignore you, avoid you, and revel in joy every time you get in trouble and even point out to your father when you have misbehaved." But this is catty and childish behavior. It is also reactive behavior to the testing your stepson is doing with you. This is exactly how he wants you to react, so he can say, "See, I told you so, she is wicked." So don't fall for it, no matter what.

Handling Hostility

How can you deal with all the hate and nasty comments? The first stage is recognizing them and kindly and patiently commenting that you really wish he wouldn't say those things to you because you find them hurtful and you were just trying to be as kind as possible. The second stage, if the nice approach doesn't work, is to ignore the comments. You can point out that you will be ignoring them by stating, "I am ignoring your comments. I told you I found them hurtful and I really don't find them helpful to our relationship."

If ignoring does not work and cruelness persists, you are at stage three. Here your partner can have a conversation with his child that does not blame the child, but instead validates the child's feelings and acting out but also asks that he find a better way to deal with his anger. An example would be: "Simon, I know you are really angry, and your stepmother certainly understands, too. It seems like you are constantly angry and taking it all out on her. Is there another way we can deal with your anger? If there is something you think I could do to make it better I would like to know. I think it might be fun for the two of you to get to know each other better, but it seems hard to get to that point with all this anger." This way, the father is putting it out there that both of you hear loud and clear that he is angry and you would like to help him deal with this so you can move on and do more fun things. If the other biological parent is aware that your stepchild is being cruel and wants to help fix it, it can be quite powerful to have the other biological parent speak to the child as well, along the same lines as your partner.

If all of this does not work, you have reached stage four, calling a truce and staying out of one another's way. In this stage, you can plan visitation for times that you are not around, or have visitation at sites other than your house. If you live with the child, you can have certain zones of the house that are stepmother-free or stepchild-free during certain times. If, however, this persists, it is time to move into counseling for the child, and potentially, family counseling for everyone. Hopefully, with time, and you as the adult showing enough respect to keep your distance from the child when he needs it, your stepchild will recognize that you are not out to get him, but simply can't have a relationship with him when he is belittling or insulting you.

ALERT!

You can't hurry love, so don't try. People don't get along with each other overnight, and if anything, you have time to work on this relationship. Maybe it will be after the terrible twos, terrible teens, or terrible twenties. Have patience; don't try to force the relationship.

A stepchild of any age may harbor great dislike for you, and it may affect you a great deal or not much at all, depending on age and situation. If your adult stepchild does not like you, but you only see him once a year, it may not bother you or create an issue on a daily basis. If you interact frequently with your stepchild, you are going to have to find a way to exist in the same room as one another. As you are both adults, hopefully there will be a way that you can respect one another enough to be cordial. Keep in mind, however, that this child, whether four or forty, is a part of your partner's life and family, and you married your partner knowing this. A marriage will not necessarily change a child's attitude toward you or force him to respect you. The only way you can garner respect from another adult is to treat him with respect. This still might not work, but at least you are not doing anything to create more strife.

Overall, make every attempt you possibly can to show your stepchild that you understand his feelings, are open to discussing his feelings in an appropriate way, and want a relationship with him, even if it takes ten years. Remember, you are the adult in the situation, so you may have to swallow some pride by not reacting to nasty remarks. This is a hurting child who wants to test you and see if you really are in it for the long haul. If you thought long and hard before getting into this relationship, you should feel confident that you are in it for the long haul and be able to work with your stepchild on how to form a positive relationship.

CHAPTER 2

Dating a Parent

Chances are you will date a parent before becoming a stepparent. You may have an interest in someone you don't even know is a parent, only to find out once you begin dating. Or, you may know he is a parent but be a little nervous about dating him because he has children. Before getting into a relationship with a parent, you must do some self-investigating and decide whether you are prepared to be in a relationship with someone who has a child.

Be Ready for What You Are Getting Into

Dating a parent when you are not one can either seem like a piece of cake or completely intimidating. It should be somewhere in the middle. All of your time with each other shouldn't be consumed with the fact that your new beau has a child; however, it should be at the back of your mind with every decision you make about your position in the relationship and every decision you make as a couple concerning your relationship.

Honesty Is the Best Policy

This is what you need to be ready for and willing to accept before moving to the next level and possible stepparenthood. If you do not like children or see them as part of your future, it is up to you to be respectful enough to tell this person before pursuing the relationship. Children will always be a part of his life, and if you do not like children, he may not be the right match for you.

If you are simply nervous about dating a parent because it is uncharted territory for you, don't be hasty; think about giving it a chance. It is important to listen to these fears, but more important to investigate why you have them. Are you afraid that you will go from single to Mommy? Are you afraid that the ex will hate you? Are you intimidated because your new boyfriend will always be tied in some way to a significant other from the past? These are all valid fears and concerns; however, most can be put to rest with some solid communication between the two of you. No one should expect you to take the place of a parent who has died, moved away, or is no longer in the picture. That is not going to happen no matter how badly anyone wants it. You are not the child's mother, and never will be.

Will the ex hate you? Maybe, and this is something to be openly curious about with your new boyfriend. Is he using you to make her jealous? Are games going on between the two of them? Is she dangerous? If you answered yes or even maybe to any of these questions, it sounds like he isn't ready and may not be the best boyfriend right now.

Are you intimidated by the idea of another woman? You need to get over that one because he will always be tied to her in some way, and your potential stepchild may look and act just like her. You need to shore up your self-confidence and recognize that he is with you for certain reasons, and things did not work between them for some reason.

E-QUESTION

What if I can't get past the fact that he was intimate with someone else and I hate that they get along so well?
It may be time to look into counseling or self-esteem building workshops. This is not going to go away once you are married—marriage won't change your self-image, self-esteem, or insecurities.

The number one thing to realize and understand is that you are dating someone who may have emotional baggage, but more importantly, he brings a whole other person to the relationship. If you are not prepared to include this other person in your decisions and life in general, then you may not be ready to date a parent. This other person, your potential stepchild, brings another biological parent, another family, a range of emotions, history with your new boyfriend, and the opportunity for an incredibly rewarding relationship. But please, for the sake of everyone's emotional health, think hard about your readiness to take on a relationship with an added person to consider.

Being Okay with Second Place

If you are used to relationships where you are always number one, realizing you are number two might be a little difficult. When dating a parent, you need to respect the fact that there is a child in the mix who has needs, and those needs are going to come before yours. If the child is sick, you may have to cancel a date or spend it flattening ginger ale and opening crackers. This can be a tough adjustment to make. Plans may get canceled because of the child; plans also may change because the other biological parent has a conflict and needs to cancel visitation or send the child home earlier than expected. Unfortunately, if you are not prepared for such changes, you may resent the child for disrupting your dating life.

Preparing Yourself

To prepare yourself to be number two, envision yourself as a parent. If you had a child with the person you are now dating, how would you want her to treat that child? If your child were sick, would you want her to ignore the child and go out to dinner with you? If there was an emergency, would you want her to groan with annoyance? Of course you wouldn't. This is how you should look at your current situation. If your new girlfriend is putting you before her child, that is a warning flag. What is going on with her that she is not responding to this child, instead making you her first priority?

There will be times when you may feel you are getting blown off and the child is being used as the reason, when in fact it is not the child's fault. The other biological parent may try to disrupt plans or make dating difficult for your new girlfriend out of jealousy. If you see this occurring, recognize that this is not the child's fault, but an issue between the parents. You can certainly explain to your girlfriend that you feel as though the relationship is getting difficult because her ex is constantly refusing to take the child at the last minute and disrupting your plans, but be sure to point out that you do not hold the child responsible. Although the father in this situation is using the child as a pawn to ruin your girlfriend's attempts to move on, it is not an issue of your girlfriend having a child, but an issue of your girlfriend having an ex who is not ready for her to be dating.

FACT

While you do have to learn to be okay with second place that doesn't mean that your relationship should always suffer. It is important to make sure you and your partner have some time together without the kids, either by making regular dates or by taking short trips. Don't forget to nurture your relationship. Having a strong bond between the two of you will also benefit the children by giving them a stable home environment.

This is a tough issue, and it can lead to the demise of your relationship if the adults in the situation are not able to come to some sort of agreement. If you find it is getting to that point, you may want to try scheduling your dates when the child is in the care of a babysitter who is a neutral party in the relationship between your girlfriend and the child's father. If you find that your girlfriend is still letting the child's father manipulate situations, it may be that your girlfriend in fact is not ready to move on from her child's father and needs some time to figure out what she wants.

If you can approach all situations with the child's best interest in mind, you will have better success in your relationship. You will also learn to be relatively selfless, and you may be surprised at how good this feels. When you do spend time with your girlfriend that is solely your time, you will appreciate it more and know that the two of you found this time while still considering her child's feelings and well-being.

Know the Circumstances

How did you meet your new girlfriend? Maybe you met her at work and didn't know she was married. Maybe you knew she was married and was not happy in her marriage, and one thing led to another and you are now in love. Maybe your new love was married before, had a friendly divorce, and her ex is fine with her dating. Maybe your girlfriend had a great marriage and her husband died and she is just starting to date. All of these situations happen every day and can take a toll (positive or negative) on every person involved. It is important for you to figure out exactly what the status is of your new girlfriend's relationship with the father or fathers of her children.

You Didn't Know

You may have begun dating a woman you believed was single, and, a few dates into the relationship, you learned that the woman is married and has children with her husband. Now it is up to you to decide what you want to do. It is concerning that she was not up front with you. Consider her lack of honesty very seriously. Is she really someone with whom you want to have a relationship? If she kept you in the dark about being married and having children, she may keep you in the dark about a lot of other things, too.

If you still want to have a relationship with her, think about your long-term plans. Do you want to pursue a serious relationship with her? Is she planning to leave her husband? If so, put yourself in his shoes for a moment. Even if she has told you he is the worst person ever, consider how being "the other man" may affect your relationship with her and other future relationships. Her children, her parents, her extended family, her friends, and people you may not even know may think of you forever as the one who broke up their marriage. You may be referred to as a home wrecker—or worse. Are you willing to live with that or similar labels as a stepfather? Building a relationship with your stepchildren is likely going to be extremely difficult—especially if they are hearing from everyone around them that their parents' divorce was your fault.

If you decide, in spite of the obstacles, to pursue a relationship with this woman, it's best to find a way to do so that is as respectful as possible under the circumstances. Talk to her about your concern for the children. Let her know that you do not want to be viewed solely as the other man or a home wrecker. Consider taking a break from your relationship until she is able to appropriately end the relationship she has with her husband. Then, after some of the wounds of divorce have healed, think about reconnecting in a relationship.

You Knew

This is one of the toughest situations, and one that is constantly in the spotlight. If you knew your girlfriend was married with children, then this is all on you. Yes, she took part in it as well, but you knew, and ultimately you made a choice to get involved with a married woman. At this point, it is important to figure out the future of your relationship. Is she planning on leaving him? Is she planning on staying with him, and keeping you on the side? If she is planning on leaving him, it would be kind of you to put the relationship on hold until the divorce is over. She may tell you that the divorce or separation is tough and she needs you more than ever right now, but take a step back and think about the other parties involved. She has a husband, who is likely to be very wounded, and a child or children who are going to be traumatized by the divorce—even if it is for the best. So take a step back, and give her space to focus on the end of her marriage and how she will make sure her children are best cared for during this time.

If this divorce is messy and there is proof of an affair, and you are part of that affair, you are in for some difficult situations. You may need to deal with court dates, custody battles, and many angry people. The best way to deal with this is to remove yourself from the situation for a while. Think about everyone involved. If you are truly in love with this woman and she is truly in love with you, taking time away from each other is unlikely to disrupt your future together; instead, it may be a way of showing respect to the other parties involved. It is always wonderful to find true love, but unfortunate if the relationship disrupts others' lives.

FACT

The Internet has opened up an entirely anonymous world at our fingertips. According to research done by the Fortino Group, "one third of all divorce litigation is caused by online affairs." Online chatting can seem rather benign, but check yourself before it escalates into an affair.

Think about how you want to be perceived and how you will be perceived. Act with dignity and respect for yourself as well as for the people you may be unintentionally hurting by following your heart.

Everyone Is Cool with It

The father of the children is already remarried and wants your girlfriend to find love as well. At least that is what they let you believe. Maybe everyone really is okay with it. That is great, but even if he is okay with it, he still may feel a little tug at his heartstrings when he recognizes you are here for the long haul. He may also be more wary of you when he realizes that you are going to become a key figure in the lives of his children. It is natural for him to want assurances that you are capable of a healthy relationship with his children. If her ex is really fine with everything, keep in mind that there are still children who might react to you in a variety of ways. Be sure you are ready to be a potential stepfather, and stay honest with your girlfriend about your feelings.

There Has Been a Death

If you are dating a woman whose husband and the father of her children has passed away, you should make sure she has had time to deal with the passing of her husband, and that the family has had the opportunity to heal from this loss. When someone has lost a spouse, it is important to give her the room to remain completely in love with the person who passed. She may love you as well, but you need to respect the love she still holds for her husband and understand that she will always have that love. It is not a competition. It is not about loving you more, or you becoming a reincarnation of her husband; it is a different relationship with a different person. It is just as important for you to recognize this as it is for her to recognize it. If your relationship progresses, this attitude of respect for her husband will also help you create a positive relationship with her as well as with her children.

What Is Expected from the Relationship?

This is a good question to ask yourself no matter what the relationship. Are you in it for fun? Do you want a long-term relationship? Do you even know? If this is a fling, be up front and honest; if you want a serious relationship, be up front and honest. Someone with a child needs to know what your intentions are in order to plan accordingly. If this is a fling, fine, but then you probably don't ever need to meet the children, it would just confuse them and open the door for a lot of uncomfortable questions. If the relationship is heading in a serious direction, you should be sure you are ready to be a potential stepparent. Regardless of the type of relationship, it is important that your expectations match your significant other's.

What Does the Parent Expect?

Does your new boyfriend just want a fling? Does he want a new mom for his children? Does he see you as his future wife? He should let you know as soon as he knows. If he simply wants a fling, all you need to worry about is not meeting the children and making sure no one accidentally stumbles upon the two of you in any compromising situations. If your relationship is just a fling but he insists on introducing you to his children, ask him what they will gain by meeting you. It really won't benefit them in any way, unless of course he has changed his mind and is looking at you as more of a long-term relationship.

If your boyfriend is looking for a replacement mom, talk to him about this being an impossible task. You will never be Mom—maybe a stepmom—but not Mom. His children have a mom; you need to respect that and help him respect that if he doesn't. His ex could be the most horrendous person in the world, and he could have sole custody, but, at the end of the day, she is still their mother, and you are not. You can model appropriate adult behavior for them and step into the role of a stepmother, but you cannot make up for mistakes or misgivings of his ex.

The belief that you can change a partner in a relationship is troublesome enough; if you think you can eventually move into the number one spot in your partner's life if you "put up with" your partner's children, think again; once a parent, always a parent. If you are determined to be number one, you should not be a stepparent.

If he would like to be in a long-term relationship with you and wants you to be involved in his life, you need to tell him where you stand. If that is not what you want, if you don't like children or have little interest in getting to know his children, you must tell him. It is not fair to him or his children to be involved with someone who does not plan on being around for very long. If you also would like a long-term relationship, then you can move on to meeting the children!

Meeting Friends of Both Parties

When you date someone, it is often not long before you meet one another's friends. This can be a time to bring up the fact that your new girlfriend has a child, or a time to let it pass. Before introducing your girlfriend to your friends, talk about the situation—is it something he would prefer they know beforehand? Is it a topic he likes to avoid when first meeting someone new? Many single parents, while proud of their children, prefer to get to know others as mutual adults before introducing the fact that they are a single or divorced parent. It is often uncomfortable for a parent to be whispered about as "Jenny, Bob's girlfriend who has the kid." It is much nicer to be referred to as "Jenny, Bob's girlfriend; we talked for a while the other night and she has a son that she is so proud of!" Someone is bound to say something or assume something inappropriate; addressing the situation with your girlfriend prior to going out with friends can decrease the chances of this.

When you go out with her friends for the first time, you may find that they grill you about your relationship with her child, or how you see yourself in the child's life. This is normal; they are her friends and have her best interests at heart. It could be helpful to form a united front with your girlfriend where she says to her friends, "Bob hasn't met my son yet, and we will tackle that when the time is right" or "Bob and I are just enjoying getting to know each other right now." There are many ways of stopping the inquisitors without giving out much personal information or sounding rude.

No matter whose friends you are meeting, it is nice to have a bit of a plan in place for those potentially awkward questions or comments.

When and How to Meet the Child(ren)

3

When you went on your first date, most likely as a teenager, you were probably nervous about meeting your boyfriend's parent or parents for the first time. You probably worried about such things as how you looked, if you were saying the right things, and if you were eating with the correct fork. Welcome to having those feelings again—wanting to impress but not seem fake, to be friendly but not say the wrong thing. Meeting your boyfriend's child can also be quite stressful—especially if the child has preconceived notions of who you are and what you represent.

Who Has a Say?

Determining when you should meet your boyfriend's children is up to your boyfriend, their mother, you, and the children. If there is court involvement, the courts may have say in this as well; however, if the biological parents feel the time is right, the courts will usually agree. If the other biological parent is deceased, there may be another custodial figure or involved family member (such as a parent or the parents of the deceased parent) who has input.

Deciding When It's Time

You may have seen pictures of the children and think they are cute. You may be eager to meet them. However, by meeting the children you are suggesting quite a bit about your relationship with your boyfriend. Meeting his children brings the relationship to an entirely different level. At this point, you haven't really existed in the children's lives and have likely been brought up in a conversation, but that is it. Once the children have met you, your role changes as well. Now you are someone who is attached to their father and may be around more often.

Your boyfriend may want to wait to see where he thinks your relationship is going. If he sees a future for the two of you, he may feel that the time is right to bring you into his children's lives. If he doesn't want you to meet them, it doesn't necessarily mean he doesn't see a lasting relationship for the two of you. It could be that they aren't ready to meet you, their mother isn't ready for them to meet you, or simply that he is waiting for a time he thinks is right for everyone.

Be sure to find out if the child has any food or insect allergies. If there is an allergy, ask to be trained to use an epi-pen and double check that it is with you or your partner at all times. Also, educate yourself about where and what the child can and cannot eat.

Their mother may have concerns about you meeting her children for many reasons, but most likely she wants to protect the children's emotional well-being. When a parent lets a child form a new relationship with another adult, the parent usually wants to be sure that the benefits of this relationship outweigh any negatives. Some parents may even wish to meet you first to see if they think you would be an appropriate adult for their children to meet.

The children also need to be ready to meet you; they are perhaps the most important people to ask whether they are ready to meet their father's new girlfriend. If they meet you before they are ready, it is going to be more difficult for them to form a positive relationship with you or for you to make a favorable impression on them.

Once your boyfriend, their mother, and the children are ready to meet you, it is your turn to determine whether or not you are ready.

Are You Ready?

If everyone else is ready you probably are, too—right? Not necessarily, and that is okay. If you do not feel ready to meet the children, then speak up before it happens and before any sort of conversation about meeting you occur between your boyfriend and his children. Let him know if you are nervous or have concerns about meeting them. If you are simply nervous in a way similar to the way you might have been in high school when you met a boyfriend's parents, then you may just need to get over the initial meeting. If you are concerned, however, because kids aren't your cup of tea, you don't really want to stay in a relationship with your boyfriend, or you are already half way out the door of the relationship, tell him. By agreeing to meet his children, you are basically agreeing to be a positive part of their lives and someone who will be around for a while.

Your boyfriend should be relieved that you are concerned about the feelings of his children; however, this could bring up sensitive subjects around what is going on in your relationship, so be prepared. If your boyfriend thinks having his children meet you is no big deal because his children have met his last fifty girlfriends, you may want to speak up on behalf of his children and point out that introducing them to a revolving door of girlfriends may be extremely confusing for them. Children need and crave consistency. If you can't be consistent, don't meet them.

Taking Everyone's Feelings into Consideration

Just like everyone gets to decide whether or not the time is right for you to meet the children, everyone is also allowed to have feelings about you and the meeting. The feelings may be unfounded or unfair; however, if you can consider everyone's feelings prior to meeting the children, you may find that you have an easier time being accepted into the family.

The Other Biological Parent's Feelings

The first meeting may be anxiety provoking for the other biological parent. For example, if your boyfriend had a long relationship before you and his children grew attached to that person, the biological mother may be worried that her children will be hurt again if your relationship with the biological father does not work out. This is a reasonable concern for the biological mother to have, as she is concerned about protecting the feelings of her children. If this is the case, it might be helpful for you to speak with her about when she would feel most comfortable with you meeting her children. It might mean waiting a little longer to meet the children, meeting the children as a friend of their father's and not necessarily a girlfriend, or limiting your contact with the children to certain occasions.

Be kind to the other biological parent. Be tolerant. You do not know the circumstances of the breakup; you know only one side of things. No matter how much you trust or love the person you are seeing now, you were not in their relationship. Try as hard as you can not to judge the other biological parent. Any breakup is difficult; when a child is involved, it tends to be much harder.

The biological parent also may be concerned about her children's safety. For example, if your boyfriend has made poor choices in the past in terms of who he exposes his children to, it would be natural for the biological mother to be concerned. This is another instance where meeting with her might put her fears at ease. If you do partake in risky behaviors such as excessive drinking or partying, you should think twice about whether you are capable of making a positive contribution to their lives.

A third hesitancy the biological parent may have typically arises when you are the first person to meet her children as a potential stepparent. In this case, the biological parent is likely to feel a range of emotions including fear, jealousy, sadness, or anger. The emotions felt might depend upon how the relationship with the other biological parent ended. Whether the biological parent has begun dating also may be significant. If she is successfully dating someone, she might not be as upset as she might be if she hasn't started dating or has endured a recent breakup.

The Child's Feelings

The age of the child is likely to have a great impact on her readiness to meet you and the emotions she has going into that meeting. How the breakup between her parents affected her is also likely to have an impact. Was there a lot of fighting? Is there still animosity? If so, the child may be meeting you with a negative outlook. No matter what the attitude of the child, it is your job to be the adult in the situation and be as kind as possible. This is a child who has, at the very least, suffered the breakup of her parents or a loss of a parent. Most children will form their own opinions of you, regardless of what people around them are saying. If you are genuinely nice to her and her parents and don't get involved in any drama, name calling or disputes, you will at least earn the respect of the child.

The Family of the Deceased Parent

In cases where the other biological parent has died, other family members, such as grandparents, may be closely involved in the care and upbringing of your boyfriend's child. If this is the case, it is likely they will have some input into when it is appropriate for you to meet the child. They may be dealing with feelings of fear and concern. First of all, they have lost a child; their connection to their child is the child you are about to meet. This could bring up concerns of abandonment for them: What if you replace their daughter as Mom to their grandchild? Will you take time away from their time with their grandchild? Will you somehow make the child forget about his mother and therefore not need the grandparents in his life anymore? In addition, they know this child has been through a painful experience already. How can they be sure you won't somehow hurt the child? Will you be around for a long time? Are you ill in any way?

This situation is another in which meeting with the grandparents or family members can be very helpful to their emotional health. It also provides an opportunity to learn about the other biological parent, which may be very nice for everyone. Be considerate; there has been a major loss, and everyone is simply trying to protect the mental health of the child.

Your Boyfriend's/Girlfriend's Feelings

Your significant other might seem fine with the meeting at first, and then get a little freaked out right before the meeting or after the fact. Keep in mind, this meeting also has implications for your relationship with your boyfriend. You are now on a different track relationship-wise, and this can be disorienting in its own right. It is akin to telling someone you love them, and then wondering if you should have said it. There is some finality to it once it has been said, and this can make people start acting weird or nervous. Be patient with your boyfriend. If he thought long and hard about having you meet his child, he may just need to revisit those thoughts to remind himself of the reasons he felt it was time for you to meet each other. Even if you don't get along well with his child at the first meeting, he will probably feel better if he knows you are open to continuing a relationship with him and his child after the meeting.

Appropriate Activities for a First Meeting

The first meeting is best held in neutral territory. The idea is to create a situation that is not too stressful for you or the child. If you will be meeting the other biological parent for the first time as well, it is important to find a place where everyone is very comfortable. If you are meeting a younger child, a bowling alley, playground, or paint-your-own-pottery store would all be great places. This would give you an opportunity to chat while also providing a distraction, if needed. With a teenager, an outdoor activity, baseball game, or even a movie would probably work. Although a movie does not provide much opportunity for talking, some teenagers may not want to talk much anyway; the ride to the movies and home may provide plenty of opportunity to talk. Teenagers vary so much in terms of maturity that they may be fine with activities such as bowling or going out to eat, which both offer ample opportunity for talking.

FACT

Try an activity in which your stepchild has an interest. For example, you may think laser tag is absolutely terrible, but it is his favorite activity and this is what he chooses. Go for it, and don't be embarrassed to be awful at it or make a mistake. Instead, show him that you are open to trying new things, you aren't afraid of looking goofy, and you are willing to do something you really don't like just to spend time with him.

On the other hand, they may not enjoy speaking much at all, which means that an activity with a lot of distractions, such as a sporting event or the movies, might work best for all of you. Older teenagers or adults should be fine with a dinner date at a restaurant. If this is comfortable for you, it is nice to give the child the choice of where and how to meet. This will give him more control over the situation and perhaps make him more open to meeting you.

Fielding Questions from Potential Stepchildren

Questions from potential stepchildren can come at any age and are often embarrassing, horrifying, blatantly honest, thought provoking, or food for thought. The motivation behind a question determines whether or not it is insulting or inquisitive—and you may not always be able to gauge the true motivation. In these cases, it is best to answer honestly, and a simple, "I don't know. That is a tough one, can I think about it?" is perfectly acceptable.

Listen and Respond Appropriately

Examples of questions that may be valid but insulting include: "Are you going to dump my mom after a few dates too?"; "Do you hate my dad?"; "Do you always date married women?"; "Now that you broke up my parents, are you going to try to have a baby with my mom, too?" Questions such as these may sound terrible, but they also have validity behind them. Try to find the meaning behind the insulting part of the question. Children are trying to figure out your intentions. Are you here to stay or are you yet another in a long line of boyfriends? Should they get close to you? Are you going to say mean things about their mother? Are you yet another person who will be joining the parent bashing?

Hidden Meanings

All of these questions have hidden meanings. As the adult, it is your job to take a breath before simply reacting. No matter how snide the question may sound, think for a minute about what the child might be feeling that is causing him to ask you questions like this. What might have caused him to ask a question like this? When you have considered possible factors, answer questions as honestly as possible.

For example, suppose Jenny, your potential stepdaughter, asks, "Are you just another !@#@ my mother is sleeping with who wants to have a baby with her?" Before reacting to the expletive, think for a moment: Has your girlfriend had many other boyfriends who have come in and out of Jenny's life, perhaps taking attention away from her? Is mom a serial dater who had a child with another man, and is now paying less attention to Jenny? Is Jenny simply trying to rattle you and scare you away?

After thinking about all possibilities, a reasonable answer may be, "Gee, Jenny, I'm sorry to hear you think I'm not a very good person. I do enjoy your mother's company, but you are part of your mother's life and I would really like to get to know you. I would like you to get to know me, too, but if you don't feel comfortable with me being around yet, I understand. Would you like to try this again another time?"

Of course, your speech won't be quite so scripted, but something along these lines may help Jenny see that you are not going to feed into her anger; however, you recognize she is angry and appreciate that her anger is real.

She will also hear that you are genuinely interested in getting to know her better. She may think you are full of it for months, but if you maintain a non-confrontational manner and remain open about getting to know her, you will eventually make headway.

Including Potential Stepchildren in Your Single Life

Now that you have met your potential stepchildren, how do you have a relationship with your boyfriend that is separate from, but still inclusive of, the children? First of all, it is important to schedule family time as well as date time. If on Thursday nights, for example, you have time to eat dinner with your boyfriend and his child, consider making Thursdays family oriented. If you do this, try to avoid having date nights on Thursdays. Also, check out how you feel every week. Are Friday nights tough for you to spend with children because the workweek is so long? If so, have Friday be a child-free night for you—whether that means hanging out with your friends, taking time to yourself, or having a date night. Reserve days and nights when you have energy to be child friendly for your boyfriend's children. If Sunday afternoons are relaxing for you and your boyfriend's son enjoys family hikes, make Sunday family day.

It is important to take your emotional temperature. If you feel too exhausted on Fridays to deal with kids, then don't! Are you energized and bored most Saturday mornings? Plan something fun with the family. Check in with yourself frequently to determine your peak family times and date times.

You need time for yourself—just like in a dating relationship without kids. You need time to be alone and just veg out. Give yourself that time. Just because there are kids in the picture does not mean you need to fill every moment with family and kid-friendly activities. Kids have lives, too and will want to spend much of their time with friends, not their parents.

After checking your own emotional meter, check your boyfriend's and his children's. You may find that your boyfriend doesn't really want to deal with you on the weekdays since he is busy getting kids ready for school and sports. Or maybe the kids treasure Sunday mornings with Dad and don't really want to share that with you just yet. That is fine; everyone has a different level of patience and tolerance for one another.

In time, you will find a pattern that feels right for everyone. Be patient, as it may take a good amount of trial and error to figure out what works.

CHAPTER 4

The Other Biological Parent

If the other biological parent is not ready for your significant other to be in a relationship, then you may find getting along with this parent difficult. In the best-case scenarios, where both parents are involved in the lives of the children, you will likely have at least a disagreement or experience a little frustration, but hopefully this will be minimal. If not, and you are dealing with a person who is having difficulty dealing with you or with your relationship with her ex, remember three words: grace, dignity, and respect.

4

Meeting the Other Biological Parent

If you are not yet married or on track to be married to your boyfriend, your contact with the other parent will probably be minimal. If, however, you are in a long-term relationship and the children are under eighteen, it is likely that you will encounter the other biological parent. It is important for your boyfriend to take the lead in introducing you. He will know when he is ready for you to meet his ex, and you should let him know when you are ready. He should also check in with his ex, and be respectful of her feelings about when it is appropriate to meet you. It doesn't need to be a huge production, and is certainly on a different level than meeting the children. It is possible she will just want to say hi when you pick up her son if she is used to the idea of her ex having a significant other. If, however, she has a small child and is nervous about the child staying with you, she may want to have a more formal meeting. If there are hard feelings around the whole breakup, she may not want to meet you at all right now, and that is something you will need to respect.

Your boyfriend should inform you whether his ex is very angry about the situation or is fine with it. This can determine where you meet her for the first time. When the situation is still strained, meeting her in a neutral territory such as a park or playground can be more comfortable for both parties. Hopefully, the situation is amicable and you will be able to meet her at her house or at your boyfriend's house at a time that is convenient for everyone.

How to Deal With the Other Biological Parent

A few possible scenarios exist: Out of sight out of mind—he is fine with your new relationship and is inclusive of both of you. Or he hates you and lets it be known.

The Other Biological Parent Doesn't Mind

In the first scenario, follow the lead of the other parent. If he is not concerned with you and is cordial when you bump into one another and that is that, great. There may not be a need for you two to communicate or interact. Maybe he deals solely with your girlfriend and is not bothered by you and does not want to bother with you. This is fine, and there is little need to force a friendship. If everyone is friendly and attends functions for the children together, he may be interested in being friends or at least somewhat more involved with you than you might have imagined. In this case, you can follow his lead. Forming a positive relationship will not only make you more comfortable when you interact with him, but will also make situations more pleasant for the children. These relationships are the easiest and don't take much explaining; the worst-case scenario, however, can be damaging to everyone.

Doing small things, like baking cookies and sending them over for her birthday or framing a picture of your stepchild for her, can be nice gestures to break the ice and should not be construed as over the top. If she throws them at you or tells you she does not appreciate the gestures, respect her wishes and gracefully stop. Do not bad mouth her or judge her for being disinterested in forming a relationship.

The Other Biological Parent Does Mind

If the breakup was difficult and the ex hates you and blames you for everything, you definitely should not follow his lead. He may be rude at family events, glare at you, bad mouth you to his children, or even threaten you. In any of these situations, do not buy into the behavior or support it; it will only make things worse. If he bumps into you every now and then and lets his presence be known, ignore him and gracefully stay out of his way. If he bad mouths you to the children and they tell you, do not dignify his words with a response; instead tell them you hope they form their own opinions of you as you spend more time together. If he threatens you or harms you in any way, have respect for yourself and the children and do not become physical with him. Instead, discuss with your significant other that it is clearly not the time for you to be around the ex, and come up with an arrangement where your paths do not need to cross.

THE EVERYTHING GUIDE TO STEPPARENTING

When to Keep Trying and When to Quit

If at first the ex wants nothing at all to do with you, that is fine; but it doesn't hurt to offer a simple hello every now and then. Also, it can be helpful to remind your significant other and his child of the other biological parent's birthday or certain holidays such as Mother's Day. If you are particularly impressed with the ex's parenting skills, sending a card for Mother's Day from you acknowledges this in a kind and not too over-the-top way, and is a nice gesture. If she rolls her eyes at it, fine, but you have made a nice gesture and that is that.

If the ex has made it clear that she does not want a relationship with you and never will, you may want to ask, through your significant other, if you should say hello if you bump into one another or simply avoid her at all costs. At this point, it is up to her to make the move, and you can be respectful of her wishes and leave her be.

If the ex is somewhat hostile, you may want to meet at a neutral location to attempt to mediate the situation enough so the children are not affected by the animosity. If she does not wish to meet, again, respect her wishes; you gave it a try. If she will meet with you, and you find the conversation is heading to a negative place, stop the meeting and ask if you can agree to not interact with one another for the time being and potentially revisit this at a later time. If she continues to be negative and becomes hostile, leave the situation before it escalates. Do not try to reinitiate contact. Again, you made a solid effort and the timing was just not right.

You may find that, in time, emotional wounds heal and everyone will be able to set aside differences for at least small periods of time for the sake of the children. Unfortunately, there are some situations that do not get better with time. It is best to leave those relationships alone and remember to act with grace, dignity, and respect.

If Your Stepchild Wants You to Take Sides

Parents and their children fight, argue, disagree, and even can't stand each other's company at times. If your stepchild is going through this with the other biological parent, it is important that you listen to your stepchild. However, no matter how much you agree or dislike the biological parent, it is not your place to collude with your stepchild and agree that his mother is a ridiculous control freak with bad style.

Tread Carefully

If your stepchild would like to rant and rave, you can certainly absorb some of this and even be the voice of reason, but do not agree with him. If you do, you are setting yourself up for a negative relationship. Your stepchild will most likely tell his mother that you agree with all the negative things he is saying if you have given him reason to believe this is true. He may also decide the following week that you are the enemy; after all; didn't you say his mother was a ridiculous control freak with bad style?

ALERT!

If your stepchild is fighting with your significant other and is trying to get you on his side, it may be very tempting to agree with your stepchild—especially if you believe it will put you more in his favor by doing so. Do not do this. It is never okay to undermine any parent.

In a situation where your stepchild is alienated from his other biological parent, it is still not up to you to encourage the alienation or bring the two together. You can certainly be there as someone who can listen to your stepchild's concerns; however, getting overly involved in this type of situation is not recommended. Your partner will likely have some advice to give you as far as how he has handled the relationship in the past. If you sense that it is still a very stressful scenario for your stepchild, you can certainly speak with your partner about finding a counselor with whom your stepchild can speak.

Be the Voice of Reason

As the stepparent, you are in the glorious position to be the voice of reason. You are not the parent, so your emotions are not tied up with your stepchild in the same way as his parents'. Instead, you can listen to all the anger and unfairness that your stepchild feels and point out noninflammatory observations. For example, your stepson Joe is grounded by his mother for being one minute late. He had called to inform her he would be late, and she still grounded him! You agree (silently in your head) that this is pushing it on Mom's part, but it would be wise to just listen and agree that being grounded stinks, or jokingly say that he will probably never be even a minute late again. Perhaps give him a few strategies to avoid being late again, such as setting an alarm on his cell phone that signals him it is time to leave to go home.

By listening to his venting but not colluding with him or saying anything negative about his mother, you are modeling positive behavior, letting him get his anger out, and allowing him to experience a positive relationship with an adult in his life. He will have respect for you because you are respecting his emotions and his relationships with his parents.

In situations where the other biological parent is being unfair to the child and you are concerned, you could inform your significant other and let him work it out with his ex without getting involved yourself.

According to the National Stepfamily Resource Center, it is important that a child be "given permission (by the parent and the stepparent) to love the other biological parent." This does not have to be a direct verbal consent but more of an emotional permission that you can model by treating the other biological parent with respect and speaking of her in positive terms. Likewise, it is also important for the child to be given permission by both the biological parents to like the stepparent.

When Others Are Acting Undignified

If there are hard feelings about the breakup, someone may behave poorly at some point. It may be the ex or it may be your significant other. When people are hurting, they can say and do things they would not do under normal circumstances. If the ex is continually saying negative things about you to his children, it may become tough to ignore. There may come a point where you find this is overwhelming and having an impact on your relationship with your significant other. If this is the case, you can try to reason with the ex first, either by calling a truce or simply asking for the ex to voice his complaints to other adults and to leave the children out of it.

Asking Your Significant Other to Intervene

In a situation where the ex continues to say negative things to the children, your significant other may have to sit with the ex and attempt to mediate the situation to the extent that the ex is at least not harassing you or trying to manipulate the children. If this is unsuccessful, your significant other may have to speak with his children and explain to them that sometimes adults don't get along well and say things to one another or about one another that are mean. Instead of blaming their mom for being cruel and telling his children that she is trying to make them hate you, he should take a nonblaming approach and explain the situation in terms that the children will understand. It is often helpful for children to have a situation familiar to them with which to compare what is going on between the adults.

E-QUESTION

What if my husband's ex makes a scene in an attempt to ruin our wedding?
You may want to see the other biological parent try and embarrass you at your wedding, so that you can finally show everyone how awful she is. Do not let it happen. Think about your stepchild and protect him. By acting civilized you are not just protecting your stepchild, but you are protecting the other biological parent and her relationship with her child. If the other biological parent snaps out of it, she will thank you in the end (even if she doesn't say so).

For example, Timmy, your potential stepson, is convinced that you keep saying mean things about his dad and it is your fault that his dad has trouble getting out of bed in the morning and is cranky more frequently. Your girlfriend can say to Timmy, "Remember when you lost to Bill in wiffle ball and he told everyone you were the worst player ever? This is kind of like that. Bill said some things that weren't very nice, and then you told everyone Bill was stupid, which also wasn't very nice. Now we all know that you aren't the worst player ever and Bill isn't stupid, right? Sometimes our anger gets in the way and we say things we don't really mean, and it takes a while for us to realize some of the things we are saying aren't really nice or fair. This is what is happening with Dad right now. He is not mean or bad, but he is a little angry with me right now, so he is saying some stuff that isn't very nice about my boyfriend. Hopefully, in a few months, he won't be so mad and everyone will stop saying things about each other."

After giving an example he can comprehend, opening up the discussion for any questions or worries he has would be helpful.

Don't Blame

It is important to avoid the blame game, and for both you and your girlfriend to avoid pointing fingers—even if someone is pointing them at you. Kids are clever; they get it. Maybe not right away, but as time goes on, they figure out who is instigating all the issues. It may take years and they may never tell you that they realize their dad was acting ridiculous, but they usually come around and at least form their own ideas about you—separate from the ideas their dad has put in their heads. And, if you remain as neutral as possible, their dad may form his own ideas about you—separate from the ones he formed based on his emotions. He may channel his anger elsewhere or at least stop feeding negative things about you to his children.

Stress reduction is important in life, and finding techniques that work for you can benefit you and your relationships. Exercise, such as yoga, running, or walking, can be great for your emotional and physical health. Seeing friends and being social can give you time away from stressful situations and also feed your friendships. Volunteering is another great way of reducing stress and doing something beneficial for the community.

If he becomes harassing or dangerous at any time, you may have to involve the authorities to protect yourself. This would also need to be explained to the children in a manner similar to the explanation above. If you or your girlfriend can point out that the police are simply trying to make sure no one gets hurt, and again don't blame Dad, the situation will be less traumatizing for the children. Framing the situation as one where Dad needs help keeping himself safe is better than saying Dad is dangerous and might hurt someone. Try to protect the relationships the children have with the adults in their lives.

Be Aware of Your Own Feelings

As far as your stress level with the whole situation goes, be sure to check in with your emotions frequently. Is this getting to be too stressful? Is it exhausting? If so, take a break from the chaos. You may need to take some time away from your girlfriend and the children. Remind yourself frequently that you need to be looking out for and protecting the children. In order to do this, you need to be taking care of yourself. If their dad overwhelms you, you may take your stress out on them, which is not what you want.

FACT

Need to talk? Find groups supportive of stepparents and stepfamilies. In these groups you can find people who have overcome many of the same hurdles you are facing and can offer advice to help you succeed. Your community may have an ongoing support group or you can find one on the Internet. If there is no group in your area, the National Stepfamily Resource Center (*www.stepfam.org*) can provide assistance to help you organize a local chapter.

Find someone to talk to about everything—someone to whom you can vent your frustrations. This might be your girlfriend, a friend, a therapist, or one of your own parents. Your girlfriend may seem like the natural choice since she knows the whole situation; however, a more neutral party would be better. There is no need to fuel any burning fire. If the two of you talk about how crazy her ex is, you may just feed into his behaviors and fall into negative behavior patterns. A therapist, friend, or parent can help you cope with your emotions and also provide feedback as a neutral party.

Whomever you decide to confide in, make sure you do so in a place that is free of the children. Otherwise, they might overhear you, and it is likely to be disturbing to them. It is normal for you to rant and rave occasionally; just be sure to do it privately so there is no chance that they will hear you.

When You Are Acting Undignified

If you are acting undignified and know it, then knock it off. You may be thinking, "But she is so mean to me." Do not play into that; two wrongs do not make a right, and you are not only acting undignified, you are an adult who is setting a poor example for a child. If you recognize you have been acting atrociously, stop what you are doing and apologize to everyone who was affected by it. That may mean you apologize to your stepchild, your significant other, and the ex. Even if your negative behavior was nothing in comparison to something she has done to you, apologize anyway. You have behaved in a way you would not want your stepchild to mimic, so you should try to rectify the situation by apologizing and explaining to your stepchild that you let your emotions get the best of you and acted in a way you wish you hadn't. It may feel awful while you are apologizing, but in the end you are the one who is acting with self-respect and respect for those around you. This will gain the respect of others and perhaps help them look at their own actions and see how they have behaved in unhelpful ways.

Acknowledging the Other Biological Parent's Position

No matter how difficult the breakup or amicable the relationship, you must always acknowledge the other biological parent's position. It is easier to see in many ways when there is animosity because you are looking for reasons why people are behaving badly. When everyone seems happy, however, it is easy to forget that the other biological parent may even have a position. When it comes down to it, your stepchild is their child, their flesh and blood. By allowing you to form a relationship with their child, they are trusting you; even if the visit is court ordered and they have no choice—they still have to accept the fact that their child is going to have a relationship with another adult that they have no control over. This can be threatening, anxiety provoking, sad, great—it can be just about anything at any time. It is part of your job as an adult to be mindful of this.

Many possible scenarios exist. You might be younger and in better shape; what if their child likes you more and thinks you are more fun? You may have a great job and seem to bring out in your significant other what she could not. Their daughter likes to talk to you about her new boyfriend. Their son would rather play football with you because you are more athletic. Even the most benign moment between you and your stepchild could bring up all sorts of emotions for the other biological parent. It is important that you keep this in the back of your mind at all times.

Children always adjust better to change if they can have access to both biological parents. This means not only seeing the other biological parent but also thinking well of her. Sometimes visitations can be painful and revive old wounds for the other biological parent, but such visits are important for your stepchild's emotional health and well-being.

Even the kindest ex may be sad every time she sees you because you have a relationship with her daughter that is more about fun and less about discipline. So remember the emotions of the other biological parent. You never know when these emotions might flare up. You will be better prepared to manage any out-of-character behaviors if you keep in mind that this parent, no matter how wounded, cruel, or distant, is trusting you with her child.

No one knows her child better than a parent. A parent often knows the simplest solutions—a solution that is often so subtle they may not even realize how valuable and needed it is. They may, for example, know of a solution that is as simple as rocking a child to a certain rhythm or pouring his juice in a certain way. This is part of the priceless information a parent brings to the table, so try to respect that parent.

CHAPTER 5

Moving In

Moving in together is a huge step in any relationship. It may occur before or after marriage or without plans to even be married. Hopefully, by now you've met your partner's children and started forming relationships with them. No matter where your relationships are in terms of stability, you may find that everyone's emotions—yours, your partner's, the children's, and the other biological parent's—become a bit rattled at the tune of the two of you moving in together. This is to be expected, and can be prepared for and dealt with successfully.

Making Room in Your Home and Heart

Hopefully, you have made room in your life for your stepchild by this point and you feel relatively comfortable with him. Upon moving in with your significant other, you may find that you need to open your heart a bit more, now that you are sharing a bathroom, television, sofa, food, and kitchen with your stepchild. Depending on the custodial situation, you may be sharing your home with your stepchild anywhere from two hours a week to twenty-four hours a day. The more time your stepchild spends at your house, the more you will need to adjust and be flexible.

Adjusting to Your New Life

Most people have a rhythm of some sort in their daily routine. Maybe you get up at five every morning, run for an hour, shower, make your coffee, and enjoy your coffee in peace and quiet. This will change, not only because of your stepchild, but also because of your significant other. Perhaps the most difficult part of moving in with your significant other isn't really the addition of a stepchild, but the readjusting of your relationship with another person. The added responsibility of a stepchild living with you only adds to the stress of an already stressful situation. This is not to say that adjusting to moving in is a negative experience, but even happy experiences cause stress when they include a major life change.

The most stressful moments in someone's life include death, marriage, divorce, moving, changing jobs, gaining a new family member, and having a major illness. Life-event stress can be measured using the Holmes Rahe Social Readjusment Scale, found at *www.cop.ufl.edu/safezone/doty/dotyhome/wellness/HolRah.htm*.

It is likely that this pleasant morning routine of yours will change. If your stepchild is with you in the mornings, your morning run may turn into packing lunch and getting him out to the bus on time. Your seat on the sofa may be taken by him or your significant other when you get home from work.

Your television time may become homework time or time to adjust to a new television show.

Even though these things may seem like no big deal, they will put a crimp in your daily routine, which can eat away at you quite a bit. If you find you are becoming irritable or feel that your space is invaded, talk with your significant other about how to change the schedule to better suit everyone's needs. You may realize that not running in the morning means a bad day for you and anyone around you. To remedy this, maybe you can pack lunches the night before and your significant other can take on bus duty. Another solution might be waking up earlier and figuring out a better bathroom schedule.

All of these adjustments can take a toll on you, your significant other, and your stepchild. The best way to handle this is by reminding each other this is something you thought long and hard about prior to buying matching key rings, and that it was a decision that took everyone's happiness into account. Make room in your mind and heart for your daily routine to be disrupted. Accept that you will have to change some of your habits and your schedule. The more open you are to being flexible, the more open your partner and stepchild will be as well.

If you find you are the one making all the changes, this is a big red flag. Everyone should be making adjustments to benefit the new family unit. Just because you may be the odd one out doesn't mean you should make all the adjustments to accommodate everyone else. Keep in mind that you are all defining yourself as a unit for the first time and will all have to make changes.

Making Room for Your Stepchild

Aside from making room mentally and emotionally for your stepchild, you also need to make physical room for him. Even if he is only at your house for two hours a week, he still deserves a place of his own while he is there. Having a room to himself is ideal. If you have more than one stepchild, children of the same sex can share rooms, but children of the opposite sex should not be in the same room after one or more pass the age of eight years. If the time your stepchild spends at your house is limited and you are moving into a small house or apartment that does not have another bedroom for your stepchild, consider how to give him a space in the house that is his and his alone while he is there. This doesn't mean he will go sit in his space while at your house, but knowing he can have his own space is very important. Ideas for space include the kitchen, living room, your bedroom, or even a nook in the hallway. He should have a spot that has privacy and that he feels is conducive to his needs. Keep in mind he may need a quiet space to read or work on homework.

If your stepchild will only be sleeping over occasionally—a child who is in college or lives far away—he should still have a place to sleep when he does visit. He should always feel like your home is his home. He is not a guest, and certainly not a burden. If you do not have two bedrooms, a pull-out couch or futon in the living room or another room in the house may suffice. If this is the case, privacy is key. Your stepchild deserves to have privacy. Instead of grumbling that he takes up the whole living room when he is there, enjoy the fact that he is visiting and declare the room in which he is sleeping off limits to yourself and your significant other until he is up and about.

In situations of full or shared custody, where your stepchild will be at your house with greater frequency, it is important the child has a consistent place to sleep and stay. In tight situations, this may still be a futon or air mattress; however, make physical room for the child to be a child. This may mean toys all over his bedroom, which is really your living room with a pull-out couch. It could also mean the child sleeps in the living room but uses a room with more privacy, like your bedroom, to change clothes or talk on the phone to friends. The more welcoming the physical environment is for your stepchild the more settled he will feel at your house.

Give Your Stepchild Time to Adjust

If you are moving in immediately following a marriage, it is probable that you explained both situations at the same time. If, however, you are simply moving in and marriage may be in the future, then the moving-in discussion should happen before the move-in date has arrived. It is best for your significant other to tell his child alone or with the other biological parent. No matter how well you get along with your stepchild, he may feel pressure to act happy or excited if you are there during the moving-in conversation. If he is immediately excited and thrilled, you can plan to go out and celebrate later that day or week, but for the actual conversation, it is best that he have private time with his parents to react in a way that he needs.

If your stepchild is not happy that you will be moving in, it shouldn't stop your plans; however, this new concern may change the timeline or housing configuration you had in mind. This is why it is best to start the moving-in discussion earlier, instead of close to the move-in date. In case your stepchild is extremely upset, you may have to delay moving in or figure out a visitation schedule that will ease the child into the idea of you living with his parent. You do need to respect your stepchild's feelings, but you also need to live your life and respect your relationship with your significant other.

Give your stepchild space to adjust, but do not let him manipulate the situation and make you feel as though you cannot spend time in your own home. It is important that you also feel comfortable at home and get to spend time there!

With teens and tweens especially, you may find that you need to work out a system at the beginning of the relationship where you are not as visible when the move-in occurs, but as time goes on, you spend more and more time together at home. With younger children, you might need to make your presence known a bit more, and encourage more time spent together either with you alone or as a family. Younger children might have a hard time getting used to you and the idea of everyone living together. By being present with him and consistent about when you will be home and what your routine will be, your stepchild will have an easier time understanding what to expect from you as a part of his household.

Involving Stepchildren in the Process

A great way to involve your stepchild in the moving process is to include him in the selection of a new home, a bedroom in a home that is new to him, or even picking paint colors. Every child should have input into where the family will live, even if it is not a deciding factor. Moving can be quite disruptive to a child, so you need to handle this with care. The whole moving process can make for great bonding and a true feeling of inclusiveness for your stepchild.

Keep Parent Time Alive

Another way to make your stepchild more comfortable is to be sure his alone time and time with your partner do not decrease. He may feel like he is being pushed out of the picture and doesn't know if he is still important in his parent's life. Many children are nervous that they will somehow be replaced or forgotten about once their parent is in a serious relationship. When you do move in, this can inadvertently happen. Try to notice if it is happening. A trip to the grocery store for your significant other may now involve you, where before he used to go with his son. Keep little things like this in mind, and try to keep rituals consistent—especially at the beginning. Over time, you will develop your own rituals as a family, and past rituals may change to include you.

Remember that there are other adults in your stepchild's life who might be able to help support him through all these changes. School teachers, coaches, and any other supportive adults can be helpful to your child if they are aware of the situation. It doesn't mean the adults should intervene; however, making them aware of any changes can prepare them for any out-of-character behavior by your stepchild.

If your stepchild is already feeling threatened, however, do not intrude upon these rituals. Your significant other may insist that you join in with certain rituals, but if you notice your stepchild is not happy about this, refrain from participating for now. It is a great time to have a conversation with your partner about how you have noticed that his child really treasures time with his father, and you wish to respect that. In his haste to have everyone getting along and being a family, it will be easy for the biological parent to forget that one-on-one time with his child is also important to the success of this new family unit.

Food and Mealtimes

The refrigerator and pantry could actually have their own book. Food is central to most people's lives. It is how we live, socialize, celebrate, reward, and nourish. Food really shouldn't be used as a reward, and even using it to celebrate can lead to future eating habits that are not conducive to one's health. Food is, however, very important to the household. In many instances, you may not only be stirring a pot of different personalities, but also of different diets. You may be a meat and potatoes guy; your wife, a believer in high protein diets; your stepdaughter, a cheese lover; and your stepson, an organic vegan. How on earth do you shop for all of these different tastes? Do you really need to buy that organic tofu? Yes! You need to feed everyone, and you want to build a happy, healthy kitchen. In order to do this, you cannot only cater to yourself—shop for everyone in the family. It is very likely you will have to encourage everyone to compromise a bit, but catering to everyone's needs will be worth it.

Food is something people find comfort in, and having what you want to eat is a way of feeling nourished and included. If your stepchildren are only there on the weekends, make sure you stock the kitchen with foods they enjoy. They will know you didn't forget about them if there is evidence that you thought of them while grocery shopping. Regardless of how often your stepchildren are there, mealtime is a key time for the family unit. It is a way of bringing everyone together to share the goings-on of the day. When cooking dinner, incorporate everyone's needs into the meal. This may mean some major creativity, but it could open up many new tastes for everyone. If you live with your stepchildren full time, consider assigning cooking duty once a week for each member of the family. If your stepchildren are too young or too busy, have them pick out a meal they would like to try and cook it for them.

There are ways of compromising that will make everyone feel included and respected in the house. It is amazing how much food can impact someone's comfort level. Food is a way of connecting with people and taking risks with one another on new meals. Creating a kitchen and mealtime that are all encompassing will help build stronger relationships within the family.

Setting Yourself Aside

Similar to making room in your heart, you may recognize that your position as number two on the totem pole becomes more pronounced once you move in with each other. It may also open up more time for you to spend with your significant other, which may counteract the feeling of being in second place. When kids are a factor in a move, you need to think through every decision. Maybe you live in the city but the schools don't have the programs you are seeking, so you move in with your significant other in a town far from the city with a school system that offers the kind of programs you are seeking. This is the kind of situation where you will have to consider what is really best for the child and the family, not what is best for you.

FACT

Incorporate some routine into your lives at this time of change. Set up a standing date of everyone doing an activity together at least once a week. It can be anything from playing a board game, to going out to eat, to a trip to the local park. Let each person give suggestions as to what to do each week so everyone can have a say.

Once your stepchild has moved in with you or is visiting consistently with you as a housemate, you will see new issues arise that you were able to avoid before. Your stepson may be a terrible sleeper or a sleepwalker. You may find that you can no longer take part in your "secret single behaviors" because there is always someone around with whom you are not yet comfortable. It is difficult enough adjusting to a significant other moving in, but having your stepchildren move in makes the adjustment even more difficult.

With your significant other, there is more opportunity for compromise. With your stepchild, you may find you and your significant other are the ones who need to make the sacrifices. For example, if your stepchild is sick, one of you is staying home. If the three of you now share a bathroom, you and your significant other will be the ones to get up earliest to shower in order to leave time for your stepchild. You can still compromise with your significant other on certain things; however, when it comes to a child, you have to put yourself aside and make decisions and adjustments that benefit the child.

Whose House: Yours, Theirs, or New?

Everyone knows you are moving in together, but where will that be? Can you fit in your house? Is her house close enough to the other biological parent? Is this an opportunity to move to a new home or even a new city? Deciding where to live can be difficult, while also being one of the most fun activities to do as a family. There are many aspects to consider when moving and children are involved; you may find the final decision depends on something relevant to your stepchild.

Your House

Your home may seem like the perfect option if it is big enough and close to where the children and the other biological parent already live. If the situation is one where your girlfriend's house was too small and your house is bigger and in the area, yours may be fine. The other biological parent may agree that your house is fine as well if he realizes his children will still be just as close if they move in with you. If you have also suffered a recent marital breakup, you may find that you don't want to stay in your home either if it holds negative memories.

Their House

When one of you lives in a house in which you lived with an ex, or in a house that has bad memories, it is a good idea to consider a different house. It may feel uncomfortable for you to move into a house with your significant other that she used to share with her husband. This situation may also be uncomfortable for the children, as you are literally moving in on Dad's turf. Seeing you sleep in a bed Dad shared with Mom or sitting in Dad's seat in the living room can be a lot for your stepchildren to stomach, and may be difficult for you as well. Their father may also have issue with this, and if the divorce is going to be a battle, you may find you must move due to court decisions.

No matter which house might seem the best, moving must be weighed against the disruption it will cause the children. If your partner feels the need to maintain as much stability as possible by staying in her current home, you need to agree for the sake of the children, no matter how inconvenient. Once the children are more comfortable with the marital change in their lives, they might be ready to move to a new home.

If the other biological parent moved out a long time ago and has moved on with his life, it will be less difficult for everyone to see you in that setting. The difficulty of the breakup and timing of the breakup will have a lot of impact on how comfortable it will be for you and your stepchildren if you move into their home.

A New House

A new house can be costly, but if you have the means to move into a home that is new to all of you, you are all on a more equal playing field. If you are bringing two sets of children together—yours and your significant other's—and you will be living together full time, a new house may be the necessary solution.

Moving one set of children into a house that already belongs to other children can be very difficult for all the children. It will be difficult for the children moving in to feel like this house is theirs; the children who already live in the house may feel and act territorial. Asking a child to share a room that was once his and his alone will be tough for both children, and symbolizes both children's greatest fears: The child moving in will never feel like the room is really his and the child whose room it is will feel pushed aside and imposed upon. Both children will feel forced together. It is best to avoid these situations if possible.

Consider Location

When deciding where to live and which housing option is best, geography is a factor that requires much consideration. For the adults in the situation, concerns such as being close to work and convenience to health clubs, friends, and social activities may be very important.

For the children, the following are important:

- They can easily go between parental houses if custody is shared.
- They can visit with relative ease if custody is only on a visitation level.
- They will not be too disrupted as far as friends and social interests are concerned.
- They have access to a good school district.
- The neighborhood or complex is safe and child friendly.
- The house has enough room for them to have privacy when needed.

These are issues your stepchildren may not think of on their own, but something you and your significant other should keep in mind and even bring up with them while deciding on the best place to live.

Involve Your Stepchildren in Decisions

Regardless of where you end up living, it is unlikely the choice will appease everyone. Keep in mind that this move symbolizes a huge change in your stepchildren's lives. Involve them as much as you can in the decision making. If you house hunt together, ask your stepchildren for their opinions. And then, really listen to their answers—children notice funny things about houses and neighborhoods that can be very useful. Did they like the neighborhood? Would they like to live in the house where they have to share a bedroom but have an extra bathroom or would they prefer to share a bathroom but have individual bedrooms? What bothers them about the area?

Once the move has happened, have them help make decisions about the little things, such as where the toaster should go or what color the bathroom should be. All of these little things will help your stepchildren feel like they are part of the process. You and your significant other will have the final say; however, considering your stepchildren and respecting their opinions will make it a true family decision.

How to Involve the Other Biological Parent

The other biological parent will have more involvement when your stepchild is school age and younger. Once your stepchild is no longer living with either one of her parents, where you live is not as much of an issue. Prior to informing your stepchild of your move-in plans, it may help to talk with the other biological parent. Similar to discussing dating and your initial meeting, it is respectful to talk to the other biological parent about your plans. If you have a relatively open relationship with her, you and your significant other could ask her input about timing, geography, and other questions regarding your plans. She may have some very helpful advice or opinions about school districts or what she would consider too far away in terms of distance between parental homes.

When the Other Biological Parent Reacts Badly

If there is still animosity between your significant other and his ex, this move may represent too much of a change in your relationship, and she may not react well. In a case where the ex does not react well, be patient, and consider putting the move on hold or slowing down the process if you think this will benefit the child. If she is going to withhold visitation or try to jeapordize your stepchild's relationship with your significant other, work as hard as you can to protect your stepchild in the situation. Unfortunately, your significant other may have to involve the courts if there is no other way of resolving the issue at hand. If the courts are already involved, they will likely have some input into how far you can move from the other biological parent.

With all these factors, you could have many different choices of where to live or be restricted to a small area. If this is difficult for you because you had planned to move far away or follow your career to different parts of the country, you need to remember that by moving in with your significant other, you also agreed to take on his moving restrictions. Put your stepchild's best interest first and you will find moving in an easier and potentially rewarding process.

Finding Alone Time

There are many different types of alone time. There is alone time with yourself, in your house, not worried about anyone wanting to change the channel or needing a ride somewhere. There is alone time where you escape the house and find somewhere to be alone. There is alone time for you and your significant other. There is alone time for you and your biological children. And there is alone time for you and your stepchild. It sounds like a great deal to balance, but it actually isn't. The hardest one to find, by far, is alone time to yourself in the house. Second place would be alone time with your significant other. Alone time with children is important to have, but is often easier to find time for than other types of alone time.

FACT

Date time or alone time is important to keep your relationship fresh, but it is hard to schedule. You may find you feel guilty spending time away from your stepchildren, but they need time away from you, too. Plus, your time away will invigorate you and help make you a more engaged stepparent when you are together.

To create alone time for yourself, make a plan with your significant other on how you can obtain this treasured time. Perhaps he can take the kids for an entire day for his own alone time with them. This way, he is creating alone time for the kids as well as providing alone time for you. If he does this once a month, you could do the same for him. It is important that you both have time away from the children and from one another. If you don't, you can become worn out, overextended, and resentful of your children or each other. Make finding alone time a priority.

To create couple alone time, you may have to seek out help from in-laws, your children's friends, a trusted babysitter, or the other biological parent. If the other biological parent is in a relationship as well, you could alternate weekends with her. If you both have children, plan your weekends so that your children and your stepchildren are visiting their other biological parent during the same weekend. If working out a schedule is not feasible, then you can usually find friends of your stepchildren who will host a sleepover one weekend, as long as you reciprocate the favor. This can be a great way to get to know your stepchildren's friends and their parents while also providing you with a scheduled date weekend.

CHAPTER 6

Getting Married

Getting married is an exciting time in anyone's life, and a huge life change no matter what the circumstances. If you are already living together, you may not be prepared for the impact marriage might have on your relationship with each other and on your relationships with others. If you are not yet living together, you are probably expecting a big change because getting married will also include moving in with your significant other. This chapter will stick exclusively to discussing the wedding and your changing role once you say, "I do."

Involving Your Stepchild-to-Be in the Wedding

Picking bridesmaids, groomsmen, china, and locations can be fun, but also frustrating. When stepchildren are involved, it can be a matter of not stepping on anyone's toes, including everyone appropriately, inviting people you may not have any desire to ever see unless absolutely forced to, and remembering the reason you are going through all this pain and suffering—to marry the person you love. Including your stepchild may bring the level of anxiety up a little bit, but at the same time, it may bring the level of joy up as well. Just like a wedding without stepchildren, it is a balancing act between frustration and fun.

Factors to Consider

There are five main factors that will help you determine how and if your stepchild should participate in the wedding:

- The age of your stepchild
- Your relationship with your stepchild
- Your partner's relationship with your stepchild
- Your stepchild's desire to be a part of the wedding
- The other biological parent's feelings about your stepchild's involvement

Each one of these should factor into your decision on the best way to include your stepchild. They should also help guide you in deciding on a role for the stepchild that will make everyone feel the most comfortable. It can be rather tricky, and feelings can get hurt even if you are extremely careful. One thing that may help is that weddings have become a little less formal in terms of who takes on which position. There is even room for you to create a special position if you are struggling too much with fitting your stepchild into the wedding. Instead, fit the role to your stepchild.

Age Considerations

As far as age is concerned, if your stepdaughter is six, the role of flower girl may be perfect. If your stepdaughter is fifty-six, the role of flower girl would be insulting; however, a reading role may be perfect. Age is one of the most helpful factors in determining where your stepchild fits. Very young children can be flower girls and ring bearers, preteens can be junior bridesmaids and groomsmen, and older children can be bridesmaids or groomsmen. Preteens and above can have an extra part in your ceremony, like reading, singing, or performing a church-required duty. There is a way to incorporate everyone, no matter what the age.

With younger children, you may have to invite the other biological parent. If the child is extremely young, you may actually need the other biological parent to help the child down the aisle or for caretaking purposes.

Difficult Ages

The toughest ages to deal with are teenagers and young adults, the fifteen to about twenty-three year olds. Not only are they at a difficult age in general, they could fit into a number of roles and could be quite offended if you put them in one they don't find suitable. For example, if you have a fabulous stepson who you would love to have as a best man, it may seem silly to have him as anything else. If your stepson is only seventeen, however, and he is consumed by school and has no organizational skills, it may be very overwhelming for him, his other biological parent, and you to have him as the best man by himself. To remedy this, you could have two best men, one who will take over control of the rules and requirements that come along with the job and the other, your stepson, to be honored as a best man on your wedding day. You could even call them Best Man and Honorary Best Man. This is where creativity is needed and can really make your wedding planning fun.

With a stepdaughter, you may also find you struggle with a role for teenagers. Should she be a bridesmaid or your maid of honor? Maybe you don't have a maid of honor at all, but instead name your bridesmaids according to your theme or their personalities. For example, you could have a Maid of

Making You Laugh, a Maid of Keeping You in Line, and so on. This is your wedding; you have some creative license in determining roles for people you wish to involve in your special day.

Consider the Relationship

Your relationship with your stepchild will also play a part in how you choose her involvement in the wedding. This is strongly influenced by your partner's relationship with his child. It is with these two relationships that you may need to compromise the most. If you are very close to your stepdaughter, it is less likely that your partner's relationship with his daughter will cause you to find some sort of middle ground. In this situation you would probably place her in a visible role in the wedding and it is unlikely your partner would argue with this.

E-QUESTION

What if my stepdaughter is out of control and might do something atrocious and embarrassing if I have her in the wedding?
This is a conversation your partner needs to have with her. He should stand up for you in this situation as well as advocate for her to behave in a way deserving of a role in your wedding. If she has been cruel to you despite all your efforts to get along with her, he will need to step in and consider not including her in the wedding party if she is not capable of acting appropriately.

If, however, you do not get along well or feel very comfortable with your stepdaughter but your partner feels strongly that she hold an important role in the wedding, you may need to compromise. Although this is your wedding, it is also your partner's wedding and he should be able to include those he cares for in ways he finds suitable. If he wants his daughter to be your maid of honor and you really don't want her to be, you could suggest she be his best maid. This way you are including her in a positive and important role for your partner, and you are still able to choose the person you feel best fits the maid of honor position.

If You Don't Want Your Stepchild to Participate

If you don't want to have your stepchildren in the wedding at all, you need to think about what this means as far as the future of your relationship. Your stepchildren are going to be there forever; not feeling as though they should be a part of your wedding, while your partner does, is a very strong sign that you may not be ready to share your life with these stepchildren. You and your partner need to agree on how these children will be a part of your lives. Will they hold a central role? Will this negatively affect your marriage? If so, now is the time to figure that out, not after you walk down the aisle.

Your Stepchild Does Not Want to Participate

Some children may not wish to be in the wedding at all. Some may not even want to attend. However, this should not alter your wedding plans or change your wedding, unless it is possible that your stepchild will change her mind about the wedding in the near future. If you give her too much control over marital decisions, you might be allowing her to run the show for years to come. Forcing a child's participation or attendance is a huge mistake and has the potential to make everyone miserable.

If your stepchild was able to tell you or your partner that she is not comfortable being in the wedding, you should respect her feelings and not make her be in the wedding. A child may decide not to be in the wedding for a variety of reasons. She may simply be terribly shy and not want to be on display. In this case, you could thank her or acknowledge her in a more private way.

Your stepchild may not be happy about the wedding, and she has the right to feel this way. Hopefully, her feelings will change in time. In these cases, be sure to explain to the child and the other biological parent that you would love for her to participate and will hold a spot for her if she changes her mind. You can also give her options. She may not want to be a bridesmaid, but might like to sit at the head table. She may decide at the last minute that she wants to be a part of the wedding to support her father, and tells you this the night before. If you are prepared for this possibility, it will not be a problem.

If the breakup between your partner and his ex was particularly difficult, your stepchild may not want to support the marriage by even attending, and this is fine as well. Similar to a child who doesn't want to participate, be sure to keep the opportunity for your stepchild to attend open. Instead of grumbling if she decides to attend at the final hour, thank her for coming and enjoy her presence.

The Other Biological Parent's Role

The other biological parent also has some say in how your stepchild participates, more so when the child is younger and/or if the other biological parent is a primary custodian. If your stepchild is six years old and your partner only has visitation rights, the other biological parent will have a lot of control over whether the child participates in the wedding. If he is absolutely against this new marriage, he may tell you that the child cannot participate, and there may not be anything you or your partner can do about it.

An idea for your partner may be to involve his child in the marriage process by asking permission from the stepchild before asking you to marry him. This can provide a child with a feeling of power because she was not only able to voice her concerns, she is in on the surprise, which can be quite exciting for her.

If the other biological parent is open to the wedding and your stepchild's participation, asking the other biological parent's opinion about how to include your stepchild is a nice way of acknowledging the other biological parent and finding out how your stepchild will feel the most comfortable. As children become teenagers, they will probably be more vocal about how they want to participate, and the other biological parent may not be as much of a factor.

Involving Your Stepchildren

Since you are not only getting married to your partner but also creating a new family unit, you may wish to recognize the creation of this new unit by giving your stepchild a memento of the day. You and your spouse can have your stepchild come up at the end of the ceremony so you can give him a chain with a family medallion or give your stepdaughter a ring, symbolizing her part in your new family unit. You may choose to do this prior to the ceremony, at a different time entirely, or during the ceremony. If you do decide to include your stepchild in this way, you may want to run it by her to see if she would be comfortable receiving this gift in front of everyone at the ceremony. You may want to give it to her in front of everyone but she may not, and you don't want to ruin a special moment because you have humiliated your stepdaughter.

Wedding planning can be fun and stressful at the same time. You must be willing to be creative to cut down on stress and increase the fun. You also need to practice the flexibility you will need to use the rest of your life when it comes to involving and dealing with your stepchild. Your stepchild will be involved in your life from now on, and the list of people to consider when making a decision for your future will be similar to the list of people who factor into your stepchild's role in the wedding. This is good practice for the rest of your life together.

Who Has a Say in Your Wedding Plans?

As if there weren't already enough people telling you what to do, you will need to consider even more people's opinions when a stepchild is included in the marriage. First and foremost, you and your partner do have the final say. What you decide is best is what will ultimately occur. People will have their opinions, reactions, and grumblings, but it is you and your partner who have to make the decisions and live with the fallout. To avoid excessive fallout, it is important that the two of you listen to at least some of the opinions of those most affected by your marriage: your stepchild, any children of your own, the other biological parent, your parents, and your partner's parents.

It is highly unlikely you will please every single person involved. If you have never planned a wedding before, you may be surprised just how important a choice between asparagus and green beans may be to your mother-in-law. But these are disappointments everyone can deal with and will eventually forget. What you need to be cautious about are decisions that may harm someone or injure relationships for a long period of time.

Stepchildren

You and your partner will have disagreements; she may want roses and you may want lilacs. Your stepchildren will have opinions about the wedding plans as well. If your relationship with your stepchild is positive, or at least neutral, you may decide to give her a voice in some decisions or even base some of your own decisions around her choices. If you appreciate her input and want her to feel as much a part of this as possible, you could have her help pick the type of flowers, the color of the dresses, or even the perfect cake.

Perhaps your stepson is in a band; maybe you could let them play a quick set at the reception, even if they sound like howling coyotes. Decisions like these will make your wedding a celebration of your new family, not just the relationship between you and your partner. Your wedding guests may suffer through your stepson's music, but at the end of the day, you and your stepson and many others will appreciate how you included him in your special day.

ALERT!

If your stepdaughter can't stand you, then be careful how you involve her. For example, if you allow her to pick out the flowers, she might deliberately choose ones you are allergic to just to see how you will respond to her choice. Use reason when including your stepchild in these decisions; don't just let her take over the decision making because you want her to like you. You are still the one getting married!

If you can't stand your stepchild and he can't stand you, you may not give him much input on the wedding, but he probably won't want to give you any constructive feedback anyway. No matter what your relationship is like, there are certain courtesies you need to consider.

When you think about your stepchild, think about times in his life when he should have all the thunder. If you come in and steal his thunder by announcing your wedding date is the same date as his first gig at a bar somewhere, you are going to do some serious damage to your relationship with him. Here are a few more considerations:

- Don't plan your wedding for the same time your stepchild is graduating from high school or college.
- Don't plan your wedding for the same time as your stepdaughter's due date.
- If this is your stepson's senior year in high school or college, take note of prom dates, senior week, final's week, and any vacations.
- For your stepchild's sake, do not plan your wedding for the same month his other biological parent is getting married.
- Do not plan your wedding too close to your stepchild's wedding date.
- Leave Father's Day, Mother's Day, and any biological parent or stepchild birthday wedding-free days.
- Yearly vacations your stepchild takes or special anniversary celebrations should also be left untouched.

Have your stepchild write a calendar of events for the year, and when you choose a date, clear the date with your stepchild. This is a common courtesy. If your stepchild is young, you may have to check his schedule with his other biological parent to make sure you are not disrupting any other plans. These thoughts should also come to mind if you have children of your own; don't steal their thunder either! If you are trying this hard to respect your stepchild, practice this same respect with your own child.

The Other Biological Parent

The other biological parent actually does have some say in the wedding plans—to a degree. If she holds your stepchild's schedule, she needs to tell you a date that works. If she is getting married as well, you will need to plan around her wedding date, shower date, bachelorette party, and honeymoon.

She may make certain requests about how you are going to incorporate her child into the wedding. Maybe she doesn't want you to use a certain song to dance with your stepson because that is the song she wants to use when she dances with him at her wedding. Maybe she doesn't want you to get married at the local hall because that is where she married your partner years ago. These are all valid requests to take into consideration. It doesn't mean you need to heed them; however, they are simple requests that will benefit your relationship with her and your stepson in the long run. If she sees you trying to appreciate her feelings, hopefully she will respect this and nitpick as little as possible.

Parents

Your parents and your partner's parents will probably have concerns similar to those of any other parent of a child who is getting married. They may have even more concerns, however, when it comes to how you are planning your wedding in regards to your stepchild. These can come out of nowhere and be very surprising to you; their concerns may even seem totally ridiculous. Your partner's parents may want you to have your five-year-old stepson as the only groomsman in the wedding. Your parents may tell you to include only your own children in the wedding and not your stepchildren. Parents and grandparents can get a little bit demanding when it comes to protecting their own. If they don't like what is going on, they will probably speak up, even if everyone else feels okay with the plans. What is important for you to remember if they make an off-the-wall request is that they are probably trying to look out for someone—you, your child, your stepchild, or your partner. Handle them gently and listen to their complaints, which may contain some nuggets of great information. Be sure the decisions you make are decisions you and your partner can defend with integrity. If you feel any pangs that might suggest your decisions are unfair or may cause irreparable harm, rethink and rework them.

When the Other Biological Parent Interferes

If the other biological parent seems to be throwing up roadblocks, it can be tough to manage and very stressful. Sometimes it can be difficult to tell the difference between coincidence and purposeful interference. Hopefully, you have shown respect for the other biological parent when planning your wedding; however, this does not always mean he will offer you the same respect. If it seems that there are a lot of conflicting dates or requests from the other biological parent, take them at their word at first; they may just be coincidental issues that are appearing. The first three dates you throw out may really be impossible for your stepchild to take part in, so be as flexible as possible. If the roadblocks keep coming and seem contrived, do not cater to the other biological parent's every whim.

Don't let the other biological parent claim expense is an issue in order to prevent you from involving your stepchild. Avoid this by paying for your stepchild's clothes, food, babysitter, or any other wedding expense the other biological parent might incur.

Taking a Stand

If the other biological parent is making it impossible for your stepchild to take part in any of the wedding festivities even though you have changed the date eight times to suit him, you and your partner may have to take a stand. You could involve the courts if they are already involved. Or you could tell the other biological parent that it seems as if every date you pick is just impossible for him, so although you hate the thought that your stepson won't be a part of the wedding, it may have to be that way. You or your partner could attempt to point out that the other biological parent could compromise on dates as well. It might not work, but try to come to a compromise instead of being stubborn, even if the other biological parent is stubborn or was stubborn about his own wedding. Another option is to involve the other biological parent's parents and see if they can help mediate the situation.

It may seem as if the other biological parent will stop at nothing to ruin your wedding. If this happens, try ignoring his actions; however, do document them for your own records. Ignoring his actions may anger him even more, and instead of giving up he may continue to act out. The next step would be to have a civilized conversation with him, asking him to stop his actions since he is not only hurting you but also hurting his own child.

Again, he may only become more obnoxious. If this is the case and you fear he may be dangerous consult an attorney and the local police.

Who Is Invited?

Ultimately, you and your partner will create the guest list; but just like at any other wedding, you will probably wind up inviting some people you hardly know and some people you don't really like. Depending upon the age of your stepchild, you may have to invite the other biological parent. If your stepdaughter will not walk down the aisle unless she knows her mother is there, then invite her. She may decide to come only to the church or decide to stay for the whole party.

Your Stepchild's Family

Your stepchild has another biological parent, aunts and uncles that you may not even know, and grandparents totally unrelated to you. All of these people may want to see your stepchild in the wedding. They may have no issue at all with your marriage, but really want to see how beautiful your stepdaughter is in her bridesmaid dress, or hear the performance of your stepson's band.

You have a few options in these scenarios. Most people understand that weddings are expensive, so they may not expect to be invited just to witness your stepchild. Call the other biological parent and let her know it is okay with you if the relatives want to come to the ceremony to see your stepchild, but that you cannot afford to have more guests at the reception because of money or capacity constraints. If they would like to see something that will occur at the reception, it is appropriate to let them in for that piece of the reception with a similar explanation. If they just want to take pictures of your stepchild, tell them the time and place the pictures are being taken and invite them to come along. If you really enjoy their company and can afford to have them at the reception, then go ahead and invite them. These are a few solutions that are meant for situations where the relationship between you and the other biological parent is at least civil. If you hate each other and think her family will do anything to disrupt your day, use your judgment and only include them in situations that will be safe for everyone.

If your stepchild is a teenager or older, you may want to let him invite a friend or two to have at the wedding. This will help him have a better time and allow you a chance to get to know his friends a little better. If your stepchild is much older, you should invite him with a date if he is not participating in the wedding.

E-QUESTION

Do I have to invite the other biological parent If she Invited us to her wedding?
Not necessarily, but you probably should, unless you think she is going to do something dangerous or cruel. If she invited you to be courteous, extend the same courtesy to her.

Unless your partner is completely estranged from his children, you will want to include his children in the wedding, even if it is just as a guest. If your partner's ex passed away, let him and your stepchild determine which members of her family they wish to invite. If they feel it is important for her parents to attend the wedding, they should be able to invite them. If the parents feel it would be too hard for them to attend, it is their option to decline. Guest lists are not easy, and you should invite people who are important to you, your partner, and your stepchild.

Can You Have a Honeymoon?

Your ability to have a honeymoon depends a lot on the age of your stepchild, the other biological parent, and your schedule. Should you have a honeymoon? Absolutely! Will you possibly need to cut it short or go somewhere close by because of your stepchild? Absolutely! You can still have one—it just might take a little flexibility on your part. If your stepchild is very young, you may need to have a quick weekend away instead of the fourteen-day trip to Greece that would be your ideal honeymoon. It may be very confusing for your stepchild if you leave for two weeks. If the child is preteen or younger, a long honeymoon may be too disruptive for her after such an emotionally charged event. Some children may fear that a biological parent who is getting remarried is abandoning them. If your stepchild feels this way, taking her father away for two weeks is only going to reinforce this fear. Consider taking a few mini honeymoons throughout the year and going away on weekends when your stepchild has plans or is with her other parent. You could also consider taking your honeymoon at a different time, like when your stepchild is away at camp, on a trip with her other biological parent, or somewhere else.

FACT

On January 9, 2006, *Newsweek* published an article entitled "The Family-moon," which discussed the new trend in taking the whole family along to celebrate a second marriage instead of just the bride and groom. The article can be found at *www.newsweek.com/id/47392.*

You may find that you do not want to go on a honeymoon right after the wedding, but instead opt to take a family trip. This is a great idea for some families. It is a way of celebrating your new family and not just your marriage to one another. You should, however, have a honeymoon that is solely for you and your partner, even if it is just one night. It is important to celebrate your union as a couple as well as your coming together as a family. Don't forget about yourselves because you are so busy trying to incorporate or please everyone around you.

Establishing Your Role as Wife or Husband

Now that you are officially married you are officially a parent, with all the benefits of the kids listening to you, respecting you, and calling you Mom, right? Wrong. You may find that not a thing changes once you are married. Or you may find that you are, in fact, treated with less respect, and no one listens to you or even speaks to you. Establishing your new role does not happen once the ring is on your finger; it has been happening during your engagement and will continue throughout your marriage. You are now legally a wife and stepmom, but emotionally this is an adjustment that will take time for everyone—including you.

First of all, you need to get used to the idea of being married and thinking of yourself as a wife or husband. You are still the same person, but now you are officially in your partner's life. You may have been acting much like a wife for the past four years, but now you are legally married. This might feel kind of strange at first, but you will most likely get used to it, and you should definitely make time to enjoy it.

Second, others need to get used to the idea of you being a wife. Your husband now has a wife and is a husband. Your stepchildren may not look at you as their stepmom, but you are now their dad's wife, no matter how they feel about you. Third, your financial position may now be different in the relationship. Sometimes when people are married they combine everything, and your name and your spouse's may now be on the house, the checking account, the bills, and your stepchild's emergency contact information.

Should You Change Your Name?

Many changes may come with your new role. If you are considering changing your name, or if you would like your partner to change her name to your name, this is a conversation that should take place well before the wedding. A biological mother who shares her last name with her children might wish to keep her last name to make things less confusing for her children. She might also decide to hyphenate her name. Try not to take this personally, but instead look at it from her perspective or her children's perspective. It might be quite a struggle for your stepchildren to suddenly have a parent who no longer shares their last name.

Conversely, if you are considering changing your name to your partner and stepchild's last name, find out how they feel about this first. To a child this might feel like you are trying to take the place of their mother. If their mother was always Mrs. Marshall and now you are Mrs. Marshall, it might not sit well with your stepchild. You can always change your name later or find out if hyphenating would be a more comfortable situation for everyone.

Another factor to consider is how the other biological parent might react or feel about you taking on the same name as her children. This doesn't have to be the deciding factor, but if she is keeping the last name, it might help if you don't take it until the children are done with all their schooling so it is not as hurtful for her or as confusing for them.

New Responsibilities

Thinking of yourself as a wife or husband may take some time, whether this is your first marriage or you are becoming a spouse for the fifth time. How you define yourself as a wife or husband is really up to you, and everyone does it a bit differently. There will be outside expectations, and might people will expect you to know certain things about your spouse and your stepchild now that you are in a spousal relationship. You may also be counted on for things you may not have been expected to do before, such as planning your husband's birthday parties, contributing financially to the family, and sending out holiday cards. If this is how you see your role as a spouse, then this should be a rather fun adjustment for you. Many people do not see their role changing much as they go from fiancé to spouse. Instead, they feel it is just a title, and expect things to go on as they always have. Oftentimes, this is because a spouse has already been doing some of the actions typically involved in spousal relationships before the actual wedding date.

Ease Into Being a Family

As mentioned earlier, your stepchildren may not look to you as a stepmom but acknowledge you as their father's wife. Regardless of how your stepchildren think of you, it is important that they show respect by either engaging with you in a positive way or by being courteous enough to avoid you if they cannot stand you or do not approve of your marriage. Your husband may have to talk to them and others about the fact that you are now his wife and he expects some level of civility from them. If they have never been civil to you, they are not going to start now. They may feel that they have to accept you now that it is official, so your relationship may get easier. They may also be so angry that it is official they actually get worse before they get better about accepting you. It can play out in many different ways, and every situation is slightly different.

Now that you are the husband, do not try to change everything and expect everyone to respect you. Do not make your stepchildren start calling you Dad; that is not your choice. Change as little as possible so everyone can get used to their emotions regarding you becoming a husband. For now, keep the house consistent and ease into any changes that may need to happen.

Don't force your stepchildren to accept you immediately; it will take time. Keep being respectful of your spouse, your stepchildren, and the other parent, and hopefully things will fall into place.

CHAPTER 7

Creating Memories with Your Stepchild

Memories are made every day. Most of us strive to attain happy memories, particularly when it comes to our children. Laying the groundwork for creating happy memories can help set the stage for positive moments between you and your stepchild. In order to create these memories, you need to bond with your stepchild in your role as stepparent, which can be fun but also a bit tricky. How do you create new traditions without taking away from old ones? Is there room for you to spend time with your stepchild on holidays? Fitting yourself into your stepchild's life is the key to creating these memories.

Developing a Bond While Respecting the Biological Parent-Child Relationship

Now that you are officially a stepparent, hopefully you are ready to take on this new mentor/parent role in the relationship. What you do not want to do, however, is take the place of a biological parent or compete with the other biological parent for your stepchild's affection. Remember that your relationship with your stepchild is distinct from his relationships with his biological parents.

This goes for the other adults in your stepchild's life as well. His relationship with his mother is their relationship. His relationship with his father is between the two of them. Each relationship is different and there is no need to compare them. Also, if you have more than one stepchild, your relationship with each stepchild will differ. There is no need to compare these relationships either; all you can do is control how you behave in your relationship with your stepchild or stepchildren. It shouldn't matter if your stepchild currently hates his biological mother; your relationship should not benefit because someone else's is suffering.

E-QUESTION

Now that I am a stepmother, shouldn't bonding come easier for me? Not necessarily; in fact, bonding may halt for a while because you are now truly a stepparent. No matter how well the wedding went, your stepchild still has to adjust to you in this new role. She may take a step back before she is ready to bond with you as a stepparent. Be patient and don't hurry the relationship.

Respect Everyone's Feelings

How do you do this? You should be sensitive to the biological parents in the situation. It is not likely your stepchild will pit you against your partner during times when your partner and stepchild do not see eye to eye. It is likely, however, that your stepchild, often unknowingly, will pit you against the other biological parent. If you have a fifteen-year-old stepdaughter who hates her mother because, "she is stupid and I hate her because she is stupid," then she may come to you to vent about how stupid her mom is. This is fine in some respects, because you are an adult from whom she may be seeking feedback, and venting may help her do this. However, if you agree with her that her mom is stupid you have crossed a line and will be disrespecting her relationship with her biological mother. Instead of agreeing that her mom is stupid, tell her that you understand she is feeling angry with her mom but you are sure her mom is trying her hardest, and maybe they are just going through a rocky time in their relationship. You can be supportive of your stepchild by listening to her and suggesting ways to better communicate with her mother, and at the same time respect her relationship with her mother by not saying anything negative about her mom or her actions.

What if your stepdaughter's mother did something mean and you want to agree with your stepdaughter to make her feel better? You can tell your stepdaughter that you understand why her mother's actions made her feel sad or mad, but avoid saying that mom is mean, stupid, bad, or cruel—even if she is. The way to avoid this is to focus on your stepdaughter's feelings in relation to her mother's actions. This way, if you speak with her mother, you can say, "When you called Tricia a brat, it really hurt her feelings" instead of, "You are so mean; I can't believe you called Tricia a brat. She thinks you are cruel, and so do I." By doing this, you continue to respect their relationship even if you disagree with the way her mother handles things.

Forming a New Bond

Once you have the respect piece of the relationship down, you should work on how to bond with your stepchild. If you have been involved with your stepchild for years, this may have already happened and will probably continue. If, however, it has not been smooth sailing, you may have to force the issue. Don't deceive your stepchild into bonding with you, but you may have to plan some outings or activities that are out of the norm. One of the best ways to bond with your stepchild is to take an interest in something that interests her. If she loves horses, read about them so you can converse with her about them. Let your stepchild further educate you about the topic. Mention that you have read about a new method of training horses, and ask if she knows anything about it, or simply ask what kind of horse is her favorite.

Kids love to have a captive audience—even if they generally hate you. Any adult who will listen to them without judging, looking bored, or acting like they already know the information or know more information will gain points with most kids. Not many people really listen to kids and hear what they are saying. If you do this, you are on your way to creating a bond even if your stepchild doesn't think she wants one. An ear that is willing to listen is hard to resist.

When you listen to your stepchild, do not try to solve her problems. Listen; don't cut her off, and don't tell her you know how she is feeling. Listen to her and keep your mouth shut. Tell her you understand that she is feeling sad or mad, but don't tell her you know exactly how she feels—you don't. Listen to her, and you will speak volumes without saying a word.

If you have a hard time even getting your stepchild to sit in the same room as you, offer to drive her somewhere next time she wants to go out. Car time is precious, especially with teenagers. The car is nonthreatening; there is an end in sight, a radio or scenery for distraction, and she is not even required to make eye contact with you. You may even find that the only time you seem to get along with your stepchild is in the car. For now, that is fine. Build your relationship however you can. If she offers you five minutes, take them and don't push for ten.

What Should the Child Call You?

What your stepchild calls you depends more on you when the child is younger and more on her as she gets older. It also depends on the entire family situation. If your stepchild never knew her mother and you are the only mother figure she has, she may end up calling you Mom, if it is okay with you and everyone else. If it feels weird for you, it is fine for you to ask her to call you something else. Don't suggest your stepchild call you Mom if no one else has suggested it. As much as you may want to be called Mom, you are not her mom and there is someone else who is—deserving or not.

Some ideas for what your stepchild might call you may include: your first name; your initials; a nickname (not a mean one!) she made up for you; whatever garbling a toddler may come up with; or an agreed-upon term of endearment.

If your stepchild is calling you Mommy and it makes you cringe in dic comfort, do not have an obvious negative reaction, if at all possible. Your stepchild may be trying to let you know she respects you and thinks highly of you. Be gentle when you approach her about what she calls you, and make it a positive change by letting her create a fun nickname for you.

Depending on your relationship, your stepchild may not want to address you at all, except to mutter a few choice nicknames under her breath when she passes by. If this is where you are in your relationship, let it go for now and don't react—at least by calling you Stepmonster or Wicked Witch she is acknowledging your existence. Although these nicknames are far from your hopeful nickname of CJ or Rock Star, you have to start somewhere. In the future, you may even laugh about being called Stepmonster, and it could turn into a term of endearment.

Holiday Ideas with Your Stepchild

Who spends which holiday where will depend primarily on the custody arrangement. It is likely that these arrangements have been made prior to your arrival. It is helpful for everyone to know the plan ahead of time so they can schedule their holiday festivities. If you can plan holidays far in advance, you will prevent a great deal of confusion and avoid potential arguments. Once you have planned them, put them in writing and remind each other who goes where before the holiday arrives.

Sharing Holidays

Most parents want to be with their child on the big holidays. If the court is not involved and there is no fixed schedule, you may have to compromise. Perhaps the child can spend Thanksgiving with Mom one year then Dad the next, or he could spend every Thanksgiving with Mom and every Christmas with Dad. Families choose different plans for different reasons, but you can still celebrate the holiday with your stepchild even if he is not there on the actual day.

Stressful holidays require creativity. If you know your holiday schedule for the year, it will be easier for you to be creative. If you will not see your stepson on Thanksgiving, consider having a second Thanksgiving by cooking a turkey a week or even a month before or after. When he goes to his other biological parent's house, you could call and ask if you could send over a dessert or flowers. If the answer is no, respect that, but if it is yes, this can be a way of being involved and contributing to your stepson's holiday without being there.

FACT

Lizzie Capuzzi, a daughter and stepdaughter, is credited with creating the official Stepmother's Day. Lizzie wrote a letter to her state senator requesting a holiday to celebrate her special relationship with her stepmother. His response was to announce on the Senate floor that the "Sunday after Mother's Day would now be Stepmother's Day." To read the story, go to *www.annieshomepage.com/stepmothersday2.html.*

Holidays also provide a perfect opportunity to get your stepson involved with your extended family. If Easter is a big holiday for your biological family, see if you can incorporate your stepchild into your family's traditions. Maybe your parents have a huge egg hunt in their neighborhood for all their grandchildren; if so, bring your stepson along and begin to include him as part of the family. It may seem awkward at first, but, after a while, he may become one of the regulars and even look forward to spending time with your extended family.

Mother's Day and Father's Day may be the most emotionally loaded holidays in stepfamilies. Cards and gifts designated for stepmoms and stepdads are available; however, it isn't a holiday you should expect to be all about you. Instead, remind your stepchild that these holidays are coming and help him brainstorm ideas for his biological parents. If he happens to buy you a card or gift enjoy it; but if he does not, don't worry—it may only mean that he thinks of you in a way that is different from the way he thinks about his biological parents.

Combining families of different faiths can be challenging, but it can also open up many possibilities with respect to celebrating holidays. Encourage children in the family to educate other family members—stepsiblings, stepgrandparents, and other biological parents—about different religious traditions celebrated in their families. This can be very fun for everyone. If the biological parents are arguing about which religious traditions to celebrate, let the biological parents handle the decision making.

Stepsiblings

If you have brought a biological child into the relationship as well, be sure to work on coordinating the holidays so this child has an opportunity to celebrate at least some holidays with his half-siblings and/or stepsiblings. Holidays can often help half-siblings and stepsiblings bond by providing celebratory time together. Unfortunately, holidays can also be difficult times for stepsiblings. If a stepchild is only there during visitation and your biological children live with you, your stepchild may feel that he doesn't fit in at the house and holidays may feel more stressful than happy.

This brings up the importance of your stepchild feeling as if your home is his home as well. If he has somewhere to sleep when he is there, a toothbrush that stays at the home, and his favorite foods in the kitchen, then he is probably in a good frame of mind to enjoy holiday celebrations. This same scenario can unravel in the opposite way as well. If you feel as though you do not see your stepchild enough because he doesn't live with you, you may overcompensate by buying him extra gifts, cooking only what he likes, or paying more attention to him. It is a tricky balance. Your child and your stepchild will usually point out if they are feeling left out, but be sure to learn from your mistakes!

New Traditions with Your Stepchild

One way of bonding with your stepchild is to begin creating your own traditions outside of the holidays and other celebrations. These traditions may come about naturally. You may already have established traditions that you don't even recognize as such. Perhaps on Thursday nights you and your stepdaughter watch *Jeopardy!* together and keep score. That is the fun part about traditions; they often come out of something you already enjoy doing together. If you cannot think of any traditions already in place, you can create some.

New ideas will have a greater chance of sticking if everyone involved finds them enjoyable. If you know your stepdaughter enjoys art, you could make every second Sunday of the month a Visit-an-Art-Museum Day. The two of you—or everyone in the family—could participate. It is a good idea to have some that include everyone in the family and some that are enjoyed just between you and your stepchild.

Taking the Lead

Creating and nurturing these traditions will be primarily your responsibility. Remember, you are the adult, and children often get bored or act a little lazy. If your stepchild seems bored and annoyed every time you go to an art museum and doesn't perk up once you are viewing the exhibits, it is time to decide whether this is a tradition you want to pursue. Talk to your stepchild; it could be that going to the art museum on Saturdays instead of Sundays might help because Sundays are homework days. Everyone has natural high and low points during a day; perhaps your outings are occurring at a time of day when your stepchild typically experiences low points. Be sure to have fun during outings, and don't take them too seriously. If it feels forced your stepchild will sense it. You may try ten trial traditions that don't work before you find one that does work. Laugh about it; you could even create a Bad Tradition Day. More than finding the perfect tradition, time with your stepchild is what counts. She will recognize your effort (she may never tell you this!), but she will appreciate it.

Appreciating Past Traditions

Families often have traditions they don't recognize as such. If a divorce or death derailed your stepchild's original family, many of these traditions may have been disrupted. Your stepchild will not only miss the consistency of his original family unit, but also the traditions that they practiced together. It is important to talk to both biological parents, if possible, about traditions they think he may be missing. The biological parents may recognize he misses going to his favorite ice cream place every time the Red Sox play the Yankees, like they used to do when they were all together. Instead of copying this tradition exactly, think about creating a similar tradition. For example, you could put the radio on at home whenever the two teams play and grill hamburgers. After the game, your stepchild may go out to the ice cream place with your partner or the other biological parent. Traditions that are saved should be saved in ways that are respectful of everyone involved. By attempting to save traditions, but perhaps adopting them in slightly modified form, you are also helping to maintain consistency in your stepchild's life.

ALERT!

Don't take over old traditions. If you try to push your way into sacred traditions, you will do more harm than good. If a tradition seems particularly sentimental for your stepchild, let her invite you to participate before barging in.

If a parent has died, your stepchild and your partner may do something every month to celebrate the parent who has passed. Instead of trying to get involved in the tradition, you may give them space to continue with this tradition on their own. If you would like to acknowledge this tradition, you can ask your partner if it would be appropriate to have flowers on the table every time they take part in the tradition or if you can add a bouquet of flowers to take to the gravesite. Ideas like this may seem innocent and unobjectionable, but depending on where your stepchild is in the grieving process, they may not go over well. To avoid mishaps, speak with your partner first and follow her recommendation.

What Not to Do with Your Stepchild

This list could go on forever, unfortunately. Some items on the list are obvious and some may not be obvious. The tough part for you is that you probably want your stepchild to like you, and acts that seem relatively harmless can be horribly detrimental if they play out poorly. The top ten don'ts are the following:

1. Do not buy your stepchild alcohol or drugs.
2. Do not provide your stepchild with birth control unless approved by a biological parent.
3. Do not lie for your stepchild (unless you are planning a surprise party or something along those lines).
4. Do not party with an underage stepchild.
5. Do not discuss your marital stress with your stepchild.
6. Do not criticize either biological parent to your stepchild.
7. Do not become involved in a sexual relationship with your stepchild or his friends.
8. Do not undermine anything the biological parents have said or done.
9. Do not use your stepchild to get back at either biological parent.
10. Do not physically or emotionally harm your stepchild.

Although some of these may sound ridiculous, they may not be in some situations. For instance, suppose you are at a family party and everyone is imbibing. Your sixteen-year-old stepson asks, "Can I have just one beer?" You may think, "What is the harm? One beer is fine. Everyone else is letting their kids drink a little, plus I've seen his mother give him a beer before, so why not?" His mother may then show up at the party earlier than expected and see her son with a beer. When she asks where he got the beer and learns you said he could have one, this won't help your relationship with your stepson or his mother. Do not get sucked into these sorts of predicaments. Before making decisions, think about how everyone would react if you did any of the above, and how you would feel if someone allowed your child to do any of those things.

Children who feel they have an adult to talk to about issues such as sex and drugs are less likely to engage in high-risk behaviors than children who feel as though they cannot talk to the adults in their lives. Be that caring, communicative adult if you can.

Birth Control

The issue of birth control is one of the most challenging issues for stepparents. It may seem like common sense to provide your stepchild with birth control, whether condoms, pills, or any other contraception, but this is a shaky area. At least one of the biological parents should know before you help your stepchild obtain birth control. It is likely that your stepchild feels more comfortable talking to you about birth control since you are not his parent. It's great that he feels he can trust you. You don't want to break his trust by running to one of his parents to tell them he's having sex.

You can act as a mediator of sorts if your stepchild is okay with you discussing this with either parent. If he is unsure, you can bring up to either parent that Johnny's friends seem like they are talking about sex a lot, or spending a significant amount of time with their partners. You can then suggest that you have a discussion with your stepson if the biological parent is comfortable with you having such a discussion. This can open up the lines of communication and may help your stepson speak with his biological parents. If there is no way you can talk to either biological parent, you can encourage your stepchild to see his doctor, school counselor, or school nurse, who can have that type of conversation with him and provide contraception or tell him where he can access birth control.

If you think for a second that you may be providing your stepchild with something either biological parent would not approve of, then don't. It may appear to disrupt your relationship with your stepchild at first, but as time goes on, it will only earn you the respect of your stepchild and the biological parents. Being consistent, safe, trustworthy, and open to new experiences is the best way to set the stage for bonding with your stepchild. Give it time and enjoy the process.

CHAPTER 8

Rules and Discipline

Everyone has different ideas about establishing rules and disciplining children. When stepparents are involved, rule setting and discipline can become even more confusing. There are more adults in the mix telling your stepchild what to do, and each adult may have a different set of rules. When there is more than one child, you may find that not only are the rules different for each adult, they may also be different for each child. It is important to create a consistent plan of rule setting and discipline so that your stepchild knows what to expect from everyone involved with her care.

Who's in Charge?

Children usually spend more time with one parent than the other; the parent who is with them the most tends to be the disciplinarian. When stepparents are introduced into the mix, there may be one or more of four people at any time in charge. If you are in the custodial home, you will probably be in charge of discipline at some point, especially if you are caretaking a younger stepchild. The chance of being the only adult with your stepdaughter is greater in this situation.

As the child ages, you will have less time alone with her, simply because of her calendar of school schedules, social events, and other activities. If you are not in the custodial home and your stepdaughter visits only on weekends, your time in charge is likely to be minimal since your partner is likely to be with you when your stepchild is present. Again, as your stepchild ages, you will be even less likely to be the disciplinarian.

Great ways to decrease negative behaviors include: ignoring the behavior; redirecting your stepchild; removing your stepchild from the situation; and praising positive behaviors. Start with these first and see if they work. It can be helpful if there is more than one child in the house. Each child can witness what behaviors you praise and, based on such observations, work to obtain positive reactions from you.

When You Are Often in Charge

There are many different scenarios, and they can all be rather tricky. If you are going to be alone with your stepchild often, then you are going to end up being in charge. To make sure your stepchild is aware that there are times when you will be in charge, you and your partner should discuss this with her. Explain that you are the adult in the house and need to enforce the rules in order to keep her as safe as possible. Your stepdaughter may tell you she does not need to follow your rules since you are not her mother. You can agree with her that you are not her mother, and explain to her that these rules aren't yours, but rules of the house that you are enforcing since you are the adult in charge.

It is extremely helpful if you have your partner back you up, and if he continues to back you up when you try to enforce the rules. If you also have the support of the other biological parent, it will be easier for you to follow through on enforcing the rules. Discipline is much easier, even for the child, when everyone is on the same page.

When You Are Rarely in Charge

If you are rarely in charge and most of your time with your stepchild is spent with your partner as well, then let him handle discipline. You can be supportive of his discipline, but there is little need for you to become the main disciplinarian when a biological parent is around. During times that you are the only adult, look at it as a babysitting type of discipline. You are in charge in the moment and will enforce the rules; however, any long-term consequence can wait until your partner returns. Hopefully, you will not have to be the lone disciplinarian in any situation, and you will have support from both biological parents in instances where both are alive and involved with the rearing of the child.

If You Married the Lenient Biological Parent

You may have caught on early in the relationship that your partner is the lenient parent. However, it can be relatively easy to miss if you haven't spent much time with your stepchild, so this may come as a surprise for some stepparents. Watching how your partner disciplines his child can explain quite a bit about your stepchild's behavior. It can also help you prepare for challenges you may face if the two of you choose to have your own children.

If your partner is lenient, you are going to have to figure out why he is lenient. Does he avoid disciplining his child because he has limited time with his child and doesn't want to spend that time disciplining? Is he lazy about discipline and doesn't enforce a long-term grounding because it is just too much work for him? Has your partner given up on discipline since nothing has ever seemed to work? Getting to the root of why your partner is lenient will help you figure out the best way to approach him about changing his ways.

Your partner's lenience is not something to blame on your stepchild. If he is lenient when your stepchild does something awful to you but tough at other times, this is still not your stepchild's fault. This is an adult issue and should remain that way.

Having a nonconfrontational conversation with your partner can help you figure out his motivation. If you simply note that he doesn't stick to grounding, or that he lets his child get away with things that surprise you, you are likely to create an open dialogue. If you approach your partner in the heat of the moment by expressing with exasperation, "You never follow through on your consequences! No wonder your daughter is such a monster!" the lines of communication may not flow. Once you have this conversation, you can then have a conversation on the importance of discipline and consistency in your stepchild's life. He may not believe you at first, and he may resist becoming the bad guy; however, over time he will find that by enforcing rules and disciplining his child consistently, he will not be a bad guy, but a safe parent.

Creating a Consistent Pattern of Discipline

Consistency in discipline is the key to success. It can be challenging to implement, but very rewarding once it has become a pattern. The biggest obstacle to consistency is not kids, but adults. Adults get lazy, tired, and frustrated. It can be a lot easier to give in to a child when you have had a long day. You cannot be lazy about discipline, and neither can the other disciplinarians in the child's life. Will you have an off day every now and then? Probably, but the less this happens the easier it will be to discipline your stepchild.

One of the best examples of consistency in discipline is seen in classroom management. If you reflect on your own schooling or have recently visited a classroom, you may have noted that teachers who are clear about classroom expectations often have calmer classrooms. The teacher who always makes his students raise their hands before asking a question will have a quieter classroom. If he consistently does not respond to students who talk out of turn, the students will learn to raise their hands. Teachers often have charts or posters on their walls that break down expectations and describe in detail exactly what will happen if those expectations aren't met. As long as these signs are not just for show, this teacher probably has a well-managed classroom.

E-QUESTION

You don't really expect me to write these rules down, do you?
Yes! They don't have to be displayed for the world to see at all times, but having a written rule book that is easily accessible can be helpful to everyone. When someone does slide, you may be surprised to see who points out the consequences in writing.

When kids know the expectations and the adult is consistent, kids feel safe. Feeling safe creates an environment where even the most hyperactive student doesn't feel the need to act out. Classrooms that are poorly managed, with teachers who let kids slide here and there, do not feel safe for students. They do not know when they will get in trouble for certain actions or when the teacher will look the other way.

Implementing a strict but fair code of discipline is exhausting at first, but more so for you than for your stepchild. Is he going to push every limit and test you to see if you are consistent? Probably. Will he "tell on you" if you do let something slide that his biological parent did not, even if he begged you to let it slide? Absolutely. This is one of the reasons it is important for everyone to maintain the same rules and consequences. Any variation in the consequences is an issue you will have to deal with on an adult level. Kids crave consistency and order, and you and your partner need to stay united when you discipline.

Including the Other Biological Parent in Discipline Decisions

In a perfect world, you will have the same exact rules with the same exact consequences in each house, and you will communicate after every visit so consequences are enforced and everyone is on the same playing field. However, this probably won't happen; it is hard enough to be united in one house. If the consequence is small and will only occur at your house, you can mention to the other biological parent that it happened, but there isn't much reason to tell him prior to implementing the consequence. On the other hand, if you are working on decreasing a specific behavior of your stepchild's—like kicking or biting—and everyone is on board, it is important to keep the lines of communication open about the behavior. The other biological parent should be informed that Dylan bit four people over the weekend, and only stopped biting when he lost his video game privileges in addition to a time-out. This will help him enforce consequences at home. It may also lead to a change in consequences. All the parental figures may need to get together and figure out a new consequence for Dylan's biting behavior. It is also important that the other biological parent shares your stepchild's behavior with you and your partner. This will help you maintain consistency.

Don't postpone your stepchild's consequence unless he is old enough to understand. When children are young, they won't make the connection between the consequence and the behavior if they are too far apart. Teenagers can manage a bigger lapse, as long as they are informed in advance that there will be a consequence if they engage in a certain behavior.

It is extremely important to involve the other biological parent in discipline decisions when it may affect him. If your stepson sneaks out of your house on a weekend and you and your partner want to ground him for the next week, you need to talk to the other biological parent about this before setting forth the consequence with your stepson if your stepson is going to be at the other biological parent's house for part of the grounding period. You may discover that the other biological parent was planning a night out on Thursday and was going to leave your stepson home alone. In this case, you can volunteer to have your stepson come back to your house for that night or come up with a consequence that will not include Thursday, so the other parent's plans are not disrupted. Also, the other parent may have already planned a fun weekend getaway for himself and your stepson. If this is the case, you don't have to take this away from him, but be creative with the other parent to create an appropriate consequence for your stepson.

Behavior Plans

Behavior plans are fun and useful. Involve your stepchild in creating a behavior plan—it shouldn't be something you come up with on your own or with the other biological parent. Your stepchild should be part of the process, and can give suggestions on consequences. Many times, you will find that the consequence your stepchild chooses will be harsher or longer in duration than what you may have chosen. When creating behavior plans, keep in mind that you want to provide opportunities for your stepchild to earn rewards as well. Focusing primarily on negative behaviors is discouraging for everyone.

Ideas for Creative Behavior Plans

What should a behavior plan look like? It can be a notebook that travels back and forth with your stepchild from house to house, a poster board with a sticker chart for positive behaviors, or a calendar with marks representing good and bad behaviors. Brainstorming as a family will help everyone figure out an effective format. Maybe your stepdaughter is a huge baseball fan. If so, then you might create a chart that has baseball terms or even a baseball field with a figure of her that can be moved around on the field (Velcro works great for this). When she does something positive like brushing her teeth without being asked, she earns a single. You can record her single on a chart and also move her figure to first base. If she then bites her sister, she may go back to the dugout for getting caught trying to steal a base.

This is definitely the fun part about behavior charts, and kids really get into them and will check to see that you are doing your job by keeping track of their behaviors. Make sure that you have a cheat sheet of what her behaviors will earn. For example, brushing her teeth might be a single, biting might be a stolen base as well as a time-out that she must serve while her Velcro person serves time in the dugout, etc. A day with no negative behaviors may earn her a homerun, which could mean choice seating on the couch the next time her favorite team plays.

When thinking of rewards for your stepchild, try to avoid using food as a reward, as this can set your child up for issues related to food and eating later in life. Rewards can be time alone with a parent, first choice next time you go to the movies, time at the park, or an extra trip to the library for a new book. Make rewards as inexpensive as possible for your own sake, and so your stepchild doesn't come to expect gifts for good behavior.

Visual charts are the most useful and fun for many children. You can make them less childish as your stepchild gets older, but even adults enjoy seeing their progress visually, if possible. Simple charts with star stickers can work wonders for any age. If you are trying to change a behavior, you could even use a behavior chart and ask your stepchild to hold you accountable. If you are trying to lose weight, for example, your stepchild can help you reward yourself with stickers on the days that you work out. It can be fun to have the whole family involved when working with behavior.

Short and Effective Consequences for Short-Term Visits

If your stepchild only visits on weekends or even less, you are not going to want to spend all of your time disciplining or following through on consequences he earned in his short time with you. Starting each visit with reminders of how much fun it is when his behavior is positive can be very helpful. If he behaved well the last time he visited, you can point that out in an observant way: "Remember last weekend? We had so much fun and you were so helpful with your little sister when we had to wait longer than we wanted to at the restaurant." If the weekend before didn't go well, don't bring up your stepchild's negative behaviors. Instead, focus on the parts of the weekend that were positive. If you start your visit by saying something like, "I hope you don't spend your whole weekend in time-out like you did last time," you may have just encouraged negative behavior. Let your stepchild start with a clean slate when he visits.

FACT

Time-out should be given in minutes and immediately after the negative behavior. If your stepchild is five years old, the time-out should be five minutes. If he is six years old, it should be for six minutes, and so on.

Young Children

It is easier to find short-term consequences when it comes to younger children. They will only connect their consequence to the behavior for a short time anyway, so any prolonged consequence will be lost on them. Time-out is a quick and efficient consequence. Make sure the time-out seat is somewhere safe, but also removed from any fun distractions like video games or television. Many parents send their children to their rooms, only to discover that is not a punishment but a reward, because they have fun toys and gadgets in their rooms or privacy to be on the phone. Consider not using a child's room as punishment so your stepchild is not confused about what his room represents. If you do have to use your stepchild's room for consequences, make sure you take any fun items out of the room before he goes up there.

Older Children

With older children, effective consequences can be to take away their access to their cell phone or computer for a period of time. It is like a time-out, but just from their most coveted possession. Talking about the problem behavior is also appropriate. Point out why the behavior is negative, what it was that upset you about the behavior, and why it shouldn't be repeated. The older the child, the longer you can wait before addressing the behavior in a conversation.

Clean Slate

Once the consequence has been served, move on and give your stepchild a clean slate. It will probably be easier for you to move on than for a child to move on, but if he sees that you still care about him and love him, he will likely move on as well. Holding grudges and being angry after the consequence is over will only punish your stepchild and disrupt your relationship.

In a situation where you cannot get over the anger very quickly or your feelings are very hurt, talk about this with both your partner and your stepchild. Tell him you appreciate that he followed through with his consequence, but that your feelings are still bothering you so you need a time-out for yourself. Be sure to reiterate that you do not hate him and will not be mad at him forever, but you just need a little more time to feel better about the situation.

CHAPTER 9

The Infant and Toddler Stepchild

Every age range comes with its own set of challenges and nuances. With the infant and toddler stepchild, you won't have to deal with a child talking back, but you may need to interact more frequently with the other biological parent than you would if your stepchild were any other age. Infants and toddlers can be a handful. If you do not have children of your own, learning how to handle an infant or a toddler may seem overwhelming. If you do have children of your own and have been through the infant and toddler years, you may need to be extra careful that you don't impose your own ideas about parenting onto the child or other biological parent.

Infant and Toddler Basics

Children included in the infant and toddler category for purposes of this book are under four years old. Taking care of children in this age group involves all sorts of fun activities, like waking up in the middle of the night for feedings and diaper changes, helping the child learn to crawl, walk, and talk, etc. There are many milestones that occur in these four years for which you need to be prepared.

CPR and First Aid

The first recommendation is to get trained in infant and child CPR and first aid. That way, if there is an emergency you will feel prepared; being trained appropriately can also give you peace of mind. Even if there is animosity between you and the other biological parent, he may rest a bit easier knowing you are serious and responsible with respect to caring for his child. Make sure you also have a list of emergency contacts handy, including the biological parent's work and phone numbers, the pediatrician's name and number, poison control, emergency services such as police, fire, and paramedics, and the name and number of the nearest children's hospital.

E-QUESTION

Where can I find a CPR or first-aid class?
You can find CPR and first-aid classes by contacting the American Red Cross or your local YMCA, fire department, hospital, or community center. They are typically very friendly, and are invested in trying to educate everyone—including those without any training or experience. They can allay some of your fears and equip you with tools you may need in an emergency.

Everyday Necessities

Take a crash course with a friend or family member on diaper changing. It takes practice, so you may not be a pro with one crash course, but at least you will know which side is the front of the diaper. You also need to learn how to operate the gear most used for your stepchild—like the car seat, stroller, swing, and carrier. These often have difficult-to-secure latches and other gadgets, and how to open and close such devices may not be obvious at all. It is best to learn how to safely and effectively use such things before you actually need them, when you may have a crying or cranky infant or toddler distracting you. Car seats can be especially tricky, but once you learn how to use the snaps or grips, you will find them much easier to maneuver.

Babyproof your house if your stepchild will be visiting or staying with you. At the infant stage, he probably won't be very mobile, but the crawling and walking stages happen so quickly that it's best to go ahead and take all the precautions ahead of time.

Baby-Proofing Checklist

❑ Check all the cabinets and drawers in the house. Buy safety latches to make them more difficult to open.

❑ Buy doorknob covers or doorknobs with locks to make rooms more difficult to access.

❑ Install safety gates to keep a child from stairwells, rooms that might have dangerous objects, or any other place you do not want your stepchild to have access to.

❑ Use outlet covers for any exposed outlet in the house.

❑ Check your furniture for sharp or hard edges, especially end tables and coffee tables. Use bumper covers to make them safer for your stepchild.

❑ Keep windows safe by installing window guards so your stepchild cannot open them on his own.

❑ If you have window blinds, cut the cord or keep it wrapped and out of reach to prevent strangulation.

❑ Lock all cleaning products, medicines, and alcohol in cabinets that are out of reach.

❑ Keep small or fragile objects out of reach or locked away. Always check your floor for any object a child might pick up and pop in his mouth.

❑ If you have furniture your stepchild might use to help him stand, make sure it is sturdy enough to support him or attach it to the wall with furniture ties.

❑ Check your fire, smoke, and carbon monoxide detectors to make sure they are working correctly.

Finally, find out everything you possibly can from your stepchild's parents:

- Does your stepchild have allergies?
- Does his mother want him eating only organic food?
- What is his schedule for naps, eating, and bedtime?
- Does the parent have any helpful tips for getting him to burp, sleep, or stop crying?
- What do you need when you take your stepchild out and about?

These are probably the most important things for you to learn. Every child is different; it will take time for everyone to figure out what this baby's different cries sound like, when he is sleepy, or when he wants to play in his swing. For now, especially if you are new at this, taking notes will be a good idea. You may deal with some ridicule from your partner or the other biological parent, but it is better to be prepared than to be stuck with a crying baby at the grocery store with no diaper bag and no idea how to soothe her.

Have two of everything. If you are caring for the child for visitation only, buy everything that the custodial parent has in the diaper bag. Buy a second of his favorite blanket, toy, pacifier, etc. If you can afford it, purchase another car seat, stroller, and carrier. Being equipped as if your stepchild is with you full time will help you avoid desperate phone calls to the other biological parent when you realize that you left his favorite blanky at the other house.

If you are really uncomfortable about taking on an infant or toddler stepchild, be honest with your partner about this. Don't stay alone with your stepchild until you feel comfortable doing so. It is much better to delay your first time alone with the stepchild than to try to prove that you are ready to take on this responsibility when you are not. The infant and toddler section of the bookstore is extensive; at the outset, pick one or two well-respected books and read them, but reading too much information can be confusing instead of clarifying. You can always return to the store later and buy more books. As mentioned earlier, every child is different; give yourself time to get to know your stepchild and you are soon likely to feel comfortable.

What Is Your Role with a Child Under Four?

A child this young is not going to understand who you are in relation to him or his family. He also won't understand why his parents don't live together, or even notice that other people's parents do live together. Since he doesn't have much of a social circle yet, you probably won't need to address questions like this until he starts preschool and starts recognizing that some parents live together but his do not. For now, you are an adult in his life who helps take care of him. The amount of caretaking you do will vary greatly depending on your custodial situation. If you are married to the custodial parent, you will take part in more parental activities. If your partner does not have custody but does have visitation, you may never have to change a diaper or wake up four times a night to attend to your stepchild. You may feel more like a babysitter and less like a parental figure. No matter how often you see your stepchild or how much you are involved, it is just as important to be a safe and healthy adult for your stepchild.

E-QUESTION

What if my toddler stepchild is sick? Is it my responsibility to take him to the doctor?
If your partner is not available, reach out to the other biological parent. Ask how she would like to proceed. She may want to take the child to the doctor herself, or she may request that you meet her with the child at the doctor's office. In case of emergency, make sure you have your stepchild's emergency phone numbers at all times. If this is an urgent emergency, call 911 and the biological parents.

As the stepparent to a child under four, you may end up taking on a significant piece of child rearing that you have no familiarity with at all—such as teaching the child to use a potty, eat with utensils, and to walk. Hopefully, your partner will play an active role, allowing you to follow his lead and support the lessons he is teaching his child. If you feel you are the more hands-on parent, make sure you follow the same patterns that the other biological parent would like implemented. For example, if she asks your stepchild if he needs to use the bathroom fifteen minutes after he eats or before leaving the house, make sure you do this, too. This will help establish consistency between the two houses at an early age. The more consistent you are, the less disrupted his life will feel.

Since he probably doesn't understand who you are in relation to his biological parents, he may be confused about what to call you. He may accidentally call you Mom or Dada, not realizing that you are neither his mother nor his father. Discuss with your partner, and maybe the other biological parent, what your stepchild should call you. If the other biological parent is not involved or is deceased, it may be more appropriate for your stepchild to call you a parental name than in other situations. If you do not want to be labeled in a parental way, you can come up with an alternative name that feels comfortable for everyone involved.

Being Sensitive to the Other Biological Parent

If your stepchild is an infant and the other biological parent is not deceased, it is obvious the breakup was rather recent. As a consequence, emotions may be running higher than in other stepfamily situations. It is important for you to be sensitive about this, and to parent in a way that keeps in mind the heightened emotions. If you are in a noncustodial situation, the other biological parent may request that you not be present during visitations, which the courts may approve for the time being. Keep in mind that she is probably hurting and is also afraid you may somehow bond with her child in a way she doesn't feel she can deal with at the moment. Although you may not see it this way, it is possible that she sees you as someone who stole her husband and could potentially "steal" her child, too.

Seeing you bond with her infant would probably be painful even if the breakup had been a mutual agreement. You cannot completely understand how she is feeling, and you should try to be as respectful as possible of her emotions. In time, she may feel more comfortable with you being involved with her child, especially if she can see you as someone who wants what is best for her child. If she sees you as someone who is in competition with her for her child's affection, it isn't likely she will want you around her child.

Even if everything with the breakup was fine and both biological parents are happy they are no longer together, the other biological parent may still have fears about leaving her child with you. Infants cannot speak or verbalize to their parents what happens in their day when their parent is not there. This is a big fear for a parent; not only is she letting you care for her child, she is trusting that everything is safe while her child is with you. Once a child is older, he can tell his parents if someone hurt him, but for now, when your stepchild is in your care the other biological parent has to trust that you are a safe person to care for her child. This alone is a huge obstacle for any parent; if there is any history of abuse within the family or if the breakup was emotionally charged, this obstacle will be even bigger. Time to get over wounds and getting to know and trust you as a caretaker may be the only factors that will make the other biological parent more comfortable with the situation.

Drinking, using drugs, and having all-night parties should not even come to mind when you are caring for your stepchild. If you feel you cannot stop these behaviors in yourself, be responsible enough to tell the other parent that you are not ready to care for his child because of these issues. Consider going to counseling or talking to your primary care physician if you are having a hard time giving up these behaviors.

As the other biological parent does try and trust you, be flexible when it comes to her calling to check in and make sure everything is going well. Also, if there were any guidelines to follow, be sure to follow them. If your stepson is to go down for a nap at three in the afternoon, don't wait until four o'clock because you are playing or put him down at two o'clock because a good game is on television. The more you comply with the other biological parent's schedule for her child, the more likely she will be to feel comfortable with you caring for her child.

Keep a Notebook

Since your stepchild is so young, try to share with the other biological parent how following the schedule went and maybe even note it in a notebook. Having a notebook that travels back and forth with an infant or toddler can help everyone feel more involved when they are not able to be with the child. If your stepson looks like he is about to take his first steps, put that in the notebook. You can share this notebook with your stepchild when he grows up as a fun memoir. A notebook can also be a respectful way of sharing information when the relationship between you and the other biological parent is somewhat tense. It may lead to opening up the gates of communication so you can move on to speaking to one another.

FACT

Dr. Peter Marshall, author of *Cinderella Revisited*, says that it's important to recognize the differences between blended families and nuclear ones. "I think the biggest mistake that stepparents make is trying to make the stepfamily just like a carbon copy of a nuclear family. Stepfamilies are not the same as nuclear families. They are very different. The biggest mistake people make is having a preset notion of what a stepfamily is and forcing it to fit into a mould which very often it cannot fit into."

When You Disagree with How the Biological Parents Are Parenting

You may find that you were not raised the way your stepchild is being raised, or that you did not raise your own biological children the way your stepchild is being raised. In many cases, you don't have the right to say much of anything. If your children were raised on breast milk only, it is not up to you to tell the biological mother of your stepchild that she is any less of a parent for using formula. It is her decision. If your partner would prefer your stepchild be entertained with classical music instead of television, do not "sneak" television time in when she is at the grocery store. The biological parents are still the primary decision makers in the child's life. If you are bringing a great deal of experience to the table, you can suggest certain approaches if they seem to be struggling, but don't be a know-it-all or try to impose your ideas on them when they are not invited.

Abuse

One of the only times you must make a stand as far as commenting on parenting is if you suspect or know there is some sort of abuse going on by either one of the biological parents. If it is the other biological parent, you need to discuss the situation immediately with your partner. In a case that already has court involvement, call your attorney or court-appointed social worker to make them aware of the situation. Follow their guidelines as far as continuing visitation or keeping the child with you. If the case does not already have court involvement but abuse is occurring, you can call the child protective services agency in your area and report the abuse. If you do not call or take steps to protect your stepchild, the office of protective services can find you guilty of neglect or abuse.

Remember, you are protecting the child, and in abusive situations the child is your number one concern. Do NOT try to mediate the situation yourself or go to the other biological parent's house and threaten her or hurt her in any way. It is best to have outside agencies deal with these situations. Often, they will lead to court proceedings, and it is best to follow whatever the outside agencies recommend.

Not all states have toll-free or twenty-four hour hotlines for reporting child abuse. If you do not know who to call, or if you and the abuser live in different states but the child travels between both houses, call the National Child Abuse Hotline at 1-800-4ACHILD or 1-800-422-4453.

If the abuser is your partner, you must tell the other biological parent, or tell the authorities and have them tell the other biological parent. Remove yourself and your stepchild from the situation immediately, either by leaving the house or calling the police. Similar to the above situation, if you allow the abuse to continue, you are guilty of abuse and neglect as well, and may have your own biological children removed from your care. Your partner may be very angry if you report him, and you may feel that you have betrayed him; however, you must continue to do what is best for the child, and if necessary, put your relationship with your partner on hold until he has gotten the help he needs.

Dealing with Extended Families

Your stepchild may have four very involved extended families: his biological mother's, biological father's, the other stepparent's family, and yours. Juggling all of these families can get rather hectic, but can also be a great base of support for your stepchild. It will probably make holiday planning a bit time intensive, but it can also force everyone to spend time together for the sake of spending time with your stepchild.

FACT

Whenever you are planning a party always be sure to find out if there are any food allergies amongst any of the guests. This is especially true for guests from the other biological parent's side. You don't want anyone to accuse you of trying to purposely harm anyone else. It doesn't necessarily mean you need to avoid certain foods all together, but you may need to label all food items clearly so people know the ingredients.

Family Get-Togethers

Birthdays may be the event that brings everyone together each year. You may decide to have separate birthday celebrations if you really do not get along well, but if you can manage, attempt to have one all together. This is a great way to learn tips about your stepchild that you do not know but his stepfather's mother noticed. It is an opportunity to get to know the other important adults in your stepchild's life and for them to get to know, and hopefully appreciate, you. It also represents to your stepchild that he has many people who care about him. Hopefully, this will start a pattern for the adults where they set their differences aside to celebrate the child.

As far as your extended family goes, include them as much as is comfortable for the biological parents. Since this is your stepchild, he is technically their stepgrandchild, stepniece, or stepnephew. He may be at family get-togethers and events, so your extended family should know who he is and welcome him when he is in attendance. If any of your extended family has issues with him being around, you will need to stand up for your stepchild as you would your partner. By entering into this marriage, you accepted your husband and his child, and they need to work on doing the same. Hopefully, they will welcome your stepchild and include him in the family as they would any other child.

If your extended family is going to participate in childcare or babysit from time to time, it is important that both biological parents feel comfortable with this. In this case, the other biological parent may want to meet your niece or your mother before you have her babysit. If she does feel comfortable with your choice of babysitter, she may even use your niece herself or ask if you know any other capable child-care providers.

Merging Toddlers

Bringing a toddler into your life can be sleep depriving enough, but bringing a toddler into your own children's lives has the potential to be either very challenging or life enhancing. Depending on the age of your own children, you will have to deal with scheduling conflicts.

Teenagers' Concerns

If you have teenagers, they may look at this new toddler with angst, thinking their social lives are now over since they will become built-in babysitters. Talk to your children about this and any other concerns they may have. They should not become your default babysitters, and you should try to make this merge as undisruptive as possible for them as well as for your stepchild. Teenagers who fear their lives will be negatively impacted by their new little sister may not be willing to spend time with her. They may resent her and avoid her at all costs. If you do try to set up babysitting with other family members so you do not disrupt your teenagers' lives, you may find that they actually want to babysit, and develop a strong relationship with their stepsibling.

Concerns for Children Between Toddler and Teenager

If you have children who are between toddler and teenager, you may find you face issues of jealousy. Since infants and toddlers are labor intensive, you may be spending less hands-on time with little ones of your own. Your children will be able to understand this and accept this more when they are teenagers. Prior to the teen years, however, they may see your stepchild as the reason you are not paying as much attention to them. Be aware of this, as most children will take out their anger on the stepchild, not on you. If you see this happening, address the situation and explain to your child that it is not his stepsister's fault—she is only seven months old and needs to be held frequently. It may not sink in right away, since what your child wants is your attention back on him.

Think about making a chart similar to a behavior plan chart that will reward your child with time alone with you if he can help out in some way with his stepsister. For example, if he helps wash the baby bottles, he can earn a walk around the block with just you. This will give him some control over the situation, help him develop caring and responsible behaviors around his stepsister, and allow him to earn time with you.

ALERT!

Your child may need to wait for gratification when it comes to a reward. Do not promise time alone with you at any time he wants; instead, make coupons that he can hand to you for redemption, and the two of you can then make a plan. Plan your alone time when you are 100 percent sure there will be another adult available to take care of your stepchild.

Toddler Concerns

If you have a toddler and are going to merge two toddlers or infants, sticking to schedules will help you the most. If your toddler is with you full time and your stepchild only visits, you may have to compromise both schedules a little bit to make your time together as manageable as possible.

If you can get them napping and eating at the same time, your life may be a little easier. You do not want to do this, however, if it is going to negatively affect either child's daily routine. If you disrupt your stepchild's schedule and then send her home, that is unfair to the other biological parent. If their schedules seem impossible to manage without disrupting them somehow, talk to the other biological parent and get suggestions from him. He may be perfectly fine with moving your stepchild's naptime up half an hour. Completely different schedules are not necessarily bad, however, so try them a few times before you change them. One toddler may nap 1:00–2:00 P.M., giving you time to spend with the other toddler. When that toddler goes to sleep, you will have uninterrupted time with the other toddler. It may take time to figure out the perfect schedule, but you will eventually find one that works for the whole family.

If both your stepchild and biological child live with their other parent full time, consider having visits where you have everyone together as well as visits where each child visits solo. This way, you will be able to work on your relationship and your partner's relationship with each child. The children can work on their relationship with each other when they visit together. As they get older, they may want to visit together more frequently, and may even visit each other at times when no visitation is scheduled.

CHAPTER 10

The Young Stepchild

Children between four and eleven years of age are fun, challenging, and old enough to ask precarious questions. This age group is often eager to learn and picks up on things most people don't expect them to notice. Understanding of social cues, social roles, manners, kindness, generosity, consistency, negative and positive behaviors, and family roles are all coming together for these children. With these discoveries come many questions, assumptions, and limit-testing behaviors. If you can remain as open and honest as possible with your stepchildren, all the while maintaining a sense of humor, the easier it will be to get from age four to eleven without any major mishaps.

What Is Your Role with a Child Under Eleven?

Your stepchild is now old enough to occupy himself. Hopefully, he is potty-trained, walking, talking, and feeding himself (not preparing or cooking food, though!). Your role now might be a bit more pronounced, since your stepchild may understand that you are a stepparent, not just Mom's friend or another adult that takes care of him. If you are just getting involved with your stepchild and he falls between four and eleven, he will probably enter into his relationship with you understanding your place in his family.

At this age, children are still young enough that they need hands-on care and direct guidance, but old enough to learn from adults instead of just mimicking them. This can be a fascinating time in a child's life because he is starting to make his own choices, observing how others around him behave, and learning from experiences. This is what your focus will be with your stepchild; the focus has also shifted for the child. With infants and toddlers, you are primarily focusing on them. With children between four and eleven your focus is on them, but theirs is also now on you. They are constantly observing you and your choices and actions. This shift in focus is what will primarily define your role with your stepchild.

E-QUESTION

This seems overwhelming. What if I make mistakes while they are watching?
Own that mistake. Explain to them that your behavior wasn't great in that moment, and that you are not perfect, but you try to behave as best as you can. For example, if you slam the phone when you are angry, you can explain that you let your anger get the best of you and didn't think before reacting. You can also explain how you will handle your anger differently in the future.

Model Good Behavior

Since you are now in the spotlight with your stepchild, it is important to behave in a way that you will be proud of if he goes home to his father and gives him a run down of your daily activities. As an infant and/or toddler, it was important to behave in a way that would keep your stepchild safe and out of danger. This remains true, but now you also need to recognize that your stepchild can talk, and will talk about your behavior as well. Your emphasis should still be on keeping your stepchild safe, but now you should demonstrate behaviors to your stepchild that will keep him safe. For example, crossing the street is something that may become entirely different now that your stepchild is older.

Behavior in cars is important. If you have road rage, get it under control. Kids will pick up on your use of the horn, your cursing, your hand gestures, and your dirty looks. They will also pick up on your use of a cell phone or any other multitasking you do in the car. You are modeling; they are taking it all in. If you do not want your stepchild to talk on the phone while driving or flipping people off when they run red lights, don't do it yourself!

Take this scenario with a child over four: You hold your five-year-old stepson's hand and begin to walk to the crosswalk. He says, "The store is right there; why can't we cross here?" You reply, "It is safer to cross on the crosswalk, because the people driving the cars are supposed to look for us and stop for us if they see us. It is still important for us to look both ways, but they should be on the lookout for us, too." You get to the crosswalk and wait to see if the cars will stop. One car goes right by without even slowing down. Your stepson says, "He didn't stop; he didn't even look." You reply, "That is why it is still important for us to look before we step into the street. Just because it is a law that cars must stop doesn't mean they always will." The next car stops and you cross the street, holding his hand. Once you get to the store, a customer who is leaving holds the door open for both of you. Your stepson marches in. You remind him, "What do you say?" Your stepson gives the customer his best smile and says, "Thank you!" You enter the store and purchase what you need. On your way out, your stepson holds the door for you, but you are checking your receipt and continue out the door. Your stepson says, "What do you say?" You are now reminded to thank him!

With an infant or toddler, you are more in control of the body of your stepchild and you might pick her up and cross the street, trusting that you can judge the cars correctly and keep both of you safe. With your five-year-old stepson, however, every moment becomes a teachable moment. He learned that a crosswalk is for pedestrians to use to cross the street, that some people do not follow the rules so you still need to be responsible, and that it is polite to say thank you to someone who holds the door open for you. He also remembered what you said about being polite and pointed out your rude behavior.

In addition to modeling good behaviors you will have to manage some unacceptable ones as well. When possible, be discrete when correcting inappropriate behavior. A good way to nip bad behavior with this age group is to have a talk with your stepchild in private. Preschoolers are becoming aware and concerned with the opinions of others and can get easily embarrassed if you discipline them publicly.

If you do slip up, it is likely your stepchild will call you out on the behavior, and potentially point it out to many people. As embarrassing as this may be, it should remind you of how important your behavior is to your stepchild and just how much it affects him on a daily basis. Also important is how you speak and what you say. If you are still spelling out "bad words" so your stepson doesn't catch on, you are behind the times. He has probably figured it out by now, and even if he can't sound out what you spell, he could get kicked off the playground for calling a classmate a "J-E-R-K." If you can keep this in mind, you will probably become a more polite and patient person and your stepchild will be polite and patient, too!

Perceptions of the Young Stepchild

Your stepchild is in the know—kind of. Her friends in kindergarten have pointed out that she has four parents and Missy has three parents, Bobby has two parents, and Simon has one. Why does she have four? How come she lives with her father and stepmother, but your own kids live with you and her mother? Why do other kids get to live with her mother but she doesn't? Did you take her mom away? What is a divorce? Bobby said people get divorced because they hate each other. Missy said stepmothers are floozies and stepfathers are idiots.

Welcome to your stepchild's perceptions of you—whether right on target or completely off base, she is going to have them, and it is only by being comfortable with yourself and your relationship that you can answer them as openly and as honestly as possible.

Figuring It All Out

First of all, it is not her fault if she thinks you are an idiot. She probably heard it somewhere else, and decided that if Missy said stepfathers were idiots then you must be one, too. The only way to change her mind is to not act like an idiot, and talk with her about who you are in her life. Second of all, scolding her for trying to figure out who and what you are to her will only make matters worse. She is probably hearing so many different ideas about stepparents, divorce, remarriage, half-siblings, and stepsiblings that she isn't quite sure what to make of it, and the only way to figure it out is to try out the things she is hearing from other kids at school. This can open up a fun conversation that also creates bonding time for the two of you. Ask her what she thinks a stepfather should be or how she sees you. Does she think you are an idiot? Why? Try not to be defensive; she is just trying to figure this whole thing out. If she feels that she can come to you and voice her concerns or questions no matter how insulting they may sound, she will be more open to trusting you and communicating with you as she gets older.

FACT

In a study of stepchildren by Constance R. Ahrons, PhD, it was determined that most children had good relationships with their stepparents, even though they struggled at the outset. These relationships improved as the children got to know their stepparents better. So hang in there; your relationship is likely to blossom over time.

Perceptions of Older Stepchildren

The older end of this age group may have very similar questions and perceptions as the younger group, especially if you are the first stepparent in the relationship. If you are not the first stepparent, however, you may find more resistance from your stepchild if she is at the older end of this spectrum. She may see you as identical to the stepmother she had last year, even if you are completely the opposite. To encourage her to get to know you as separate from any stepmother of the past, be yourself. When she accuses you of "being just like her," question her about it. How are you like her? What is she afraid will happen if you do have similarities to her last stepmother? If you cook the same dinner as she did, is your stepdaughter afraid you will then leave as well?

Be yourself, and support your stepdaughter in her worries and concerns. It may be frustrating to be compared to someone from the past, but eventually that will lessen in frequency and potentially disappear. As is always the case, if you notice your stepchild struggling, it might be helpful for you to suggest to your partner that he seek out counseling or some sort of support for your stepchild.

Being Sensitive to Concerns of the Other Biological Parent

The other biological parent may feel slightly more comfortable leaving his child with you now that his child can speak up. Also, he won't miss any major milestones if his son is with you for the weekend—most of those have already happened. The primary concerns will most likely continue to be the safety and security of the child. You may also still run into a parent who worries that his child will like you better than him, or that you will somehow win his child over in a way that he cannot. These are valid fears that the other parent is having; kids at this age may decide they like you better because they see you once a week and you and their mom buy them toys each time, and no discipline takes place with you. It can be a very tough place for the biological parent to be.

Model the Biological Parent's Rules Regarding Manners

A contributing factor to the biological parent's fears at this stage is that these are the formative years for his child. This goes along with fears parents have of their child's safety and security. Children are learning manners, respect, habits, morals, and what will be expected of them in the future. If you differ from the other biological parent in any of these areas, it may be a bone of contention. This is the age where your stepchild can reason and make decisions based on facts. She will have opinions and they may be based on your influence, even if you didn't mean to influence your stepdaughter in any way.

E-QUESTION

What if my partner and I don't have time for the nitpicky things that the other biological parent is fixated on?
Well, you may need to look at why you don't have the time. Is it truly a nitpicky thing, or is it that she is forcing you to do something you don't really care to do? Be flexible. If it is a behavior the other biological parent feels is really important to reinforce, and it is a positive behavior, work with her, not against her, and support her in her efforts by expecting this behavior at your home as well.

For example, if you don't usually put a napkin on your lap while you eat, and the other biological parent practices manners at all times, you may find your stepdaughter agrees with your way of eating—without the napkin. A simple behavior like this can turn into an argument between your stepdaughter and her biological parent that will likely include a sentence similar to this: "But my stepdad doesn't use a napkin on his lap at home. I agree with him. He is much nicer." Your stepdaughter might be sick of being picked on for forgetting her napkin and make a remark that stings. Hopefully, the other biological parent will inform your stepdaughter that as far as his house goes, she needs to use a napkin, and what you do at your house is up to you. He may also have a conversation with you about his struggles with your stepdaughter around manners and ask you to implement proper manners at your house. Practicing manners that are similar will make life easier for both of you and reward you with a well-mannered stepdaughter.

It is the simple, small, yet extremely important things that come into play for this age group. Most parents want to raise a child to be a productive member of society while they still have influence and control over the child. Those years will be gone as soon as the teen years are on the horizon.

Merging Your Children with Young Stepchildren

The smoothness of the merger will depend on your children and stepchildren, their ages, and living arrangements. Your children may be very welcoming of your stepchildren and vice versa. This would be a great scenario. Your children or your stepchildren may also want no part of one another—especially if the biological parents had a difficult breakup. In the aftermath of a difficult breakup, you are not always viewed as the only bad guy. Your stepchildren may see your biological children as more of you—the bad guy. Immediately, they will not want them around and every time you annoy them, they may take it out on your children. Also, your own children now have a stepparent and may feel similarly to your stepchildren. With two angry sets of children, you may end up with quite an angry household. At this point, you and your partner will have to do as much as you can to mediate the situation.

Stepsiblings Under Eleven

With children under eleven, it can be helpful for them to have plenty of time alone with their biological parent. Your stepchildren should have time with your partner as well, and you should have time with your biological children. You also need to make time for the entire family to be together. If the situation is particularly hostile, you may have to ease into the family time. The majority of time will be alone time, reassuring all of the biological children that they are still a priority and are actually gaining, not losing, people who love them. Once your children and your partner's children are reassured, they may have an easier time accepting each other.

Finding Commonalities

If your children are the same age as your stepchildren and you are all going to live together, they are probably going to be involved with each other more than they are involved with you and your partner. They may go to the same school, share a bedroom, play on the same sports team, etc. This forced time together may help them more than they realize. If they go to the same school, they may dislike or like the same teacher. If they share a bedroom, they may both want to paint it black (let them paint it—there are bigger arguments for which to save your energy). If they play on the same team, they may make a killer combination, or just enjoy the sport together. Any one of these commonalities can help. The one thing they do have in common is that they both have stepparents. They are not at the age yet where they may necessarily bond over this as teenagers might, but pointing it out to them won't hurt. If you can find anything for them to enjoy together, you will likely find them at least tolerating one another.

Your Older Children and Younger Stepsiblings

When your children are older and are adjusting to stepsiblings who are under eleven, you may find that it is your children who need to find a little patience. Children over the age of eleven are at an age where privacy is imperative. Children under eleven are usually excited by the opportunities to spend time with their older stepsiblings. You and your partner need to mediate the situation so both children get what they need. Make sure the teenagers have privacy, and time away from the little ones, and the little ones have playtime with the older children.

Watch out for any aggression that might appear in your biological children or stepchildren. Unfortunately, kids often don't know how to verbalize anger very well; instead, they may strike out at one another. If this happens, address the issue by talking, implementing behavior plans, or even by going to family therapy.

Your Younger Children and Older Stepsiblings

If you are bringing a younger child into the family and your stepchild is between four and eleven, it may be a little easier for everyone to adjust. Your child will probably adjust rather easily and not be overly affected by her new stepsibling. Your stepchild will probably have a tougher time adjusting, however, because he is more aware that gaining a sibling means sharing more and dealing with another person in the house.

If any of the children over four, yours or your partners, are only children, the merge is likely to be more difficult. The longer the child has lived as an only child, the more difficult blending the families is likely to be. Only children tend to be a bit more set in their ways, and not as flexible as children growing up around other siblings. This can cause frustration and annoyance for the only child. In this case, make sure that the only child has "only" time. Find a space in the house that she can have to herself for periods of time.

Check Chapter 5 for tips on moving in and helping everyone merge successfully. It is a tough part of creating a new family, but it can be very rewarding once it is accomplished. Give each other time to get used to everyone's nuances and weird habits; you might even find you appreciate them.

The Impact of Having a Child of Your Own

Some children would be thrilled to have a sibling, or another sibling; others will not be very happy at all. Children under the age of eleven are going to have an easier time adjusting than teenagers, but struggle more than a child under four. The mind of a child under eleven years of age is usually not thinking of all the underlying connections and meanings to having a stepsibling. Instead, your stepchild may come up with surprising reasons why she believes you are having a child. She may also have very unexpected questions and concerns. These are normal and can come from a variety of sources; children at this age get input from so many people around them— peers, teachers, coaches, the other biological parent, television and other media, etc.

Your Stepchild's Feelings

If your stepchild seems extremely angry, ask why. You may never know unless you ask. She may think she has to share her room, because she has to share her room with her other half-sister at her mother's house. She may think her father loves you more than he loved her mother, because an adult somewhere along the line told her you only have babies with people you love more than anyone else. She may think you aren't supposed to have a baby because you are a stepmother and not a real mother, so how could you have a baby? It is important to listen to her questions and concerns and respond to them honestly. Even if your stepchild is as thrilled as can be about a baby, she may have some strange preconceived notions about what that baby means as far as her life goes.

The more you can keep your stepchild's schedule consistent throughout your pregnancy and the birth of the child, the better it will be for him. As soon as his life is disrupted, he may have a negative feeling about the baby and blame the baby for this turmoil.

Before you sit down with your stepchild to tell her that you and her father are having a baby and she will be a big sister, plan the right time to have that conversation. If you only see your stepchild on the weekends, you may want to have the conversation first with her mother, then with her. This will give her time alone to digest the information and consider how she will handle any questions her daughter has, and it will give you and your partner time with your stepdaughter while she adjusts to the information. Prior to telling her, prepare for questions she might ask, such as: "Why are you having another baby? You already have me." "Where will I sleep?" "Do I have to share my toys?" "Will you love me less?" "Is he going to live with mom and me?" If you can, predict questions she will ask, but there are sure to be some unpredictable ones in the mix.

If she doesn't live with you, she may be very concerned about why this baby gets to live with her father and she doesn't. This is an issue you need to address with her before she even thinks she is being replaced. Emphasizing the importance of her relationship with this new baby is key. It is also important to keep her involved in the pregnancy as the day of the birth approaches. You can show her ultrasound pictures, give her some say in how the room is decorated, have her help pick out a name or middle name, etc. These gestures should help her feel that she is not being left in the dust for this new child.

Respect the Feelings of the Other Biological Parent

Remember that this may be a very difficult thing for the other biological parent. Similar to a wedding, this is another step in your relationship that solidifies your relationship to the public. This may also symbolize to the other biological parent and/or your stepdaughter that they are being replaced in some way. The other biological parent may have dealt with this more when you married your partner, but your stepdaughter may be really confused, especially if the news affects her other biological parent in a negative way.

Rumors Your Stepchild Hears

Similar to how your stepchild learns ideas and bizarre beliefs from his peers, he may also hear rumors from his classmates about what other adults are actually saying. Now that he is more social, he is interacting with more children and their parents. This makes your life more public as well. You, your wife, the other biological parent, and the other stepparent if there is one may all be on the pick up list from school. You may all go to his soccer games. It is inevitable that many adults in the community will now know the situation. Of course, one would hope that people could accept this and move on, but our need for insider information is strong, and if people don't know the actual story behind a situation, they are very likely to create one.

Dealing with Adult Rumors

It is less likely that an adult would say something horrid to your stepchild, and more likely a peer will overhear adults talking and then filter information over to your stepchild. There may also be situations where adults in the community take sides with your partner or your partner's ex and act inappropriately because of their alliance. Although this can be difficult on you and your partner, it can take a much bigger toll on your stepchild if not handled with maturity.

Rumors and bullying happen with great frequency on the playground and on the Internet. Check in with your stepchild about whether anyone is bothering him and ask if he is experiencing any cyber bullying or messages about his family situation on the Internet. This can be a very overwhelming way to be bullied, and extremely mean and harsh.

If other adults do or say things that are not true or are mean, think before you react. If you confront the adult in the schoolyard or even talk to him politely and set him straight, you may be putting your stepchild at risk in his social group. Think about how your reactions will affect him and his social life. If the adult said something offensive but didn't say it to your stepchild, consider ignoring it. If the adult says something to your stepchild or continues to say things to you or others that are affecting your stepchild, you can try and ignore it at first, but if it continues you may need to approach the person. You can attempt, without anger or hostility, to ask him not to talk about your private life. If he continues to do so and is negatively affecting your child, you may have to get the authorities involved.

Dealing with Peer Rumors

When your stepchild's peers are the ones saying negative things about your situation, you can attempt to speak with their parents. You also need to equip your stepchild with the tools he needs to successfully handle his peers while in school or in activities elsewhere. Wherever the harassment is taking place, the supervising adults should be notified. In school situations, it is important to involve the teacher, and if the harassment is continuous, school officials may be able to assist by mediating the situation with your stepson and his peers.

CHAPTER 11

The Teen Stepchild

The teenage years can be terrifying for your step-teen and you! However, along with the angst, drama, growing pains, and emotional roller coasters comes the opportunity for building a relationship with your stepchild that is closer than any you might have imagined. The teenage years are the years when your stepchild will likely require the most support. Your stepchild will have to experience most if not all of the defining events that had you breaking out in hives— first boyfriend or girlfriend, driver's license, sex, alcohol, prom, and college applications. Whatever your experience was as a teenager, you are now someone who lived through it and can lend the support your teen stepchild may desperately need.

What Is Your Role with a Child Between Twelve and Eighteen?

Your role with a child between twelve and eighteen years of age may change like the wind. Teenagers are a fickle bunch; your stepchild may decide he hates you at breakfast, and can't talk to anyone but you at lunch. Be ready to ride these ups and downs for the entire span. There will be some calms in the storm, but the next storm will always be right around the corner. With this age group, your role may feel rather unsettled. But enjoy it, really enjoy it. This may be the time you have the most opportunity to really mentor your stepchild. You have been modeling behaviors in previous years and teaching your stepchild by staying aware of your own actions. This is the time to take on your mentoring role with great gusto. It is such a great and fun time.

Be Consistent

So what is your role now? You will continue to model appropriate behavior, and to maintain a safe and healthy home through your own consistent patterns. This is a very important time to maintain consistency. Teenagers don't feel safe in these years—the temptations of alcohol, drugs, and sex are at the forefront. The best way to help them feel safe and help them make positive choices is to maintain a high level of consistency in rules and discipline. By consistency, don't just think of consequences, but also of rewards. Teenagers have more freedom than they did before and often find themselves in unsupervised situations. These situations can feel overwhelming and frightening to them, and they may make significant mistakes.

One way to alleviate these feelings is to monitor his unsupervised time; try to keep it to a minimum. If your teenager is going to be unsupervised for long periods of time, have someone drop by or check in. Have him call at certain times to tell you what is going on. Unsupervised time in this world is inevitable. Although he will have it, and should have some for his own sanity, how he handles himself during such times will increase or decrease your trust in his decision-making abilities. When he is caught making negative choices, you need to sanction him appropriately. When he makes positive choices, you must reward him just as strongly as you would have disciplined him had he made a poor choice. As hard as it will be to keep track of him, it is critical that you and your partner do so.

You must find a balance between monitoring your teen's time and giving him privacy—privacy is of the utmost importance to most teenagers, and your stepchild deserves it. Allow him time alone, and definitely unsupervised time with other adolescents you trust. This time will be less rocky if you respect your stepchild's need for alone time.

Being Part of the Big Talks

Another important role you may take on is in the difficult-conversation arena. You are far enough removed that your teen may feel more comfortable with you instead of his parent, but close enough that he trusts you and respects you as an adult. Topics of such conversations might include dating, sex, birth control, alcohol and drugs, and genuine frustration with biological parents. Some teenagers are able to talk to their biological parents about these topics without embarrassment. The more open the parent is to having these conversations, the more likely it is that the teenager will feel a level of comfort in asking them certain questions. If the biological parents are somewhat horrified by any of these topics, their teenager will recognize this and avoid bringing up these conversations with them. This is when he may turn to you.

Every teenager needs an adult to talk to them honestly about these topics. If they do not get their information from a safe adult, they are likely to look for it in other areas, such as their peers, older teenagers, the Internet, and television. While some of these sources are fine, and may be quite informative, there is a great deal of misinformation out there that could be avoided if they had these conversations with a safe adult.

What should you do when your stepchild approaches you with one of these topics? Don't become embarrassed and say, "I can't talk to you about that!" You may scare him away from ever asking any embarrassing questions again. If you really don't feel comfortable talking with him about any of these subjects, you could explain that, "I really don't feel comfortable having that conversation with you, but I am so happy that you brought the topic up. It is a topic that you really do need to learn about and the fact that you felt comfortable enough with me to ask about it means a lot. I don't feel like I am an expert in that area, but I would like to connect you with someone who is. Perhaps it would be a good idea to talk with your doctor?"

This handles the conversation in a way that doesn't shame your stepchild, acknowledges the importance of talking about the subject, leads the way to another safe adult with whom to have the conversation, and gets you out of the hot spot. It is extremely important that you don't create a feeling of shame for your stepchild and that he feels he can come to you with sensitive topics. Other potential safe adults might be an aunt or uncle, a school counselor, a school nurse, another parent with whom you and your stepchild are comfortable, or an older cousin or sibling.

In a study done by the Kaiser Family and the Talk Now Foundation, kids whose parents talk to them about difficult issues report talking to their parents 72 percent of the time when they felt pressured to have sex. Only 57 percent of teens whose parents did not speak to them felt comfortable talking about this topic.

If you do decide you are comfortable having this conversation with your stepchild, be sure to remain open to his questions throughout the conversation. If you start to have the conversation and then determine that you are not comfortable, this could make your stepchild feel ashamed about the topic as well, and that there are certain things he shouldn't be asking. This is confusing because he will not know what is appropriate to discuss, and will likely choose not to discuss sensitive topics at all.

The Sex Talk

The sex talk can take on many forms, from, "What is the deal with sex?" to "My best friend had it and I think I should, too." When their friends start having and talking about sex, they will begin to ask about it and wonder if it is something they should be engaging in. Having adults who talk openly about sex can deter them from having sex too early, and also equip them with correct information about birth control should they decide to have sex. One of the biggest myths about the sex talk is that if you talk to them about it they will have it. This is simply not true. In talking to them about it, you are able to talk to them about the consequences of having sex early, the potential to get pregnant, having a negative reputation, having their heart broken, and never being able to take it back. It can be an eye-opening conversation for teenagers, and a mind-changing one. If they were on the fence, they may think twice and decide to wait. It is such an important conversation to have with them.

FACT

A report by Advocates for Youth cites the statistic that 23 percent of thirteen year olds and 30 percent of fourteen year olds have had sexual intercourse. The Kaiser Foundation reports that almost 4 million teenagers a year contract a sexually transmitted disease.

If your stepchild's friends are sexually active, it is more likely that your stepchild will face more peer pressure about the subject, and may have already decided to have sex. This can be a tricky area for you. When you have conversations about this topic, try to avoid saying negative things about his friends who have had sex. If he knows you don't approve of them, he may not want to confide in you about his own concerns.

Another huge issue: Should you tell your partner that his son is thinking about sex? Or do you keep it a secret? Too much secrecy can create a feeling of shame, but not respecting your stepchild's confidentiality can have very negative affects on his ability to open up to you or trust you. So, what do you do? If your partner is horrified by the thought of your stepson having sex and will show it by becoming angry or disappointed in your stepson, you need to frame the conversation a little differently. Any parent may be a bit uncomfortable with the thought of it, so framing your conversation with your stepson as positively as possible is the best way to proceed.

For example, you could say something like, "Sean's friends are getting to the age where sex is coming up in conversations, in the shows they watch, and the movies they see. He asked me a couple of really great questions about sex, and I think it a great sign that he is talking about it instead of just doing it like so many kids his age. I wanted you to know that he is getting to that age where we have to think about that, but also hope that you can put your emotions aside a bit. Instead of getting angry or disappointed in him, be proud that he feels comfortable talking about it. I hope to continue having this kind of conversation with him; it is much safer for teenagers who have someone they feel comfortable talking to. I wouldn't want to ruin that by having him think I am running to you and telling you everything. But I did think it was important that you knew it was on his mind."

A conversation like this will hopefully help your partner see that this is a good thing, and not something to cause upset. It is understandable that he will have an emotional reaction to it, but hopefully, he will think before he reacts and appreciate the relationship you have built with his son.

Drugs and Alcohol

These are going to be available to your stepchild now more than ever before. It is important to have conversations with your stepchild about the dangers of drugs and alcohol, even if she doesn't approach you with them. You may feel as though you are annoying by reminding your stepdaughter how bad smoking is for her every time she goes out on the weekends, but she will have to hear you if you keep saying it. Soon she may repeat it back to you, which is exactly what you want. You may even say to her, "No smoking, no alcohol, and no drugs. I love you and want you home in one sober piece." You can say that every single time she goes out if you want. Will it annoy her? Maybe. Will it hurt her? Not at all.

Another important way to prevent drug and alcohol abuse is to watch your own behavior and the behaviors of the other adults around your stepchild. By abstaining or drinking in moderation, you are modeling appropriate behaviors for your stepchild. Coming home drunk, commenting that you need a drink after a tough day, or using illicit drugs are all actions that are not appropriate around a stepchild of any age. If you do take prescription drugs for any reason, be sure you are using them as prescribed and keeping them locked in a safe place. Misusing prescription medications is a form of drug abuse and can set a poor example for your stepchild. If you notice other adults in your stepchild's life setting poor examples, ask them to refrain from these behaviors while around your stepchild.

Boys and girls are both at risk for any drug. There are so many stereotypes, but when it comes to drugs, they don't discriminate. Your stepdaughter may become an alcoholic. Your stepson may become addicted to pills. Just because it doesn't fit the stereotype you are used to, does not mean it doesn't exist.

If you suspect that your stepchild has a problem with drugs or alcohol, you must bring it up to your partner; you need to have a conversation with your stepchild as soon as possible. She may be mad or hate you, but it is her life that you are trying to save. The other biological parent and any other stepparent need to be involved as well. Never keep drug or alcohol use a secret. It is not okay for your stepchild to be using and you to keep it a secret. If she never drinks and happens to come home a little tipsy one night, you absolutely must tell your partner. As soon as you keep a secret like this, you are no longer a safe adult in her life.

Teenagers need to know that you will do everything you can to keep them safe, even if it risks the relationship between the two of you. Your job is to keep this child safe above everything else. If your stepchild comes to you and tells you she is smoking marijuana, you need to take it very seriously, but don't be judgmental about it. When talking to her biological parents about the situation, try to be the person who keeps everyone's judgments to a minimum. You may be very disappointed, and you can tell her that, but don't let her believe you love her any less for her actions or that she can't redeem herself.

The Adolescent Years

One key to the adolescent years is reminding yourself that their bodies are filled with hormones and they haven't the slightest idea how to handle them. That is why they have parents. As far as the adolescent brain is concerned, it is being run by the ever-emotional limbic system, and the areas that are not fully developed yet are areas you would often expect to be developed. The parts of the brain that are not fully formed in adolescence are those that help in decision making, self-control, emotions, organization, and judgment—most specifically, the frontal lobe.

The Science of the Adolescent Brain

Despite the lack of executive functioning, the limbic system is in full swing. The limbic system includes the amygdala, which is a part of the brain that is highly emotional. When your amygdala is making most of the decisions without the help of the frontal lobe, your decisions will be based more on emotion than your ability to rationalize safe versus unsafe behavior. An example from Gargi Talukder's article "Decision Making is Still a Work in Progress for Teenagers" states that while adults can, "…use rational decision making processes when facing emotional decisions, adolescent brains are simply not yet equipped to think through things in the same way. For example, when deciding whether to ride in a car driven by a drunk friend, an adult can usually put aside her desire to conform and is more likely to make the rational decision against drunk driving. However, a teenager's immature frontal lobes may not be capable of such a coolly rational approach, and the emotional feelings of friendship may be likely to win the battle."

E-QUESTION

I got over my first breakup as a teenager. Why doesn't my stepchild believe me and stop crying and listening to sad music?
You may have gotten over it, but do you remember what it was like when it happened? Would you ever, in your entire life, want to go back there? Being a teenager is not easy. You may see them as having no bills, no responsibilities, and a lot of fun. In reality, they are trying to grow up; that may be the biggest job we have as humans. Put yourself back in your teenage years and you are bound to find some empathy.

This is precisely why we think teenagers are overly dramatic and out of control. If you can keep in mind that their brain has, literally, not yet fully developed, you may have a little more patience with them. This is what both you and they need.

The Age of Self-Discovery

Many of the topics adolescents are dealing with were addressed in the section on your role. Aside from sex, drugs, and alcohol, teenagers are dealing with who they are in the world. Is your stepchild the nerd who gets straight As? The jock? The middle-of-the-road kid? Does she want to be that person? This is the time when your stepchild will be pulled in many different directions. Does she hate being the smart kid? Should she prove herself by boozing it up with her friends?

It is tough to be a teenager: They don't know how to make tough choices; their social life is probably the most stressful part of their life; it is awful to know you aren't cool. But remember, you cannot protect them from everything. What you can do is respect your stepchild and love her unconditionally. If she is a dork, love her dorkiness and celebrate it by getting to know some of the dorky things that interest her. If she is a jock, appreciate this, go to her games, and help her balance sports and school. Celebrate her as an individual, and no matter who she is becoming, love her.

Dealing with Puberty

Here come the hormones again! Puberty is not a joyous occasion for anyone. It brings acne, mood swings, voice changes, boobs, periods, and all that fun stuff. And of course, puberty hits everyone differently. Your stepson may be a peanut at twelve and still one at fourteen, when all his friends have had their growth spurts and voice changes. This is tough on self-esteem.

There is so much that can be done about acne now. You and your partner may think it is no big deal, but it is worth a trip to the dermatologist. Even if your stepchild doesn't seem overly concerned by it, he may feel a lot better once it is gone. Go to the dermatologist and advocate for your stepchild; acne is something that can seriously affect self-esteem.

At twelve, your stepdaughter may be the first of her friends to get her period. She may also develop last and not really need a bra, while the rest of her friends are out shopping together for bras. Puberty is one of the things that can really affect their social lives and is really out of their control. The teenager with acne may find she has no date to homecoming. The teenager with boobs may find she is asked out on many dates and all her friends decide she is a slut. This is the kind of nonsense that puberty brings. Your most important job is still supporting your stepchild and being open to discussing concerns she may have about the changes taking place.

Your Role

Your role in the puberty of your stepchild will be greatly impacted by the gender of your stepchild and your own gender. If you are the stepfather of a daughter, leave her alone. Do not show your embarrassment when she starts developing. Do not tease her about her boobs or bras. Do not remark that she must have her period on days that she is cranky. Love her, don't be afraid of her, but don't be insensitive either. As embarrassed as you may be by changes going on in her body, she is more embarrassed. As a stepfather with a stepson, you may feel more comfortable being more involved. You can give him tips on shaving, using deodorant, shampooing his hair, and basic hygiene information.

Depending on the involvement of the biological mother, if you are the stepmother of a daughter you may do a lot of the period work. You may have to have that conversation with her and be the one to have an ongoing supply of tampons, pads, cramp relievers, or any other period-related item. You may also have to protect her father a bit from this situation. Here is where secrecy is okay. If she is mortified every time she gets her period, you really don't need to tell her father about it. If she has really bad periods, you can tell him she needs to see the doctor, but you don't need to go into detail with him. You may also get to buy her first bra. Again, Dad doesn't need to know all the details.

If you are the stepmother of a son, you may have to help him navigate the ladies, help him with his skin if it is a problem, and support him through his growing pains. If hygiene seems to be a major issue, talk to your partner about having that conversation with him. Don't tease him about girls, or his straggly mustache, or armpit hair; that can be very embarrassing. Respect your stepchild, and make puberty as painless as possible.

When You Are Close in Age to Your Stepchild

You are not your stepchild's friend. Your stepchild may see you that way and you kind of can be, but this will make it hard to draw the line between discipline and friendship. For example, if you are twenty-three years old and your stepdaughter is seventeen years old, it is not okay to check out her and her friends at the pool, or buy them alcohol, or have parties with your friends and hers. You are still in an adult role and she is a minor in your care.

It is also not okay for your stepchild to see you drunk or half dressed. The closeness in age just makes everything a little awkward, and you will need to hold yourself as an adult at all times. It can be very stressful for you. It may seem totally natural to befriend your stepchild, but you need to remember that you may be the one who grounds her when she is out too late. Or you may have to go to a school conference if your partner and the other biological parent aren't available. Not only do you need to be mature, you may also have to deal with the surprise or comments of other adults.

FACT

There is a great website, *www.bonusfamilies.com*, with many resources on stepfamilies and steprelationships. They put a more positive spin on the idea of "step" relations, by changing the word "step" to "bonus." A "bonus brother" sounds more endearing than a "stepbrother."

Many teenagers may actually have a big issue with you being so close in age to them. It may seem weird to them that one of their parents is dating someone who could be their friend. This is an issue your partner will need to work out with your stepchild. There may be some hostility on your stepchild's part. He may find it ridiculous to take orders from you or follow any of your rules because you could have been in high school with him. It is understandable that he feels this way. You will need to be firm and set clear boundaries. At this time, you are an adult caretaker and he needs to respect you as one, as long as you respect his difficulty with the situation. If he is having a considerably difficult time with this, your partner might need to step in and take over the discipline and boundary setting for the time being. However, he should not do so in a way that sends the message you are incapable or that you do not warrant respect as a parental figure. Your stepchild might not be comfortable with you as a parental figure and might respond better to your partner until you have been in the picture for a longer period of time.

Merging Teenagers with Teen Stepsiblings

This could go bad in many ways, but it can also be great. They may absolutely despise each other and fight all the time. If so, you need to let them battle it out a little bit. They are old enough now that they will probably get sick of fighting with each other and just ignore each other. They are also mature enough to know they are stuck in the situation whether they like it or not. One thing that may help is if they can have their own rooms, since privacy is so important at this age. If they do detest each other, they may find common ground in hating you and your partner for bringing them together. If you can deal with that, they may be able to come together a bit, which will be helpful for them.

You may have a situation where you have a stepson and your partner has a stepdaughter and it is love at first sight. Unfortunately, you cannot allow this, especially if they live together. Telling them this will never happen may push them closer, so be careful how you handle it. Remind them constantly that they are now siblings and it is an inappropriate relationship to have. While you can celebrate the fact that they get along, discourage any sort of sexual relationship between your biological child and your stepchild. If it seems to be a major concern, a family therapist can be of great assistance.

The Impact of Having a Child of Your Own

As teenagers, a new baby between you and their biological parent may be quite upsetting. They have been used to their family as it is, and adding you was hard enough. Now you want to add a baby into the mix? They may feel that you are pushing them out of the picture to start a new family. Your step-son may feel you are waiting for him to turn eighteen so you can start your own family, and have his mother to yourself for this new family. Try very hard to avoid this. Include him in the pregnancy and make sure he remains a central focus. If your stepchild is leaving for college and you are having a baby, there may be concern that you will forget about him and he won't be important as a child in the family anymore. Be sure to keep in close contact with him—send him packages throughout the pregnancy and continue to do so once the baby is born. Don't forget about him; this will help him, you and his relationship with the new baby.

If you have never had a child of your own and your partner only has teenage children, this may be even harder for everyone. It will take extra effort on your part to stay involved in your stepchild's life. He is still a child and needs you, even though he is not your son. If you have the baby and are consumed by the fact that you finally have a biological child of your own, your stepchild will feel that. Try very hard to appreciate and love your stepchild; he is a huge part of your partner's life and shouldn't be any less important because he is not your biological child.

This can also cause tension between you and your partner. If your partner thinks you are dismissing your stepchild now that the two of you have a child of your own, he may be very hurt and angry. There is a lot to think about when you first have a baby, but as a stepparent, you need to think about much more. Be sure to do so, or you will cause pain to your stepchild and your partner, which could result in them having negative feelings toward you or your biological child.

CHAPTER 12

The Adult Stepchild

Once your stepchildren are adults, or if you start off with adult stepchildren, you may find that you are less of an issue for them since you do not affect their daily living the way you would if they were younger. As adults, your stepchildren may have different concerns about you. They may think that you are involved in a relationship with their parent primarily because you are interested in their parent's money. They also may worry that you might plan on having more children. Either of these scenarios might feel threatening to them. Younger stepchildren might not have such concerns unless the situation is in front of them, whereas adult stepchildren may begin thinking about these things almost as soon as you begin dating their parent.

What Is Your Role with the Child Eighteen and Older?

If you were involved in your stepchild's life prior to adulthood, your role may already be set and your interactions will probably continue in a similar vein. You can take your cues from your existing relationship. Hopefully, you will continue to set a good example, be available to converse with your stepchild, be respectful of your partner's relationship with your stepchild, and be considerate of the other biological parent's relationship with your stepchild. If you are entering into a relationship with a partner who has adult children, your role may be minimal—limited to family parties and events. However, as time goes on, hopefully you will try to develop a closer relationship.

E-QUESTION

Why should I have to worry about getting along with my adult stepchildren? They don't live with us and they have families of their own. You don't need to let the idea of having a relationship with your adult stepchildren consume you; however, you are involved with or married to one of their parents. Building a relationship with your stepchildren may help you get to know your partner better, as a parent. You may miss out on rewarding relationships if you don't get to know your stepchildren.

Little Things Count

If you rarely see your stepchildren because you and your partner do not live near them, there are many small, fun ways to reach out to them. Ask your partner for their birthdays, anniversaries, and any other special days they may celebrate. Write cards out with your partner for those special occasions and make sure they are mailed early enough to arrive on time. This may not seem important, but it can make an enormous difference. Maybe your partner never sent cards before, and now she is because of your influence. Your stepchildren may really appreciate such gestures. You can also send cards for no particular reason, just to say hello, and to let them know you are thinking of them. This can be a nice way of checking in without being overbearing. With computers everywhere, even often in libraries and hotel lobbies for customers' use, e-mail also can be a quick, easy, and inexpensive way to stay in touch.

When your partner speaks about her children, remember what she says. If it will help you remember, consider writing it down. If she mentions that her daughter used to love going to the nail salon down the street or her son loves maple walnut ice cream, these are nuggets of information you should tuck away in your brain. With this kind of information, you can plan sentimental gifts and get-togethers for your partner and/or her children. For example, if your partner's birthday is coming up and her children are visiting, you could plan a nail date for her and your stepdaughter, prior to having cake and ice cream. Once everyone arrives, be sure to have maple walnut ice cream on hand. Small gestures like this can make your stepchildren feel as though you consider them an important part of their mother's life, and thus an important part of your life.

If your stepchildren are around more frequently, you will have more opportunities to find out their likes and dislikes, and simply be more involved in their daily lives. Small gestures can still be of great importance, and you will have more chances to implement them. As they get older, they may have major milestones, such as weddings, births, job recognition, and other major accomplishments. Since they are now adults, they may indicate how or if they want you involved. Your stepson may decide he wants you to walk down the aisle at his wedding with his stepmother, so his biological parents can walk together. Your stepdaughter may come to you with questions about her newborn since you have experience with newborns. Your role will be in large part determined by the wishes of your stepchild now that he has more of a voice in his own life. Remember, however, that no matter how your role shakes out, you need to always be mindful and respectful of the other biological parent and how he is involved in your stepchild's life.

Do They Even Care Who You Are?

Hopefully, they care about you. They might not, though, and if that is the case, don't push it. If they are well into adulthood, they might be wrapped up in their own lives and not have time to take an interest in you. As long as they see you as someone who is supportive of their mother and they see their mother as happy, they will probably trust her judgment and leave well enough alone. Situations where they might be more wary of you include when their mother has been married and hurt a few times by other partners, if their mother has a large amount of money, or if you have been married and divorced multiple times. They also may be rather skeptical if you are significantly younger than their mother. Hopefully, they are only looking out for their mother's best interest and not their own. If past partners have hurt their mother frequently, all you can do is be the best person you can be in the relationship. Be thoughtful, respectful, and kind. Think about how you would feel if your mother was dating or marrying someone new. You would probably want them to be nice to her and treat her well. This is how your stepchildren may feel.

Consider a Prenup

If your future stepchildren's mother has a large amount of money, you might consider having a prenuptial agreement written. If you do not plan on divorcing her, it may only help the relationship between you and your stepchildren, thus making it a happier time for your partner and you. It may indicate to your stepchildren that your desire is to marry their mother regardless of her economic status. This can alleviate so much tension that it may be well worth it.

Your stepchildren may also be worried that they will be left out of their mother's will, or you will end up spending their inheritance. In this case, they may not be looking out for their mother's interest, but for their own. You may not get very far pointing this out to them or arguing with them about it. If they only see you as someone who will get in the way of their money and are not able to see how happy you make their mother, it won't do you much good to fight with them about it. You and your partner should discuss how best to approach this issue. If they want to fight about it, you can simply say, "I love your mother and I believe we make each other very happy. If you are concerned that I do not make her happy or that I somehow take away from her happiness, I would like to know. My goal is to make your mother happy in any way that I can. If you are concerned about your mother's money that is a conversation you really need to have with your mother." Now this may sound as if it puts a lot of pressure on your partner, but they are her children and they are taking out their disagreement with her on you. You and your partner should discuss the best approach to this issue.

FACT

If you are interested in a prenuptial agreement, talk to an attorney. Many states have different restrictions or requirements as far as what is allowed in a prenuptial agreement. It is a good idea, no matter what, to disclose all of your assets and liabilities prior to getting married.

If you have been married and divorced numerous times, a prenuptial agreement can be helpful here as well. If marrying and divorcing seems to be a pattern for you, make sure you are ready to make this commitment. Even though your stepchildren will be adults, they will still feel the effects of a marriage and then a divorce, especially if it negatively affects a parent for whom they care deeply.

Concerns Regarding Care for the Parent

Adult stepchildren have every right to inquire about your intentions regarding their parent. As children become adults, they will see their parents as people for whom they will eventually need to care. If you are going to disrupt this in any way or make it more difficult to give their parent the care she needs, they may not trust you. If, however, you can help them in caring for their parent and bring her joy, they will probably be fine with the marriage. If you are failing in health, they may be a little intimidated by taking on your care as well as their other parents'. It is scary to see your parents age for many reasons, and having more than just their biological parents to take care of may be overwhelming. You should also not expect them to care for you, although in many cases they will by choice. To be safe, make arrangements as you get older to obtain any care you may need.

When You Are Younger than Your Stepchild

This can be a bit uncomfortable for both you and your stepchildren. Although age is just a number, your thirty-five-year-old stepson may find it disconcerting that he has a twenty-four-year-old stepfather. Society usually dictates that you should respect your elders. Elders are usually our parents, grandparents, aunts, uncles, teachers, and caretakers. When you are expected to respect someone younger because they hold a position you deem appropriate for someone older, it feels a bit uncomfortable. You may have gone to the doctor's recently, only to discover the doctor is young enough to be your child. Is this doctor credible? Probably. But do you feel a bit odd trusting your health to someone half your age? Probably. It is tough to accept that someone younger than you deserves your respect. This can be especially tough for a child whose stepparent is younger.

Your stepchild may feel that getting along with you is a way of being disloyal to her other biological parent. You may find she seems fine with you one on one, but in situations where everyone is present she has an attitude or doesn't speak to you. You can address it or ignore it, but try to enjoy the times the two of you do get along.

Your stepchild may have preconceived notions of who you are simply because of your age. The more comfortable you are with your age, however, the more comfortable your stepchild may be. If you do not make an issue of it your stepchild may not either. If he does make an issue of it, you may find you need to work harder than other partners or stepparents in order to prove yourself. This may not seem fair, but it shouldn't be a problem if you truly believe you are capable and worthy of being with your partner. You need to show how comfortable you are in your new role (even if you aren't totally comfortable). It can become a kind of fake-it-till-you-make-it situation. Your stepson may also feel abandoned by his parent, and feel that she has stopped taking care of him in order to take care of you. You can help this situation by encouraging your partner to continue caring for her child as she did prior to your arrival.

If your stepchild is very upset by the situation, you can discuss with him how you view your role as stepparent. You aren't going to be a typical parental figure; your stepson could potentially be your mentor. Explain that you are not looking to parent or discipline him or expecting respect as a parent. You can ask that your stepchild appreciate you as someone else who loves his mother and respect you as another human being.

Taking on the role of stepparent with the expectation of being respected as a parent is a very bad idea; it probably won't happen. If you can gain your stepchild's respect as a person, you have made plenty of headway. To best gain the respect of your older stepchild, conduct yourself with maturity, be open to his questions and concerns, laugh at the situation if it makes sense to do so, respect your stepchild and the knowledge he has, and prove your worth as your partner's significant other by loving her and cultivating your relationship with each other.

The Other Biological Parent

The other person in the mix who may disapprove of your relationship with your partner is the other biological parent. The stereotypes of young bimbos stealing husbands or hot pool boys causing affairs still run rampant in the media. The person who is left for the newer, younger version usually feels quite awful. Aging is not fun for many people, and being replaced by a younger version only drives home the fact that someone is aging. If you are the young replacement, you may be bright, self-sufficient, capable, kind, mature, well versed in the stock market, or even an entrepreneur. The only thing the other biological parent may see is your age, and how different it is from his. This is to be expected.

As mentioned earlier, aging is tough, and seeing someone younger with a former partner may make the other biological parent feel as though his face is being rubbed in the dirt. If you want to gain the respect and appreciation of the other biological parent (which often helps you gain the respect of your stepchild), do not flaunt your youth around him. There is no reason to tell him you weren't yet born when he graduated from high school or that you can still run a road race with little or no training. You don't need to be ashamed of your age—and you shouldn't be—but you also should not brag about it or show it off.

The Impact of Having a Child of Your Own

If you and your partner decide to have children of your own, the impact on your stepchildren and the other biological parent could be huge or it could be minimal. Since everyone is an adult in the situation, you can hope that everyone handles the situation in an adult fashion, allowing you and your partner to make your own decisions.

Respect the Feelings of Your Adult Stepchild

If your stepchild is upset by the idea that her father is starting a new family, she may be rather vocal about her feelings. This can make an already emotional time in your life even more stressful. In this case, your partner may have to mediate the situation in an attempt to minimize the stress everyone experiences. Your stepchild may be feeling abandoned, hurt, and angry. If her father left her mother, she may feel that you replaced her mother, and now that you are having a child that child will replace her. If you can, reach out to your stepchild and involve her—as much as she is willing to be involved—in the pregnancy and upbringing of your biological child.

E-QUESTION

What if my partner spends more time and money on his children from his prior relationship and not enough on our biological child? Did you expect him to stop caring for his biological children once you had one with him? Is he actually neglecting the biological child you had together? If he is, you need to discuss this with him. Maybe he feels guilty for having another child now that he sees how it has affected his children. Talking about it with him may help solve this issue. Therapy could also be helpful.

If your stepchild still detests you after your biological child is born, you can attempt to build a relationship between your stepchild and your biological child. Invite your stepchild to meet your biological child without you present, if that would be helpful—your partner can be present for the meeting. If you can put her hate aside and explain to her that you think it is important for her to know her half-sibling, she may be able to develop a relationship with your biological child, and maybe even with you. Explaining that you do not wish her anger with you to be taken out on your biological child is a great way of initiating the meeting between your stepchild and biological child. You can also indicate the positive traits you see in your stepchild and how you feel those traits could positively impact your biological child. Some stepchildren still do not wish to have a relationship with their half-sibling. As unfortunate as this may be, your stepchild is an adult and has the right to make that decision.

The Other Biological Parent

Again, the other biological parent may feel slighted by the start of a new family, and concerned that a new family will mean a dismissal of the family he once had with your partner. Try to keep this from happening by maintaining consistency in your behavior and your partner's behavior when it comes to her children and the other biological parent. If you always had New Year's Day brunch together, do not abruptly stop now that you have a child of your own. Instead, include your child as part of this extended family. If your partner celebrated Mother's Day with your stepchildren, make sure she still does so once your biological child is born. Add your child to the celebration and don't forget, or postpone, the celebrations you or your partner had with your stepchildren. Although everyone in the situation is an adult, they may revert back to childlike behavior if they fear abandonment. You and your partner can safeguard against this by keeping their time with both of you consistent and inclusive.

Your Role as a Stepgrandparent

You may enter into a situation where you are not only a stepparent, but also a stepgrandparent. You may also be a stepparent who later becomes a stepgrandparent. This is a role you may or may not have the opportunity to enjoy. Since your stepchild is the parent of your potential stepgrandchild, it is in your stepchild's hands to dictate what your role will be in this child's life. If your stepchild does not wish you to be a part of your stepgrandchild's life, you will need to accept this position and hope he changes his mind in time.

As a stepgrandparent, you have the potential to gain many new peers in the biological grandparents and any other stepgrandparents in your stepgrandchild's life. You also have the potential to face even more people who are skeptical of you or fear you are somehow moving in on their relationship with their grandchild. Biological grandparents are jealous enough of each other; adding even more grandparents to the family can create more competition for time with the child. As with the other biological parent, you want to be aware of how your relationship with your stepgrandchild may affect the biological grandparents. Remember, at least one of the biological grandparents is your partner's ex. The other biological grandparents are parents to your stepchild's spouse. If your relationship with your stepchild or the other biological parent is strained, you may find the other biological grandparents feel loyalty to them and treat you as your stepchild and other biological parent treat you. There are now so many adults in the situation it can be rather tedious to navigate around them to have a relationship with your stepgrandchild.

ALERT!

If your partner decides he is going to boycott his grandchild's celebrations or activities or his relationship with his child because of the way his child is treating you, try to discourage this. As valiant as it may seem, it will hurt his relationship with his child and grandchild, and will do more damage to any relationship you could potentially have with them. He can voice his disagreement; however, he should attempt to maintain a relationship.

If you are able to have a relationship with your stepgrandchild, keep these relationships in mind when deciding what your stepgrandchild should call you. This may be dictated by your stepchild, but if not, be respectful of the other grandparents in the picture. If one is Gramps and one is Papa, you shouldn't choose either of those. You may want to avoid a stereotypical grandfather nickname altogether and come up with a special name that you and your stepgrandchild create. Once you do find a name, and it may just be your first name, run it by your stepchild to assure you are not choosing something that may hurt someone's feelings or make anyone uncomfortable.

Another way you may become a stepgrandparent is if your child or your stepchild marries someone with children from a previous relationship. The nice part of this is that you are gaining a stepgrandchild, and you have experience that your child or stepchild may need to enhance his own relationship with his new stepchild. If it is your stepchild who is gaining a stepchild, he may gain insight into how difficult it was for you to develop a relationship with him, and your relationship with each other may reach a new level. Whatever the case, it is very important to let the biological parent steer the relationship between you and your stepgrandchild. Remain available to the opportunity of a new relationship; be caring, compassionate, respectful, and patient.

When the Adult Stepchild Blames You

Unfortunately, an adult stepchild can blame you for the breakup of her parents' marriage just as vehemently as a younger stepchild. One of the most difficult aspects of this is that anger and hate from an adult can be a lot tougher to stomach than it is from a child. With a child, you can chalk it up to hormones or immaturity. With adults, hormones and maturity may still factor in, but they are grown human beings with the ability to make decisions on their own and take responsibility for their actions. Also, when they are younger, there seems to be the potential for a future relationship. When they are adults, it seems as if they are set in their decisions, and any hope of changing their minds is minimal. This is not necessarily true; however, there are many issues adult stepchildren deal with that may affect their belief that you are to blame.

In an article titled "Working Therapeutically with Adult Stepchildren: identifying the needs of a neglected client group," Sarah Corrie identified the following eight issues adult stepchildren report in therapy:

- Feeling emotionally distressed by a parent's decision to remarry
- Feeling rejected
- Feeling betrayed

- Experiencing feelings of anger toward a parent or stepparent
- Loss of self-esteem
- Struggling to accept a stepparent who is the same age as the client
- Disliking overt signs of a parent's sexuality (such as witnessing the new couple holding hands, embracing, or flirting)
- Problems coping with parental pressure to develop a close relationship with a stepparent

Taking notice of these eight issues may give you some insight into what your stepchild is dealing with, outside of trying to accept you as part of her life. If you can respect these issues and respond to them appropriately, your stepchild may be less hostile. For example, encourage your partner to continue a relationship with his child, regardless of how his child behaves. This will decrease feelings of rejection. Try to keep flirting or kissing in front of your stepchild to a minimum. If she is still hurting from the breakup of her parents, she will not want to see you enjoying her mother in an intimate way. Discourage your partner from forcing the two of you to get along. Encourage him to respect the boundaries your stepchild has put up, and give everyone the time they need. The more respectful you are of your stepchild's feelings and place in the situation, the more respect she may have for you. She may never want a relationship with you outside of a cordial greeting, but at least you are not doing anything to make her feel worse or prove her right when it comes to finding you loathsome.

If You Are to Blame

Of course, your stepchild may blame you for good reason. If you were involved with her parent in an affair, as an adult your stepchild will understand this much more than a younger stepchild. You may find that your stepchild is never ready to have a relationship with you and simply avoids you. If this is what your stepchild wishes to do with your relationship, you should give her that space. You can still send cards or gifts to her and/or her children as the years go on, but don't expect anything in return. Do not expect you can buy her love or that you can guilt her into liking you. If she tells you or your partner she does not want you to send cards or gifts anymore, respect her wishes. If you still feel compelled to do something for her, you can buy a card, sign it, and keep it somewhere in case you are able to form a relationship with her in the future.

Even if your stepchild enjoyed you when she was younger, when she is old enough to realize you had a hand in her parents' breakup, she may change her mind. She may feel guilty that she ever liked you, and see it as the ultimate betrayal to her other biological parent. To make up for liking you all those years, she may hate you with extra gusto. These feelings will take time to lose strength.

It may take time for your stepchild to experience feelings of anger, hurt, blame, and then forgiveness, but hopefully she will get through all of these stages and find a way to include you in her life. If not, you have done all you can and you will have to accept that she is not able to accept you as a part of her life.

CHAPTER 13

Legal and Money Issues

Legal factors might play a large role in your marriage and the custodial situation of your stepchild or they may be nonexistent. Money, however, is likely to be a hot topic even if you get along well with everyone in the family and communicate effectively during every interaction with the other biological parent. The legal and monetary aspects of bringing up stepchildren are not items you may find romantic enough to bring up prior to the wedding, but they really should be discussed. It is important to put your concerns and questions on the table and continue to voice them as your relationship continues.

Lunch Money

No matter how solid your partner's divorce settlement might be, how much child support your partner pays, or how tight your own monetary situation may be, you will definitely contribute monetarily to your stepchild. Even if your partner tells you he doesn't expect you to pay for anything involving his child, it is inevitable that you will. This may not be anyone's fault; instead, it is simply a natural result of having a stepchild. Your contribution may be as little as paying for your stepson's bus pass every month or providing lunch money every Thursday. You should expect to pay for some things, and prepare yourself to do so. When you married your partner you accepted his child as part of the deal, so be ready to part with some cash.

FACT

According to a survey by the United States Department of Agriculture, in 2001, the cost of raising a child between the ages of zero and seventeen in a dual-parent home was approximately $10,000 per year. This does not include college costs or expenses that are likely to be incurred if the child remains in the home as a dependent after turning eighteen years of age.

Household Expenses

Some ways in which your expenses are likely to rise once you have a stepchild are rather obvious. You may find that you are spending more money at the grocery store and on such items as the electrical, phone, and water bills. If there are more people drawing on your utilities and raiding your refrigerator, your expenses will go up. Other situations might sneak up and surprise you. If your partner never carries cash, you may find that you are always the one to part with $5 a day for lunch money. You may also be the stepmother to a stepdaughter who is too mortified to ask her father to buy her tampons or underwear, so you may end up taking on this cost. You may also be the stepfather to a stepson who needs razors or deodorant and is more comfortable asking you to buy these items. These costs can seem like nothing, but they will add up. Before that happens, talk to your partner about how to handle these little expenses.

ALERT!

> If your stepchild has a cell phone, you may want to avoid any involvement in your stepchild's cell phone bill. If your partner wants to put his son on his cell phone plan, great, but you may want to think twice before doing so. Such things as text messaging, picture messaging, and going over his minutes are all going to add up and make for an outrageous cell phone bill.

Many surveys show that money is the number one reason couples fight and even the number one reason couples divorce. If you can keep any money concerns out in the open with your partner, you may safeguard your marriage from certain arguments. When it comes to the seemingly little expenses such as tampons, extra cookies, and increased electricity expenditure, it may sound rather petty if you tell your partner you are fed up with buying tampons every month so he needs to buy them from now on. Think about your stepchild and how to best protect her from embarrassment. If you argue with her father over her tampons, she is going to be mortified. A better way of approaching it is to talk to your partner about how you feel like these expenditures are adding up in a way that you did not expect. Although you may be happy to help out and pay for items concerning your stepchild, it is perfectly reasonable to point out to your partner how much more per month you are spending. Your partner may not realize this, especially if he has nothing to do with the bill paying, and he may simply need to be shown the difference in bills prior to taking on his child and current bills. Your stepchild may visit only, but those times that she is in the house may still cause monetary strain. If this is your first time experiencing life with a child and your partner is used to all of these extra items, it may take a while for the two of you to adjust to a situation that is new for you. You may be shocked at the price of certain kid treats, while your partner always knew the expense, and was so used to it he didn't think that it would be an issue.

It is important to keep an open dialogue between you and your partner about these issues. If you do not raise these issues, your frustration will fester and you may argue with your partner or take out your frustration on your stepchild. As far as money is concerned, it is an issue to keep between adults. Your stepson should not be scolded if your partner forgets to leave his lunch money for him. You can discuss this later with your partner. You and your partner can certainly educate your stepchild about money, but avoid doing it in a way that blames your stepchild for your financial strain. It isn't his fault that he needs to eat or shower! If your grocery bill is too high, you may need to talk to your stepson about changing to generic brands of his favorite foods or saving expensive treats for once a month instead of daily. This is appropriate and can even help your stepson learn about money in a healthy way. He may find it is fun to try and find the best bargains in the grocery-store circular or to see how much electricity he can save each month by turning off his video games an hour earlier.

Child Support

Hopefully, your partner pays her child support on time and without argument. If your partner is on the receiving end, hopefully it is an amicable situation and the child support is paid on time. Child support is a legal issue that can put strain on everyone if there is any disagreement, refusal to pay, late payment, or even snide remarks made upon payment. This strain may affect you directly or indirectly, and there is not much you can do to change the situation.

Child support is meant to benefit your stepchild, yet it is often the focus of heated arguments. An angry ex may refuse to pay child support, but instead of hurting her former partner, she only hurts her son by withholding money he needs to sign up for a sports team or attend his prom. You can certainly remind your partner or encourage her to do what is best for her child and pay the child support. If she feels she got the raw end of the deal and is paying too much, you can encourage her to seek out the advice of an attorney on this matter. Stay out of using the child support money as a way to hurt or punish the other biological parent.

Refusal to Pay Child Support

The issue of child support may more directly affect you if the other biological parent refuses to pay child support, you have a biological child with your partner, or the fighting over child support is having a detrimental effect on your stepchild. If the other biological parent refuses to pay child support, it can put more financial strain on you and your partner, and therefore upset or negatively impact your stepchild.

Try to protect your stepchild from feeling as though the arguments are about her or are her fault. She may feel as though her mother doesn't love her because she won't pay child support, when in fact her mother is angry with her father and wants to punish him by not paying. If you can explain this in a positive manner and avoid talking about her mother negatively, that would be best.

If she continues to refuse to pay, encourage your partner to obtain legal advice. Do not call and yell at her or threaten her. You can help your partner by saving receipts or tracking expenses, but the argument is one that should be dealt with in court, away from any situation that may hurt your stepchild.

E-QUESTION

How is the amount someone pays for child support determined?
Each state has different laws and different ways of determining the amount of child support one must pay. To find out what the laws are in your state, contact a family law attorney. Many states offer question-and-answer evenings with attorneys to help answer frequently asked questions.

Discuss the Monetary Affects of Child Support

If you have a biological child with your partner and money is tight and he has to pay child support to the other biological parent, you may end up arguing a bit. You might feel as though he is showing preference to your stepchild by continuing to pay child support when you are struggling to pay for formula and diapers. If you don't talk about this and find a way to remedy the situation, you will risk not only fighting with your partner but also with your stepchild. It is not your stepchild's fault. It is also not his other parent's fault. It is an issue that may need working out or changing with the help of an attorney. If your partner is struggling to financially support your stepchild and the child you have together, it would be wise for him to seek the advice of an attorney.

If your partner seems to be financially strapped by the restraints of child support, you may find yourself feeling angry or frustrated by the whole situation. For example, if you would like to build an addition on your house but can't because the only extra money your partner has goes to your stepchild, you may really feel as though you are in an unfair situation. After all, this is his situation, why are you feeling the punishing effects? Shouldn't you be able to spend money on yourselves and enjoy your marriage?

This is a tough one to swallow. Feeling as if you come second financially can be very difficult; you do come second financially. Spending money on each other comes second to making sure your stepchild is fed, clothed, sheltered, and happy. Don't blame your stepchild for this. Try not to put the blame on anyone. As much as you are in this marriage to celebrate each other, you are also in this marriage as a stepparent, and your stepchild takes precedence. If you are not a parent, try to think like one. Wouldn't you want your child's other parent to make him a priority financially? Most likely, yes.

To assure that you still celebrate your marriage, you can either find ways to save money for a slush fund or you can find ways to enjoy each other without spending money. To save money, you could suggest to your partner that you both set aside $5 a week to go into a night-on-the-town fund. Or maybe give up buying coffee every morning, and put the money saved into a fund for a trip you can take together. To celebrate each other without spending money, there are plenty of fun creative ideas. Have a dinner-in night, and alternate who cooks and who picks the meal. Set the table with candles and shut off all technological devices. You can call the local museums and see when they have a free admission day. It takes creativity, but you can still have time, money, and enjoyment for yourselves if you plan well and get creative.

College Tuition

Who pays for college tuition? Divorce agreements may specify how such costs shall be handled. Different states often dictate different requirements. Your own situation may depend on the state you live in, the status of your stepchild, the college your stepchild attends, and your own financial ability and desire to assist. For information on your specific situation, consult an attorney.

The financial aid process for college is perhaps the most confusing part about college for parents and students. For help with this, go to *www.finaid.org/questions/divorce.phtml*. You may also find help with these tough questions through your stepchild's high school guidance counselor.

Colleges have gotten savvier at finding out what resources their potential students have—especially private institutions. The Free Application for Federal Student Aid (FAFSA) used to be the one financial aid form every incoming student needed to fill out in order to apply for aid. On the FAFSA, your income and assets as a stepparent are required if you are married to the custodial parent and your stepchild lives with you. Recently, many private institutions have required all incoming students to fill out a form known as the CSS/Financial Aid PROFILE. On this form, all parental figures (biological, adoptive, and step) must report their income and assets. This has caused quite a stir, as many people do not consider the cost of tuition the responsibility of a stepparent.

If you have the means and the desire to contribute, then you do so at your own discretion. This is something you may want to run by every parental figure. Although it is generous, you do not want to make the other biological parent, your stepchild, or your partner feel uncomfortable or that there are strings attached to the money. If you do not have the means but would like to help in some way, you could certainly assist in buying books or sending up a small amount in spending money when you have it available. Most of all, support your stepchild emotionally when he goes off to school. Helping with money is great, but if you can be there for your stepchild as he adjusts to the demands of college, that is priceless.

Should You Combine Bank Accounts?

Many married people never combine bank accounts. Some have a bank account together and separate bank accounts for use at their own discretion. It may help your partner keep track of expenses if she has a separate account for her child that she contributes to on a regular basis. If your partner maintains an account for her child, then you may also have one joint account all of the household expenses and bills are paid from, and still have separate accounts of spending money for yourselves. There are many different scenarios. Choose one that is comfortable for you and your partner.

Separate Bank Accounts

Maintaining separate bank accounts can be a simple way of knowing exactly who is contributing to household bills and the amount. If you are considering keeping your finances completely separate, you may consider splitting your bills as well. Perhaps you do not watch cable, but your partner enjoys having movie channels for nights when your stepson is over. The cable bill could then be one to which she contributes a greater amount.

Although this can potentially decrease arguing over certain money matters, it can also create tension. Figuring out everything down to the penny can drive you and your partner crazy. If you can split everything in a flexible way, with room for compromise at times, you will have an easier time.

Combining Bank Accounts

If you decide to combine all of your money, you will need to seriously communicate when you are upset about how money is being spent or saved. If you find your partner is spending $5 a day on coffee while you make yours at home for virtually nothing, you may find you judge her spending habits. It is important to know her spending habits and for both of you to be open about how much you are spending and on what. However, you need to make compromises in this situation and not pick at everything your partner is purchasing. If you find that money is a struggle, you may both need to be put on a budget and held to it, or agree to save more. It may be that your partner needs to make her coffee at home three times a week and buy her coffee twice a week in order to stay within the budget, but if she can make this decision for herself you may argue a little less.

FACT

Talk with your partner about all the options for handling money and remember that your money management systems should be flexible and not carved in stone. As your family grows and new priorities emerge you will need to re-evaluate your plans. Discuss with your partner what is working and what is not. Money situations will be ongoing and will require compromise and renegotiation.

Separate and Combined

Since money is such a touchy subject and everyone has his or her necessary items, you may find that sharing a savings account that you both contribute to, and then having personal accounts for your own spending, is a great way to go. If you have a savings account that you both contribute to, you could decide on contributing a certain percentage of your paychecks. This way you may not be contributing the same dollar amount, but there is fairness in how the amount was determined. Your personal account may help you pay for your hobbies, any items you want for the house, gifts, your student loans, and any other discretionary expenses. Your partner's account may hold money for her child, child support, her coffee, and gym membership. Having separate bank accounts for items like this doesn't mean you don't trust each other, and it is still important to disclose your income and assets to one another. In case of an emergency, you may have to lend money from your personal account to your combined account. Having both gives you the ability to share in certain areas and keep tabs on your own expenses at the same time.

When You Contribute More than Your Share

As a stepparent, you may find that you are contributing more than your share in many ways. Perhaps you are doing most of the caretaking and driving, attending parent meetings, and paying for more than you expected. Doing more than your share can seem fine at first, but if you get to the point where you are frustrated, it may be difficult to speak to your partner without getting angry. This can be a tough issue to deal with, and like many other issues, needs to be dealt with by the adults in the situation, not the child.

Contributing More Time

Some caretaking should be expected, and there may be an ebb and flow of sorts to your caretaking responsibilities. It may just play out in ways that you do more some months and your partner does more in other months. However, if you notice that the responsibilities are truly unbalanced, talk to your partner about how you are feeling. Point out in a nonconfrontational way that you feel as though you are doing more than your share and need some help. Try not to make the conversation about how frustrated you are with your stepchild. And don't let your anger build up too long.

ALERT!

If your partner appears to be taking your contributions for granted and is not willing to see how much you are putting into his child, you may want to seek out couples counseling. Although money is blamed for many break-ups, it is often the issues surrounding the money that are at fault. Money is just paper; work on the issues regarding how money is used to resolve any disagreements.

Contributing More Money

If you find that you are contributing more than your share monetarily, talk about finances with your partner as soon as you see this becoming an issue. If you feel as though you need a mediator, you could both see a financial planner to help come up with a plan for your finances. For example, a financial planner may be able to point out, as a neutral party, how much money you have been spending on your stepchild and how to rework the situation so it is a more balanced contribution by both of you. Sometimes using a neutral party to point out discrepancies can take the emotions out of the situation and reduce or eliminate arguing.

If you are paying for your stepchild's private school, ballet lessons, or soccer practice, you can't take it back if you are angry with your partner. If you argue with your stepchild, telling her she is ungrateful for everything you pay for really isn't fair. The money conversations, agreements, and disagreements should occur between you and your partner. If you and your partner are splitting up and you have contributed monies to your stepchild that you would now like to have back, this should be addressed with your partner and not the child. It is helpful to keep track of it, but do not use it against your stepchild.

Adopting Your Stepchild

Adopting your stepchild can be a wonderful move to make, but it can also bring up many emotions you may not expect. You and your stepchild will not be the only ones with emotions. Your partner, your family, the extended family of your stepchild, and any children of your own may have feelings that take you by surprise. The more prepared you are for these emotions, the better equipped you will be to handle the adoption. To assure you are prepared and equipped legally, you should consult a family law attorney.

The Other Biological Parent

If the parent for whom you are stepping in abandoned your stepchild, the adoption can be healing, but it can also bring up those feelings of abandonment. Why did my mother leave? Why did she agree to let my stepmother adopt me? In most cases of adoption where the biological parent is still alive and there is some contact, the biological parent must agree to the adoption and give up their rights as a parent. The biological parent may not agree to the adoption even if she has had little to no contact with her child. This can lead to a legal battle for which everyone needs to be mentally prepared.

If she does contest the adoption, it can cause more pain for your stepchild, you, and your partner. Check the balance. Is your stepchild ready to go into a legal battle like this? You may be, but you need to constantly consider your stepchild's feelings and level of tolerance for the whole procedure. If the adoption seems to be smooth sailing and the other biological parent agrees or is no longer in contact, your stepchild may still have emotions arise unexpectedly. She may seem angry or withdrawn, even if she had seemed excited by the whole idea. Those feelings of abandonment may be rearing up again. As wonderful as you may be and as excited as you may be to adopt her, there was still someone in her life that left her in some way. Don't be angry with her if she is trying to figure out these emotions; she may not know how to express them or what to do with them. Being open to talking to her about them and having her talk to a counselor or mentor about her feelings can help her navigate the situation.

Make sure your stepchild wants to be adopted by you; she may not. It might not have anything to do with you, but simply that she still wants to leave that option open for her other biological parent. Do not pressure her or make her feel guilty. This is not your choice; it is something that will change her life forever and she needs time and space to arrive at a decision with which she is comfortable.

Your Own Emotions

You may be riding an emotional roller coaster of your own. Before bringing up the idea to your stepchild or even your partner, you need to do some self-exploration. Becoming a stepparent may have prepped you for this decision; however, this is a very big step and you may vacillate before you actually decide what is right for you. Are you ready to take on your stepchild as your adopted child? It would be beneficial for you to talk with an attorney, a counselor who specializes in adoption, stepparents who have had positive and negative experiences with the adoption process, and your partner. Before giving your stepchild a hint that this is even a thought in your mind, you need to make up your mind one way or the other. It would not be fair for you to bring up the idea and then change your mind once you have told your stepchild.

Your Partner's Emotions

You may be surprised by the reaction of your partner. If your relationship has gone wonderfully and the other biological parent is not involved, it may seem like a no-brainer. Your partner, however, may feel as though his child isn't ready for that step—or that he isn't ready for that step. Like other milestones—meeting your stepchild, moving in, and marriage—this one also has some finality associated with it. Your partner may remember how awful it was for his child to be abandoned or any other traumas or emotions experienced with the other biological parent. These may all come back up for him, and he may not be ready to move forward with adoption just yet. This may symbolize another severance of ties for him and his child. If he is not ready yet, it doesn't mean he is waiting for the other biological parent to return so they can all live happily ever after; it may just mean he is not ready to step back into a situation filled with so many strong emotions. Give your partner time to digest the situation and try not to take offense if he doesn't have an immediate positive reaction.

Adoption is a big step, and can be a very positive step. Just remember to have patience and expect the unexpected when it comes to emotions. You can't know what feelings will surface, but you can be better prepared for them if you are open minded and willing to communicate and wait for everyone to be ready for this milestone.

If You Have Children of Your Own

If you have children of your own, they may have feelings about the adoption that are positive or negative. If your children live with you and your stepchild, they may be more prepared for this to happen since their everyday lives have included your stepchild for a while. If they do not live with you, your children may have a more difficult time with you adopting your stepchild. They may see it as you trying to replace them with your stepchild. If you are not available for them as much as they would like you to be, they may see your move to adopt your stepchild as one more step away from them as a parent. It is important to discuss your decision with them and include them in the decision. Explaining why you would like to adopt your stepchild and that your biological children are still a priority may help. This may be another situation that requires family counseling. Neutral parties can be very beneficial in emotionally loaded situations. Your children may only need time to adjust to your decision and then feel fine with it. Give them this time to adjust.

Keep in mind that your former partner may have feelings about your decision as well, and may decide to voice them. You may feel that this is none of her business; however, remember that she may be worried about the feelings of your biological children. If she sees you as abandoning your biological children for your stepchild, you may have a more difficult time getting everyone on board with this decision.

Hopefully your children will actually see the adoption as a positive way of adding to your family. They might even want you to adopt your stepchild. Once you have adopted or even started the process, there might be feelings of your family being complete and finally in a space where everyone is on equal playing ground. There is no "step" anymore, and although it is just a change in name and legal standing, it can be a huge change emotionally for everyone. There can be feelings of acceptance and equality that you might not have gotten to without adopting.

CHAPTER 14

Managing Family Events

Family events involving your stepchild may be events with your family, your significant other's family, the other biological parent's family, the other stepparent's family, or any combination of these families. Navigating your own family can be difficult enough, but navigating in-laws and ex-law's can be even more challenging. Even in the most perfect scenarios emotions will still run high, and there are many toes on which you may step. If you handle events with caution, you are less likely to offend or be offended. You might even have fun!

Whose Picture Goes on the Mantle?

Formal family pictures, holiday pictures, school pictures, and candid shots might all be on display at your home. You might want to take a good look at them and make sure they include all of the people your stepchild sees as his family. You may see your family as including yourself, your partner, your stepchild, and your biological child. Your partner may have the same view. Your stepchild, however, may see his family as including his biological mother, his half-sister on his mother's side, his dog who lives with his mother, his stepfather, and his maternal grandparents. It isn't necessary for you to hang pictures of people you don't know all over the house; however, it might be nice to show your stepson that you respect his idea of family by including a picture that contains those people closest to him. Your stepson may have a picture of his mom and grandparents from a school event that you could offer to place on the mantle or he may prefer to have it on display in his room.

E-QUESTION

My stepson despises his biological mother and rarely sees her. Do I still have to put up her picture?
These are simply suggestions. You certainly don't have to put anyone's picture up if it doesn't feel right. Asking your stepson if he would like to display a picture of his mother or of another family member currently not on display is a great way to determine what he would like and if these pictures will bring positive or negative memories to mind.

Creating Memories for the Mantle

Creating pictures can be fun, too. Your stepson is most likely going to attend events where pictures will be taken of him and his family. But who is his family? Does he have two completely different families or does everyone join in the picture together? Events like prom, graduation, school concerts, awards ceremonies, and sporting events will bring these questions up in rather public places. It might be embarrassing to your stepson if you don't think about this ahead of time and when picture time arrives you, your partner, and the other biological parent have an argument over who is really his family.

To avoid this as best as you can, try and push any animosity aside and be a good sport about pictures your stepson would like to have. At graduation, he may want a picture with your partner and his other biological parent. Even though this may be uncomfortable for you, these are his biological parents and the people who genetically supplied him with the brain that got him through high school. If your partner makes a stink and wants you included in the picture, support what your stepson wants. Suggest to your partner that he can do both. He can take a picture with the other biological parent and his son and then you can step into the picture. Try to make your stepson's needs the priority. Maybe your stepson will want a picture with you and his other biological parent; this may be really uncomfortable for you, but try to be a good sport and do it for him. If his other biological parent resists the idea, you being a good sport may convince her to go along with it for the sake of her child. This will help give your stepson the keepsake he wants and also help everyone see that they can get along for the sake of a child.

When taking or hanging pictures, try to maintain a nice balance regarding who is involved. If your stepchild lives with the other biological parent and your child lives with you, it may seem natural to have more pictures of your biological child. Be cognizant of this and try to prevent it from happening. Your stepchild should be able to see that he is just as much a part of the family as the folks that live in your house. If you don't see your stepson often and the opportunities to take pictures are minimal, ask your partner to ask the other biological parent for pictures. There are so many ways of sharing pictures now that accessing pictures should be quite simple. You can also share pictures you think the other biological parent may enjoy.

Pictures symbolize important memories of people in our life and the lives of those in our home. Keep in mind that the more inclusive you are of your stepchild and those he thinks of as family, the more included he is likely to feel, and the more welcome he may feel in your home. Small gestures like this may even help break down any negative feelings between you and the other biological parent. It may be nice for her to hear that you have pictures up of everyone who is important to her son, and she may feel that you are truly trying to support her son and those he thinks of as family.

So no matter how much you do not want to stand next to the other biological parent at graduation, think of your stepchild and the memories you are creating with him. How would you like him to remember these moments? Hopefully with a smile; so grin and bear it if you must, but try your hardest to look genuinely happy.

ALERT!

Be thoughtful about which pictures you share. Do not share pictures with the other biological parent that may come across as "rubbing it in." If the other biological parent is still feeling wounded by the breakup, sharing a picture of you and your partner smooching wouldn't be nice. Also, if the other biological partner despises you, don't share pictures that contain you. Instead, share pictures of your stepson alone or with other people with whom she doesn't have an issue.

Who Gets Invited?

Figuring out guest lists is rarely fun, even when you love everyone involved. There is always the chance that you will forget someone or have to include people you don't really want in attendance. When your stepchild is younger, events like birthday parties, holiday celebrations, and religious milestones may bring up issues of who gets invited where. If there is a great deal of animosity between families, it might be wise to have separate parties. You and your partner can throw a birthday party one night and the other biological parent can throw one the next night. This is a perfectly fine way of doing things.

Keeping as many events as possible separate might work for a while, but there will probably come a time when the event needs to be shared or when your stepchild's big wish for the event is that everyone can be present at the same time. Events like graduations and weddings are particularly challenging. At such events, it may be almost impossible to keep everyone separate. Don't fight in public or make a scene. If other people try to make a scene, remove yourself from the situation, and act with respect. Constantly think about the event as one that will be a memory for your stepchild. Her memories should include as few fights as possible, and should be filled with people who support her, regardless of how they get along with one another.

If you are hosting a party or event for your stepchild, whom should you invite? This is a good question to ask both your partner and your stepchild. If you are the only ones hosting a celebration of this event, you should probably invite the other biological parent and key family members. In order to avoid snubbing someone, ask the other biological parent who should be invited from his family. Should his parents be invited? Should you include a cousin you don't know who is close to your stepchild? If the event is a shared event like a wedding, you may wind up splitting the guest list and both biological parents will be able to invite a certain number of guests. How costs are allocated can be a rather delicate subject. For smaller events like a birthday party, perhaps you can host it one year and the other biological parent can host it the following year. Another possibility is to split the cost of the event.

Larger events like weddings need to be decided well ahead of time, and with a mediator if necessary. You may decide that each family pays for their own guests and then splits the cost of hall rental, decorations, and wedding favors. Similar to pictures, events like these will be memories to your stepchild. The more positively memorable you can make the experience the better it will be for everyone. These are events where you really need to avoid people with whom you can't help but have conflict. Also, this is a time to be on your best behavior and be the bigger person if others cannot put their negativity aside. You may need to walk away from situations, stop conversations, or suggest to others that you leave any hot topics for later dates. Encourage others to put the happiness of your stepchild first by doing so yourself.

Where Will Everyone Sit?

Seating charts for large events are difficult, but can be helpful if you want certain people to be separated. Seating arrangements for more intimate gatherings may be even more difficult, as there is less space to put between people. For larger events, there is rarely a seat of honor that cannot somehow be paralleled. If your partner would like to sit at the table next to the head table at the wedding, it is probably possible to have a table for the other biological parent on the other side of the head table. This way you will maintain some equality in seating. This should be done with grandparents and other relatives as well. If possible, it may help to have both parents look over the seating chart if they are not the ones putting it together. For larger events, you may be able to split the room in half and give half to each parent. Each parent can then decide where to seat members of his or her family.

Seating people next to at least one person they know can decrease anxiety and make for a more pleasant experience for guests. Also, keep in mind any health conditions or other issues that guests may have. For example, a pregnant guest may be more comfortable close to a restroom or exit, while an older guest may prefer to be further away from the stereo equipment.

For more intimate events, seating may be more of a struggle. If there is only one place for a head of the table, there may be some feathers ruffled if one parent believes she should have that seat and another nabs it. Avoiding a head of the table may be necessary and can be done by using circular tables, or placing a child or a random person in the seat that looks like the head of the table seat. It may be easier in some instances to assign seating, and easier in others to let people choose for themselves. Assigned seating can help avoid awkward moments of, "Where should I sit?" But it can also provoke such responses as, "Why is my seat here? His stepmother must have done this to punish me." On the other hand, not assigning seats opens up the possibility of arguing over a seat or ending up next to someone you don't want to be near. If it is decided that seats will be assigned, try to think of equality in seating, and move yourself to the back burner if possible.

You may want your stepchild to decide the seating arrangement and then go over it with your partner. If your stepchild would like you to sit next to her and her mother to sit all the way at the end of the table because they are not getting along right now, consider her mother's feelings. You can tell your stepdaughter that you are flattered that she would like to sit next to you, but feel that it may hurt her mother's feelings. You can plan a night for the two of you where you sit next to one another and leave the event seating one where her biological parents have preferential seating. Try to avoid physically taking the place of one of the biological parents. Seating symbolizes so much, and how we habitually situate ourselves tells a great deal about our relationships with one another. This is probably not the effect you want to achieve. For your purposes, try to avoid creating any seating charts that will cause discomfort and place people where they feel welcome and at ease.

Navigating Events Without Stepping on Too Many Toes

As mentioned before, you may have to take the back burner so you don't step on any toes. If you can, put the biological parents in the spotlight, second to your stepchild. Do not use the event to put yourself in the spotlight or to prove that you are a better party planner or that you are willing to spend more money on an event. The purpose of the event is your stepchild. You would not want your stepchild embarrassing you at an event for you; extend the same courtesy to him.

If this is an event that you have planned, you are likely to feel more comfortable since you have more control of the situation. You know who is coming, where they are sitting, and have probably invited people who help make you feel most comfortable. If this is an event the other biological parent planned, you may feel like you are walking into a potentially conflict-ridden situation. If there is animosity between you and the other parent, it would be safe to assume those on his side of the family share his opinions about you. This can make you feel intimidated, nervous, and quite defensive. It is the defensive feeling that can turn into attitude. To avoid acting defensive, try to be open-minded and pleasant. Maybe everyone isn't as open-minded as you and would like to judge you based on actions they observe. If so, don't give them reason to agree with someone who dislikes you; instead, show them that your main concern is your stepchild and his happiness.

If you feel as though you are being attacked in some way or are feeling extremely uncomfortable, it is okay to excuse yourself from the situation or event. Although you may want to point out to those who are attacking you that they are being ridiculous, try to avoid confrontation during the event and save any such discussions for a time that is more appropriate and private. It is also unnecessary to tell your stepchild that his father was being a jerk. You can say that you were not feeling well and leave it at that. If he finds out that you left due to a conflict with his biological parent, you can inform him that you felt it best to leave to keep conflicts at the event to a minimum. Hopefully, everyone can get along for the event or at least ignore each other until it is over.

If your stepson loves the other biological parent's grilling ability and you are hosting a cookout, consider working with the other biological parent. Maybe he will grill if you buy the food. Also, don't unintentionally snub anyone who has an expertise. If your stepson's grandmother is the cake-decorating queen, don't forget about her and buy a decorated cake; enlist her assistance.

Get Information Prior to the Event

It is difficult for many people to make small talk or to introduce themselves to people they do not know. To make things more comfortable, ask your stepchild to fill you in on his relatives and other partygoers. Find out peoples' hobbies and changes of circumstances. If your stepchild's Aunt Nancy just got divorced, it is helpful to know ahead of time so you don't ask her how her husband is doing. Knowing hobbies can give you something to talk about if you are stuck next to a relative you don't know well. If your stepchild told you Uncle Bobby likes to skydive, you can bring that up when you bump into him. If you are talking to someone you do not know well, ask about his hobbies or how he knows your stepchild. Try to avoid controversial topics such as politics, religion, or whether or not they like the other biological parent. Making small talk is difficult, but getting out of a heated political discussion is even harder. Equip yourself with a couple of questions or topics that are benign and easy for you to discuss. If you really hate talking, ask as many open-ended questions as you can so the person you are talking to is the one doing the most talking.

Should You Go to Every Party?

It is not necessary for you to go to every party, even if you are invited. There may be times your partner attends but you do not feel comfortable or parties that you attend on your own once you do feel comfortable. If it is a party your partner feels is important for you to go to, discuss your concerns with him and make your decision based on how comfortable you feel and if it truly is an appropriate party for you to attend. Certain parties you should go to if possible, but others you can gracefully decline.

When You Do Not Need to Go

If your stepchild's other biological parent invites you to everything, that is great, but you are not obligated to go. If you are trying to build your relationship with the other biological parent or if it is a large event for your stepchild, you should seriously consider attending. If you are invited to a holiday cookout or a random get-together, you can decline. Let people know ahead of time whether you will be attending. If you decide to decline an invitation, do so gracefully and with appropriate timing. Don't call at the last minute and say you can't attend. If you say that you will attend then do so, unless an emergency arises. It is unfair to commit and then not show.

E-QUESTION

I just stuck my foot in my mouth and said something awful to the other biological parent's friend. What do I do?
Be direct and honest. Do not make excuses or try to explain yourself. Simply apologize for what was said and change the subject. The offended person will have more respect for you if you own up to your mistake than if you try to make excuses for it.

If you are not expressly invited to a party, you don't have to go. You may not have been invited for a reason. In this case, don't impose and go simply because you think you deserve to be invited. If it is unclear whether or not you should attend, stick to the least embarrassing option for everyone, and do not attend. If your partner is going, you can send him along with a dessert or bottle of wine and good wishes for the party. Certain events may be potentially more uncomfortable than others. If you think you are going to feel uncomfortable at a party, don't go. Your discomfort will be clear to your partner, your stepchild, and those hosting the party. If it is a party you feel you need to attend but you are extremely nervous, find a reason to leave and express this as soon as you arrive. You can tell the host that you had a prior commitment but wanted to support your stepchild by attending at least for a moment.

The Other Biological Parent Doesn't Have to Attend

Just like you don't have to go to every party, the other biological parent doesn't need to go to every party either. If you are hosting a birthday party for your stepchild and you invite the other biological parent even though he already celebrated your stepchild's birthday with him, it is understandable that he may not attend. If he feels uncomfortable or doesn't like you or your partner, don't be angry when he doesn't show. Respect his decision and let it be. If your stepchild is angry that his other biological parent did not come, you can inform the other biological parent and let him explain why he did not attend. Do not tell your stepchild he didn't attend because he doesn't like being around you or your partner (even if that is the truth). As your stepchild gets older, he will understand that everyone may not mix at times, but until then, he doesn't need to know that there is animosity.

CHAPTER 15

Stepsiblings

The idea of stepsiblings may immediately bring to mind thoughts of arguing, bullying, and competition. Cinderella's evil stepsisters are perhaps the most well-known stepsisters in literature, and symbolize only the negative aspects of stepsiblings. Real stepsiblings often get along quite well, enjoy each other's company, and form a great familial bond. Like in any sibling relationship, stepsiblings are likely to have disagreements and sometimes have their feelings hurt or get angry. However, if you and your partner are willing to act as continual mediators, your children may get along with each other more often than not.

A Truly Blended Family

The Brady Bunch is one of the best-known blended families to appear on television, and one of the first blended families to be portrayed in the media. The show featured a woman with three daughters who married a man with three sons, creating a family of eight. The stepsiblings had days when they got along well with one another and days when they couldn't stand each other. This is what you can expect from your own blended family.

Blended families may include families with a stepparent, stepsiblings, half-siblings, or a combination of all of these. In some cases, stepsiblings will live together most of the time; in others, one may live in the home while one lives with another parent. Some may never live together at all.

FACT

According to Bumpass, Raley & Sweet, one third of all children will live in a stepfamily before they reach adulthood. Bumpass also found that two-thirds of these children will end up residing with a half-sibling or stepsibling.

Blended Bonding

There are so many types of families now that it is not surprising to hear about a stepsibling or half-sibling. Blending families does not mean these children will all create sibling-like bonds. They may instead create a new type of bond that is exclusive to their relationship. This is one of the main reasons it is important not to force the relationship, but to let it develop on its own. If you force the relationship you think the children should have with one another, you may impose your own thoughts on how that relationship should be instead of letting it develop naturally. Blended family members develop different types of bonds with one another, which may seem like parenting, sibling, friendship, or even mentoring roles. The roles played in blended families are unique to each family.

The word "blended" suggests that everything combines together at the same consistency and without too many lumps. Blended families, however, are not made up of people who are the same consistency, and there will be plenty of lumps and bumps. Everyone is coming into the family with a different history, a different temperament, and a different attitude about becoming part of a blended family. Whatever happened to cause the blended family may have had a different impact on everyone, and no one will handle the disruption of the original family the same. Some members will go with the flow, while others will fight every step of the way. Don't expect your family to blend together perfectly. You and your partner will be integral to a successful blending of family members. Remaining patient, open-minded, and fair, and communicating constantly about your own relationships with each other and the other family members will help the two of you lead the other family members toward harmony.

When You Are Bringing Your Own Children into the Mix

If you are bringing biological children of your own into the family, you need to prepare them for their new siblings just as you prepared them for their new stepparent. If you have multiple children of your own, they will already have experience with siblings, but if you have one child he may face a greater adjustment and potentially have more fears about the new situation. Hopefully, the children have met their stepsiblings prior to your marriage and have some idea of what to expect. If moving in and marriage haven't happened yet, it is a good idea to take the children out together and start getting them acquainted. Not only will they be able to feel each other out, you and your partner will be able to observe how they will get along. This may help you prepare for any potential problems and identify any commonalities.

Preparing Yourself and Your Biological Children

By nature, you may have more protective feelings toward your biological children. Preparing them for moving in with stepsiblings will also help you prepare for your new stepchildren and any conflicts that may arise between your children and your stepchildren. You know your children better than anyone; try to think of quirky traits or habits they have which may lead to teasing or conflict. If your daughter can't stand the sound of snapping gum or your son doesn't like it when people touch his *Star Wars* collection, let your partner know about these quirks. Siblings, whether related by blood or marriage, have an uncanny way of quickly figuring out how to push each other's buttons. By figuring out what buttons might be pushed, you can prepare ahead of time for potential conflicts.

Take note of how your biological children push each other's buttons. Do your daughters like to gang up on your son and poke fun at his clothing? Does your son like to invite his friends over and tease your daughter about her childish taste in music? Once your children blend, they may find their stepsiblings can help them gang up on biological siblings or they may use tactics on their stepsiblings that worked effectively with biological siblings. It is important for you and your partner to be aware of these possibilities. Your partner should share the same insights into his children with you.

Notice how your children behave around their siblings. Point out to them which behaviors you expect them to enhance and which behaviors you expect them to eliminate with their stepsiblings. Letting them know what is expected of them beforehand will help bring clarity to their situation.

If There Was an Only Child

If you have an only child, you may find that your child is overwhelmed, anxious, or even angry at the idea of having a sibling. Generally, the younger your child is the less he will be affected by the addition of a stepsibling. However, the older your child the more time he has had to get used to being an only child. Since he doesn't know any differently, it may be tough for him to share you with another child—sharing you with an adult isn't quite as threatening as sharing you with someone who is more his peer. This may make him feel as though he needs to compete for your affection and be the "better," "nicer," or "smarter" child. If he doesn't feel as though he is getting enough attention this way, he may become the "bad" child and act out in order to gain more of your attention.

It is really hard for a child to go from being the one and only to a situation where he is one of many or even just one of two. Talk to your child about this and assure him that the two of you will continue to have the bond you have now. Give him ideas on how to get your attention, tell you when he feels neglected, or let you know when he needs more of your time. If he is able to use healthy ways of communicating to you that his needs are not being met, you need to respond to them in a timely and effective manner. At first, he may tell you constantly that you are not spending enough time with him, and he may seem to be monopolizing your time. Be patient and give him extra time. Once he recognizes that he can have your time, he may not feel as anxious about needing your time and will stop asking for it so much. Also, children don't want to hang out with their parents forever, so he will likely outgrow the need to be with you all the time or find friends he would prefer to be with instead of you.

If There Are Multiple Children

Similar to only children, children from multiple-child families may find their family role is threatened or different once they join with their steps-siblings. Your oldest child may no longer be the oldest. Your athletic child may pale in comparison to his stepsibling. Your only girl may now be one of five girls. Feeling as though their status in the family has changed can make children feel very out of control. This is something that is being done *to* them and not a change they are choosing to make. Helping them see that they still hold an important place in the family even though their status may change should assist in the adjustment. They will always have the role they had before in the eyes of their biological siblings; now they are just taking on new roles in this new family.

You might even suggest that they are taking on bonus roles and point out the benefits of these roles. For example, perhaps your son is the oldest of his biological siblings, but the youngest boy of his stepsiblings. As the oldest, he can role model for his younger siblings, but as the youngest boy in the stepfamily he can inherit all the hand-me-down sports gear and have brothers to look up to and emulate.

As long as your biological children are told, shown, and reminded that you are still there for them whenever they need you, that your love for them hasn't changed, and that they are no less a part of the family now that there are more people in the family, they should feel less anxious about the process. Keep your eye on them and watch for feelings of fear or anxiety, which may be expressed as anger or sadness. If you see the emergence of needy or concerning behaviors, spend time alone with your biological child or children. Do something you used to do together before creating this blended family. Don't lose the special relationship you had as a family and replace it with a new relationship for a new family. Keep the old relationship and use it to help new relationships in your blended family grow.

Perceived Favoritism

Most children have felt their sibling was favored over them at some point in their lives. An older sister might have better grades and earn a later curfew. A younger brother might be a track star and you might spend more time at his sporting events because he is in so many championships. Favoritism tends to breed sibling rivalry. You may not recognize your actions as favoring one child over another; however, if your children perceive it this way, they are going to react as if that is what is happening.

With stepsiblings, favoritism plays an even greater role and can feel much more threatening to your children and your partner's children. With biological siblings, children get used to the ebb and flow of who is the apple of the eye at any given time. With stepsiblings, the fear that you will like your stepchildren better is a new and valid fear for your biological children. Keep this in mind. This is a new situation for you, but it is also new and uncharted territory for your children. You left the other biological parent and are now with your partner; does this mean you might leave your children for your partner's children? Are you going to be nicer to your stepchildren to impress your partner? Will you avoid disciplining your stepchildren since they are not yours and turn all of your anger onto your biological children? These are the questions and thoughts that may be running through your children's minds.

Your stepchildren may have similar questions about their own biological parent, and others about you. Are you going to favor your own biological children? Are you going to encourage their parent to ship them to their other biological parent so you can keep the family only for your biological children? As soon as you or your partner shows a glimpse of favoritism, these are the kinds of questions that may arise. With these questions come fear, anxiety, and anger. Children need to know that they are loved and that this love isn't going to be taken away by anyone else. It is tough to create this balance and make the effort to show you love everyone, but it is very important for the sake of all of the children in the family.

E-QUESTION

Why is there such rivalry between all the children?
Sibling rivalry is natural and often occurs when resources are scarce. In nature, baby birds fight each other for food. With people, there is competition for what may be perceived as scarce—love and attention. Try to balance what you give and share as much as possible.

Actual Favoritism

What if there is favoritism? Once you married your partner, what if your children started acting out and your stepchildren were angels? It might be hard not to favor them, or to constantly point out to your biological children that your stepchildren are better behaved and have better attitudes. What if the opposite happens? What if the children are mean to one another, and you and your partner favor the one that takes the brunt of the bullying from the other siblings? Every one of these scenarios might happen. You may need to address the fact that certain children are exhibiting more positive behaviors, and because of their positive behaviors it may seem as though they are the favorites. Explain that this is not the case, but that you do appreciate their positive behaviors and wish the other children could act more like this or decrease any negative attitudes.

What is very important is to investigate why children are acting out. What is making your child or your partner's child so negative? Try to find out what is going on and address it. It could be that the child is afraid you will hate him, so he is just going to make you hate him sooner to get it over with. If you are willing to talk to him, and not just compare him to the sibling acting more positively, hopefully he will see that you are open to developing a positive relationship with him.

What happens if your partner favors his children? This issue needs to be talked about between the two of you, and addressed delicately. Try and point out specific instances to your partner where it appeared as though he was nicer to or favoring his children. Don't confront him and blame him, but point it out, commenting that when he did this it made your children feel less involved, less cared for, or unimportant. Your partner may not realize he is doing this, or he may appear to be favoring his children simply because he is accustomed to them and not as comfortable interacting with your children. Do give the relationships time; however, you can notice how things are going and gently point out how to make everyone feel included.

Strategies to Blend Well

Blending children is not going to happen because you want it to, because you tell them they have to, or because they now share a room. It will happen when you let them get to know one another, feel comfortable with one another, and have time to interact with one another without parents hovering over them. It is a bit of a hurry-up-and-wait process. It would be much easier if they would just get along with one another immediately, but the more you force it the longer it will take.

Give Stepsiblings Time to Get to Know Each Other

Before your children can blend, they need time to get used to each other. They may need to get used to sharing a bathroom, waiting at the bus stop together, or recognizing that the cookies that used to be only for them are now shared with these stepsiblings. It takes a little while for these tiny events—huge in the eyes of your children—to shake out. Once these shake out, the children can start seeing each other as stepsiblings. They are now part of each other's families. If all the children live together, this process may go a bit faster since they will spend more time together. You may also find you hit obstacles sooner and with more frequency since the children are living with one another. In this situation, it is important that you and your partner address issues immediately. If your daughter is constantly eating your stepson's favorite cookies, leaving him with none, explain to your daughter that these cookies are her stepbrother's and asking him to share them may be a better approach than just eating all of them. Maybe they will even bond over their favorite cookie.

> Consider having family meetings. You may want to have them twice a week when everyone first moves in, just to see how the adjustment is going. A formal family meeting will help all children feel like there is a place where their concerns will be heard and addressed. If your children and stepchildren believe they have a voice in this new family, they may feel less threatened and more a part of the new unit.

Include Noncustodial Children in Family Activities

If you are blending children who visit with children who live with you and your partner, you will need to be sure you include the visiting children in major events and decisions. The visiting children may feel that they are not truly part of the new family unit since they are not there all the time and don't get to participate in everything you do with each other. Try to include them by inviting them over for events such as birthday celebrations for the children who live with you or a night out to dinner. Consider saving certain celebrations for weekends when the other children will be visiting. If you make an effort to include them in special occasions as well as in daily life, they will feel that you consider them an important part of the family.

There are many little gestures that can make huge differences. Plan activities you can all take part in so you can build memories together. The more active you can be as a family when all of the children are present the more they will feel like part of the family. Keep in contact with them by phone or e-mail when they are not visiting. You may even suggest to the children who live with you to call their stepsiblings with exciting news. If your daughter who lives with you hits a homerun, suggest that she call her stepbrother at his house to tell him the good news. This will remind the children who do not live there that they are still thought of as important members of the family even when they aren't present.

When Children Live with the Other Biological Parent

When all of the children between you and your partner live elsewhere, it may take a little longer for the basic getting-used-to-each-other to happen. Daily routines may seem awkward for months since everyone has to get used to them all over again once they arrive. Opportunities for the children to interact with one another are less frequent, so it is important for you and your partner to build-in times when the children can be with each other away from adult influences. These won't be part of the day as much as they are in the other scenarios, so you may have to force some situations a bit. As much as you want all of the children to get along and feel part of a family unit, it is also important to have them visit as they did prior to your marriage or relationship. This way, each parent can continue to keep the relationship between him and his children special, and have quality time with them. If you can have time alone with your stepchildren and your partner can have time alone with your children, this may also help build relationships as a family.

ALERT!

Don't have the out-of-sight, out-of-mind attitude, only working on cohesiveness when everyone is around. Keep everyone feeling part of the family by creating a web page that everyone can contribute to, even when they are not visiting with you or living with you. Creating the feeling of a cohesive family takes work by both you and your partner—especially at times when all of the children are elsewhere.

This time of blending is also a great time to initiate new traditions and make sure everyone knows everyone else's birthdays or any big events on the horizon. Despite efforts to make the best of the new family and give it memories and rituals all its own, you may find that people are not meshing or willing to work on getting along. If this is the case, it is a good idea to see a counselor or mediator. Counseling can be a great way of working through the issues that are keeping your family from blending. This may not fix everything either, and you may end up having a family that just doesn't blend. Let it go for a while. The children do not need to be best friends; they simply need to be respectful of one another and tolerate each other when they are together. If you can accomplish this, the rest may come in time.

Stepsiblings Who Choose Sides

Children choose sides with their friends and original families. When there is a stepfamily, it gives children more sides from which to choose. This can compound issues you may have with the other biological parent, and also create situations where your stepchildren take their anger out on your children and vice versa. The best way to avoid this, although there are no guarantees, is to keep all children out of disagreements between adults. The older they get, the more difficult it will be to keep children in the dark. Also, if there is a parent who uses the children to manipulate situations when he is arguing with another parent, the children are going to be involved in the arguing.

Even seemingly benign comments about the other parent or parents can bring the children into the disagreement. For example, if you were supposed to take your child and your stepchild out for ice cream but your stepchild was not dropped off until well past the expected time, causing you to miss going out for ice cream, you may say to your angry child, "We can't go because Becky's mom is late again." Your child may hear, "This is Becky's mom's fault." For your child, this may mean Becky is at fault, too, and she may be very angry with Becky. When Becky arrives, your daughter may say, "It is your fault and your mother's fault that we can't go out for ice cream. You ruin everything and your mom can't tell time." Becky may now go home and tell her mother that your daughter said she is stupid and can't tell time. It can spiral out of control very quickly and cause strife between your children and stepchildren that they will use in choosing sides.

When They Take Sides with the Other Biological Parent

If your relationship with your partner came about from an affair the two of you had, you may find your stepchildren will always choose the side that does not include you. Even if you are suggesting the coolest activity in the world and their other biological parent wants them to volunteer to clean the gutters, your stepchildren may just clean the gutters. When your stepchildren take sides, try to put aside any hurt feelings you might be having and don't express them as anger. Your stepchildren may be facing their own hurt feelings and struggling with how to prove to the other parent that they will remain loyal. This loyalty may extend to your children. If your stepchildren express to the other biological parent that they really enjoy their new stepsiblings, this can come across as disloyalty or even finding some nugget of goodness in you.

Your children and stepchildren shouldn't be put in this kind of situation. What is going on between the adults should not affect their relationships with one another. If this is happening, discuss it with your partner and the other biological parent. Offer to take the anger or punishment from your stepchildren if it means they can build a relationship with your children. Suggesting to the other biological parent that you will take the heat may help her recognize that the children shouldn't be a part of the arguing and help her change her attitude. You can also speak to your stepchildren about the situation and tell them you understand their anger with you, but that your children were not at fault in any way and you would like it if they could leave them out of their anger. It may work or it may not, but it is worth addressing. The better your children and stepchildren can get along the better their adjustment will be, even if they dislike you forever.

When They Take Sides in the Blended Family

If you and your partner are not getting along well, you may find that your children take your side and your stepchildren take your partner's side. Even if they don't know what the argument is about they may jump to your defense and bring the argument to their stepsiblings. They may not even have something to fight about, but they will pick fights with one another to show their loyalty to you. If they see that you are upset they may try to make their stepsiblings upset to punish your partner. Although this may seem like backward logic, it is perfectly logical for a teenager or preteen to do this. Try to catch this before it happens and tell your children and stepchildren that the argument is between the two of you, and you and your partner do not want them involved in choosing sides. No matter who is wrong in the argument you and your partner are having it is not the fault of your children or your stepchildren.

When They Choose Sides Against You

Another interesting scenario that may happen is your children may choose sides with your partner and their stepsiblings. If your children are angry with you for the disruption of the original family, they may see siding with your partner and their stepsiblings as a great way of getting back at you. Unfortunately, your biological children probably know which buttons to push and share that with their stepsiblings. Although this situation is quite tough on you, it will help your children unite a bit with your stepchildren, and may actually help their relationship. Encouraging a relationship based on disliking you is not the point, but there is no need to discourage it. If they have found common ground in being angry with you, they may find other things they have in common with each other and develop a strong bond.

FACT

According to the article "Stepfamily Basics: What Do People (Like *You*) Need to Know?" by Peter K. Gerlach, MSW, children who belong to a stepfamily have up to twenty new family roles to figure out, such as step-uncle, half-sister, stepcousin, noncustodial biological father, or stepgreat-grandmother. These roles are in addition to the fifteen traditional extended biological family roles such as son, daughter, sister, and mother.

All the children involved may have a difficult time separating their stepsiblings from the biological parent. Your children will be associated with you and your partner's children will be associated with her. Every negative thing that your children see in your partner they may see in her children. Every negative thing your stepchildren see in you they may see in your children. Encourage them to see each other as individuals, and plan activities for them to get to know each other without your influence or that of your partner's.

Stepsiblings from Several Parents

There are plenty of people who have children with more than one partner. You may have three children with two different fathers, and your partner may have two children with two partners. This isn't a bad thing; it can just make things a little confusing at times, and you may have a few different surnames on your mailbox. With stepsiblings from several parents, it may be less likely that you will all live together, and more difficult to arrange for visitation days to coincide. To encourage bonds between stepsiblings, it is important to make their time getting to know one another a priority.

Give your children and stepchildren some things to say that will help them deflect any negative comments. For example, if a teacher at school makes a comment about the number of last names in the family, you might suggest that your children say, "It is so cool! My stepsister has a Hungarian last name, I have an Irish one, and my half-sister has a Cape-Verdian one. We are like our own little melting pot."

The dynamics of the family will also be a bit different than those in a blended family that only includes children from each parent. If you have two children from two different mothers, they are half-siblings. If you remarry and your partner has two children from two different fathers, they are half-siblings as well. Once you bring the four children together, one of your children will have one half-sibling and two stepsiblings. This child may also have a noncustodial biological parent, an ex-stepparent, a new stepparent, and a custodial biological parent. With all these parents come grandparents, aunts, uncles, cousins, and more. It can become rather confusing trying to remember who is related, how they are related, and if they are still related.

The most important factor is your child's relationship with extended family members and how you can help preserve those that are positive. If your child had a great relationship with your ex's niece, don't worry about her being the ex-niece; instead, find a way to continue their relationship as cousins. Who cares if they are no longer officially cousins because of a separation or divorce? What will help your child the most is seeing that all kinds of relationships can be preserved, in spite of disagreements between adults.

Dealing with Negative Judgments

The stigma that comes with stepfamilies, remarriages, and divorce can seem more intense in situations where there are multiple parents involved. If all of the children you are a parent or stepparent to have different last names, some eyebrows may raise at school when you are registering them. This is unfortunate, and even more unfortunate is how adults in the community may take this out on the children. They may judge them and assume they are from a dysfunctional family. Hopefully, they will not make comments, but if they do, you need to handle them with strength and grace. Be confident in your relationship and don't be ashamed. If you are ashamed, your children and stepchildren will catch on, and so will the adults who think you should feel shame. It is nobody else's business, but if they make it their business, talk about how lucky you are and how awesome it is to be a special part of all of your children's lives. Even if your stepchildren hate you and your children are driving you bananas, talk about the fabulousness of it until you shut down the people who are trying to make you or your kids feel bad. Being divorced four times, having children with three different people, and entering into relationships with multiple stepchildren has absolutely nothing to do with your ability to be a wonderful, positive influence on children. You can love them just as much as someone who is married only once. You can support them just as well as someone who has children with only one other person. Remember that, and protect and love all the children you have in your life.

Keeping Track

Navigating who is with which parent when can be very difficult. To help everyone know when and where everyone is or what is going on in the multiple extended families, consider using a program like Outlook, iCal or Google Calendars, or even creating a web page. This will help you plan events, check to see if there are events that your child or stepchild is supposed to be attending, and keep your children connected to people with whom you no longer have frequent contact. If your ex-wife has a sister that your child from a previous marriage got rather close to, your ex-wife may want to post her sister's birthday on the calendar so that your child knows when it is and can send a card if she wants. Having a calendar like this can be especially helpful when planning vacations. If you know your children will be at their biological parents' houses one week and your stepchildren are going camping with their uncle that same week, you can plan a romantic getaway for you and your husband during the same week. What helps you will also help the other parents, and can keep the lines of communication open.

CHAPTER 16

Adding to the Family

As with any family, the addition of another child or more children can add both stress and joy to parents and other children in the family. When you are a step-parent, having a biological child with your current partner can affect many people. What may come as a surprise is how the other biological parent having a child might affect you, your partner, your stepchild, and others.

Talking about Half-Brothers and Half-Sisters

The topic of half-siblings may never come up, or it may come up if you are considering having a child or the other biological parent is having a child. If your stepchild is under the age of five, he is probably not old enough to understand the dynamics of the family, and therefore doesn't need the idea of a half-sibling completely explained. However, if your stepchild is older he may have the capacity to comprehend the adult roles in the family, and therefore he may have the ability to understand the idea of a half-sibling. Regardless of the age of your stepchild, help him adjust to the idea of a sibling, be it a half-sibling on your side or on the other biological parent's side. Talking about the possibility of a sibling and maintaining communication are important pieces of preparing your stepchild for such an event.

Discussing the Idea with Your Stepchild

If you are considering having a child with your partner you may want to bring up the idea with your stepchild, not mention it until it is a reality, or talk about it openly. How you handle talking about it may depend on the age and maturity of your stepchild, as well as on your relationship with your stepchild. If your stepchild seems well adjusted to your marriage to your partner, but you are unsure how he would feel about a stepsibling, you may want to ask him what he thinks. Most kids will have an idea that you are asking because either you or their other biological parent is having or thinking about having another child. You need to be ready for followup questions if your stepchild is savvy. You also need to be ready for your stepson to ask the other biological parent if he has concerns about the possibility that either one of you might have a child in the future. These are not reasons to keep your stepchild in the dark; however, be prepared for some fallout before you even broach the subject. Remember, as well-adjusted as your stepchild may be, the addition of another sibling may mean less time and attention for him. No matter how much he adores you, this may anger him. The thought of having to share a parent not only with a stepparent, but now with another child as well, may bring up emotions you were not aware he felt. He may react happily, not at all, with tears, or with a tantrum.

If your stepchild is quite young or greatly dislikes you, you may want to wait to tell your stepchild until you are far enough along that it is considered medically safe to tell people. With a younger stepchild, he may not understand what is going on and will only be confused if you discuss a possible pregnancy or hint at a pregnancy too early in the process. Younger children often think that if you are pregnant they will have a sibling tomorrow. They can become rather confused when they learn they need to wait nine months. Also, if there is an unfortunate event of any sort, it is much harder to explain to a seven-year-old what a miscarriage is or that it is upsetting for you to talk about what happened.

ALERT!

Make sure you first discuss with your partner any conversation you are considering having with your stepchild. Springing thoughts of pregnancy on your partner via your stepchild is not a good idea. Also, your partner should have input on any conversation about any serious topic you wish to discuss with your stepchild before it happens. He knows his child best and may want to wait, talk to him alone, or talk with the other biological parent first.

With a child who is not your biggest fan, not telling him is not for the purpose of keeping him in the dark so you can spring it on him and horrify him more, but to protect you both a bit. If he figures it out or questions it, don't lie. You should talk to your partner about approaching the topic if you suspect he has figured it out. If you are at the point where it is time to tell him and he hasn't indicated that he knows, plan your approach with caution and sensitivity. You and your partner may want to inform the other biological parent that you are intending to have this conversation with your stepchild and would like her input, or would like her to be available for support once you have had the conversation. You may decide that it is best for both of you to tell him, for your partner to tell him alone, for the other biological partner to tell him, or for your partner and his ex to break the news.

Respect Your Stepchild's Feelings

When he finds out that you are going to have a child, he may be quite angry. He may see your pregnancy as a way of pushing him out of the picture and having your partner all to yourself. He may also be worried that with the addition of a child that is yours he will be the underdog. Instead of just going one on one with you, it will now be two on one. He may say some very hurtful things to you that can really make you feel terrible. You need to be prepared for any of these reactions. No matter what he says or does, do not react to him negatively. Remember that he is a child who is going through intense emotions and may need some time to reconcile his feelings. Don't say anything hurtful to him or make him feel badly for how he is feeling. Let him sit with the news for a while before your try to engage him in a conversation about it if he appears to be quite upset.

E-QUESTION

We are giving our stepson time to deal with the news, but I feel compelled to reach out and explain our side again. Is there anything I can do to help him accept it sooner?
There is no way to hurry it up, but you can be supportive of him and respect him while he sorts things out. Keeping his routine as consistent as possible, giving him extra time with your partner, and offering positive reinforcement when he does speak about his half-sibling are all ways of supporting him without forcing anything on him. Be sure to maintain this consistency once your child is born, and give him the same attention he received prior to his half-sibling's arrival.

Nothing will damage your relationship by waiting before you speak. Speaking too soon may cause one or both of you to say something you may regret later. You may find that your stepchild is too upset to have a conversation with you about it even after your child is born. He may need a great deal of time, and it is important that you allow him the time and space he needs. If he needs more than just space, helping him find support with a counselor or therapist can be quite beneficial.

If your stepchild is older and often asks about a half-sibling, has a half-sibling he is happy about, or you know he will be happy about the news, you and your partner may decide to tell him early on in the pregnancy. You should still talk to your partner about when, how, and with whom it would be best to have the conversation. Also, you should still prepare for the worst reaction just in case. He may have an initial reaction of anger that quickly passes or start to worry about his place in the family as the pregnancy becomes more noticeable. If your stepchild is quite close to you, he may worry that having a biological child of your own will somehow change your love for him. Be upfront about this and assure him as often as possible that your love for him will not change and the two of you will still have a fantastic relationship. Involving him in aspects of the pregnancy can be helpful. For example, you could have him help you put the crib together, pick out paint colors, or help with packing the hospital bag.

No matter how old your stepchild, how marvelous he thinks you are, or how easygoing he is, he may still encounter a range of emotions about a new sibling. Children who are angry at first may be more excited than anyone when their sibling arrives. Children who are thrilled at becoming older siblings may understand the reality of a new baby only when they have experienced their first sleepless night. Keep the communication with your stepchild as open as possible throughout the pregnancy and in the months to follow. Don't expect it to be smooth sailing, and try as hard as you can not to become angry when your stepchild has mood swings about his new sibling. If you find that he is having profound difficulty with the adjustment, you may wish to seek out counseling for him and your family.

Being Sensitive to the Other Biological Parent

Should you base your decision to have a child on the other biological parent? No, but he is someone who may be impacted by the decision. First and foremost, he is one of the parents of your stepchild and will have to deal with any emotions your stepchild feels. Also, the addition of a child to your family may mean a decrease in resources for his child, such as time spent at your house, child support, and the role his child holds in your family. Aside from how this change will affect your stepchild, the other biological parent may have his own emotions about this change as well.

You don't need permission to have another child, or even the other biological parent's blessing; however, you do need to respect him and his feelings about the situation. Instead of letting him find out through the grapevine, from your four-year-old stepson, or when your child is born, have a conversation with him to inform him of the news. Your partner may decide it is best that she tell him or that you both tell him. Since she has a longer history with him, she may have greater insight into how he will take the news. He may be absolutely fine with the news or he may be upset. Allow him space to voice his concerns. Are child support payments going to decrease? Is your partner still going to keep up with visitation? Is your partner going to retain full custody? Questions like these are normal and deserve to be answered by a knowing party, which is why it is so important that your partner be prepared for these questions when she relays the news.

Pick a place that is comfortable for the other biological parent to have the conversation and where he can react without embarrassment—his house, your house, or another place he has access to sit, leave, cry, yell, or have a long conversation. If you or your partner is afraid he may become violent, tell him in an area that is safe for everyone involved.

It is also important to think about the circumstances of the other biological parent. Is he remarried? Does he have other biological children with his current partner? Is he able to have more children? Is he still pining away for your partner? Is the birth of your child going to coincide with any important events he has approaching? Depending on his situation, he might react in different ways. Some of these questions are ones to which you may not know the answer. If he is having trouble having a child with his current partner, you may not know. He may have a surprising reaction, and still not tell you the reason; keep these thoughts in the back of your mind. If you do find out he has an important event around the time of your child's birth, work with him to allay his concerns. Talk to him about your hope that life will remain as consistent as possible for your stepchild, and let him know that his support is needed in order to create a positive experience for your stepchild.

Hopefully, you and your partner will not endure negative feedback or actions on the part of the other biological parent. The more respect you can extend to him the more he may reciprocate. Just like with your stepchild, you may find the other biological parent will go through a roller coaster of emotions. Be prepared for some changes in attitude about the pregnancy that may appear to have no rhyme or reason to you or your partner. Remember, the other biological parent may have concerns about his child's well being, and any erratic behavior by your stepchild may be attributed to his concern.

Helping Your Stepchild Accept the Other Biological Parent's Pregnancy

The other biological parent may be in a relationship and decide to have more children. You may find this out through your partner, your stepchild, local gossip, or the other biological parent. If she does not tell you or your partner and you find out in another way, obtain the facts first; rumors may be completely wrong. A shell-shocked, confused, or young child may have misinformation. Instead of calling yourself, have your partner call and verify the news you have heard. Even if you or your partner is angry, try not to take it out on the other biological parent prior to hearing the entire story. Also, the other biological parent may be celebrating something wonderful, and yelling at her or being angry at her news may disrupt everyone's mood about the pregnancy. If you or your partner is angry, figure out why this is making you so angry and address it on an adult level. Did she have a child last year and shirk her responsibilities with your stepchild? If so, address these concerns with her; don't be angry at her pregnancy.

Your stepchild may act as you expected he would act, completely the opposite, or somewhere in the middle. He may not really know how to feel about the pregnancy and may not want to talk about it at all. Either way, you and your partner should let him know that he can talk to either of you about it and that you will answer his questions. If he becomes angry at his half-sibling or threatens to hate his half-sibling, try and figure out the source of his anger. Is he angry because his mother missed his birthday because she was in the hospital having his half-sibling? Explain to him that this is not anyone's fault, and certainly not his half-sibling's fault. Try to have him direct his anger appropriately. Instead of hating his half-sibling, encourage him to express his anger to adults. His half-sibling hasn't been able to do anything to him yet, and until that time his anger should be directed elsewhere.

FACT

Some experts believe that birth order does have an impact on personality and certain traits. One interesting fact taken from Jan Landon's article "Birth Order" in *The Topeka Capital Journal* states, "Of the twenty-three first astronauts to go into outer space, twenty-one of them were oldest children. The other two were only children."

Your Reaction

Your reactions and your partner's reactions may have a great impact on how your stepchild responds to the pregnancy and to his half-sibling. If the two of you make faces, comments, or become very emotional, your stepchild will catch on and may react similarly or let your reactions affect his own. If your stepchild is already negative about the pregnancy, any negativity you show may just encourage more negative behavior. Attempt to support his other biological parent as a fellow human being, and if you have any negative comments make them out of earshot. After the news has been digested, if you, your partner, and/or your stepchild are still having a difficult time, you may want to seek the assistance of a counselor.

Including Your Stepchild in Family Decision Making

The more included your stepchild feels in your family in general the more included he may feel in decision making, even if he does not have the final word. As far as adding to the family goes, you probably will not base your decision solely on his opinion. You can, however, listen to his opinions, concerns, and comments. Listening to him may not change your plan to add to the family, but it may help everyone get their feelings out on the table. You may find out that he doesn't want a new sibling because the baby's room is going to be the room he really wanted to have. If this is his primary concern, changing the room may be an easy solution that shows him he has input into family decisions and that he holds an important place in the family unit. He may not want an additional sibling for larger reasons, and encouraging him to voice these reasons may help him deal with your decision.

You may also involve your stepchild in smaller decisions that may have a big impact on his feelings of involvement—for instance, by seeking his input on baby names or colors for the room. After you have your child, using your stepchild as a go-to expert can make him feel very important and involved in the life of the baby as well as the family decision making. Perhaps he can be involved in interviewing potential babysitters and give you his input on which one he liked best and why. He may even have tricks to help his new sibling sleep, eat, or smile. These are all ways your stepson can teach you and feel that he is an important part of the family.

Give your stepchild a duty for the day of the birth or the days following the birth. She can be responsible for calling a few people to inform them, be in charge of feeding your fish while you adjust to the new baby, or even be in charge of blanket folding. Any way to give your child an important role may help her feel included in the process.

Also important is including your stepchild in event planning. He may be a great help in planning birthday parties, holiday parties, or other events. His input and taking into account his schedule are both ways that may make him feel a true part of the decision-making process. Unfortunately, children often feel as though they don't have the power to make big family decisions because adults are always the ones making decisions and they are just along for the ride—whether they like it or not. You may find that you still make decisions that are not decisions he would make, but that they include something he suggested. For instance, you and your partner might decide that the family trip will be to visit family in Georgia. Perhaps your stepson really wanted to go to an amusement park in Pennsylvania for the family vacation. If you are driving, perhaps it is possible to visit the amusement park on the way there; this way, everyone will get a bit of what they want. Alternatively, are there amusement parks in Georgia he might find interesting? You could also print out a list of all the fun, touristy places in Georgia and let him decide what the family does for one of the days you are there. This may help him feel empowered and as if you really take his opinion into consideration when making decisions.

Assuring That Your Stepchild Does Not Feel Outnumbered

Families that include one stepchild and a number of biological children who are full siblings to one another but only half-siblings to the stepchild are often the families where a stepchild may feel outnumbered. She may not feel as if she has the bond her siblings share, she may be the only one who leaves the family unit to visit another entire family, or she may be only with her half-siblings during visitation. Visitation times under those circumstances can be challenging. If she lives with half-siblings, she may feel she is missing what may be key family time with her siblings, you, and your partner. If she only visits with her half-siblings, she may feel as though she is perpetually an outsider. If possible, your partner and the other biological parent may want to sit with her and figure out a visitation schedule where she doesn't feel as though she is missing key events or not around enough to feel like part of the family.

Keep Your Stepchild Involved

No matter where your stepchild lives, keep her involved in everything. If you are going to have a family meeting about an upcoming vacation, make sure she is there. If she lives too far away to be there, talk to her on the phone throughout the meeting. If you are planning an event, make sure it is for a day she is available. Keep her informed of everything in the works. The smallest events may feel like big deals to her if she is not able to be there for them. A quick dinner after the state science fair may sound boring to you, but exciting to your stepchild. Any time that may offer family bonding time should include your stepchild as often as possible. Extended family should also be reminded to embrace her as they do your own children. If your parents buy your biological children a necklace on Valentine's Day, your stepchild should get one as well. If you can keep the field as equal as possible for all the children in the family, everyone is likely to feel more included.

ALERT!

Work with the other biological parent to keep your stepchild's visitation days busy and fun. She is going to feel less left out of her residential family if she is occupied and having a great time with whichever parent she is visiting. This can be hard work for the parent who has visitation, but it can also help your partner or the other biological parent avoid taking visitation times for granted, and instead put effort into keeping them fun.

Help Maintain a Bond with Your Partner

It is also important for your stepchild to feel as though the bond with your partner is still strong. If she is the only child between your partner and the other biological parent, she may feel like she isn't as important now that one or both of her parents have other children with someone else and have a relationship with that someone else. She may feel ousted and that she doesn't really fit in anywhere. Try to help her see herself as a great bond between her parents and make her understand that it is a special position, not one that is negative because her parents did not stay together.

Encourage your partner to have alone time with each child, so that time alone with your partner isn't solely for your stepchild, but something every child can enjoy. You may wish to do the same. If you have a one-on-one dinner date with each child on his or her birthday, make sure you do the same for your stepchild. Making her involvement with her half-siblings as normal and routine as possible may also help her feel she is an equal part of the family. One other important relationship to cultivate is the relationship between your stepchild and her half-siblings. If they can treat her the same way they treat each other, she may feel more bonded with them.

The Impact of Half-Siblings on Your Stepchild

Age, relationship with parents, and living arrangements all affect the impact a half-sibling will have on your stepchild. If your stepchild is quite young, he probably does not have an understanding of what a half-sibling is, and will adjust to the sibling as he would any other sibling. If your stepchild lives with you, the acceptance of the half-sibling will be easier. If your stepchild does not live with you, you may find that he needs time to adjust to his half-sibling every time he visits. As your stepchild ages, if he doesn't live with you he may start to feel jealous or wonder what goes on in your family when he is not there. If he is acting out when he comes or very anxious about coming or going to your home, try and find out what is going on in his head. Does he think you love his half-sibling more because she lives there? Is he afraid you forget about him when he is not there? Address these issues and keep in touch with him between visits so he knows he is loved and thought of consistently.

Impact on Adolescent Stepchildren

Adolescents will understand the idea of a half-sibling and will probably have an opinion of the new child based upon the opinion they hold of the parent having the child. If your stepchild hates your partner, he may project that hate onto your child and not be very happy about the child. This may actually be easier if the adolescent is not living with you. If your stepchild is living with you and is struggling with the addition of a half-sibling, he may be forced to get over his anger or dislike since he is stuck in the situation. This is the age where it is very important to have open discussions about not hating his half-sister because he hates you or your partner. He shouldn't hold anger against an innocent child who is just as much a bystander in the situation as he is.

Impact on Adult Stepchildren

Young adults and adults are often busy and getting their own lives going, which can help distract them from any negative feelings they may have about their parent having another child. However, this situation has its own difficulties when it comes to a sibling bond. Instead of trying to force your stepchild to bond with your biological child as a sibling, you may find they develop more of an uncle/nephew type of relationship, which is fine. Any relationship they can build is positive and will hopefully keep them connected as they grow. If your adult stepchild is very angry about the situation, he may have a tough time seeing your partner starting another family.

E-QUESTION

I am pregnant and so is my stepdaughter. She is a little bit older than I am and not my biggest fan. How can I show my support for her as we go through our pregnancies?
It is understandable that she might be a little bit horrified that her father is having an intimate relationship with someone who she sees as too young. Try and focus on the fact that you are both enduring a life event together, and you may even be able to bond about it. You may e-mail or call to see how she is doing or send her books or articles you find helpful. Do not discuss any details about how her father is caring for you or any gripes; try and keep your conversation baby focused. Also, be sure to let her have her thunder, and encourage your partner to show his excitement over becoming a grandfather just as much as he shows excitement about becoming a father.

It may also be hard for your stepchild to see his parent having an intimate relationship with someone close to his age or even younger. Instead of worrying about your own relationship with your stepchild, promote the relationship between your stepchild and child. Send pictures, updates, and invite your stepchild to events that celebrate or include your child. He may become closer to you by becoming closer to his half-sibling. No matter what the situation is with your stepchild, help him keep his ideas about you and your partner separate from his feelings about your child.

CHAPTER 17

The Various Relationships

No step-relationship will be exactly the same as another step-relationship, and they rarely mirror the relationship between a biological parent and child. The absence of a biological relationship does not mean that the relationship cannot be strong. There are many myths and patterns that exist regarding stepparenting—some that should be dismissed and others that should be embraced. The stereotypes that exist are merely that—stereotypes that should not get in the way of you or your children creating a fabulous relationship with your stepchild.

Stepfathers and Stepdaughters

The father and daughter relationship is often portrayed as an overprotective father with a daughter who is the apple of his eye. She can get away with just about anything, and he will protect her until the end. For some odd reason, stepfather and stepdaughter relationships are often portrayed as inappropriate, with an abusive stepfather and an attractive or manipulative stepdaughter. There is often a suggestion of incest or inappropriate behaviors. In reality, stepfathers can be quite fabulous for stepdaughters.

Almost anytime there is a positive adult in a child's life, good will come from it. If your goal as a stepfather is to be a positive influence in your stepdaughter's life, you are more than halfway there. If she has a biological father who is involved and active in her life, you might find that you can develop a more positive relationship with him as well, particularly if he sees you as someone who is also out to protect his daughter and keep her safe. As the stepfather, you are far enough removed that she may feel a bit more comfortable talking to you about certain issues like dating. She may also run things by you before bringing them to her biological father.

FACT

In the article, "What to Do When Your Youngster Hits Puberty," the author cites a study by the American Academy of Pediatrics which states that the average age of menstruation for a female is now ten years of age; only 100 years ago, the average was fifteen years of age. Some doctors believe that the decline in the age at which menstruation occurs is related to diet and the environment.

Perhaps the most awkward time for a stepfather and stepdaughter is when the stepdaughter is going through puberty. Not only is this incredibly uncomfortable for her in general, but also you are a male in her life who may view her differently now that she is changing. She may now seem embarrassed in front of you or to be avoiding you. Instead of fighting this and forcing her to spend time with you, try and treat her with respect and let her have the space she needs. Treat her with the same love that you did before puberty and try not to say too many embarrassing things. For example, don't ask her if she has her period when she is in a bad mood, don't joke about her bra size, or suggest that she needs a bra. These are not appropriate ways to deal with her physical changes and will only embarrass her and make you feel like you stuck your foot in your mouth.

As your stepdaughter grows up, you might find you are a great buffer between her and her mother. Many mothers and daughters argue quite a bit for a chunk of time around middle school and high school. If you are the one living with her mother, you may be the one who can keep the peace, or at least remind your partner that your daughter is struggling with growing up and that these fights are part of adolescence. This can be a very trying time for both your partner and your stepdaughter, as most do not enjoy the fighting, but find it almost impossible to avoid. Listening to both of them may become a bit difficult for you, but it may be what they both need in order to get along. You can be a great sounding board and often the only voice of reason.

Stepfathers and Stepsons

These relationships are rarely shown in the media, and if they are the stepfather is usually drunk and abusive to the mother, and the stepson is emotionally scarred for life. There is one film that portrays such a wonderful stepfather/stepson relationship that it is worth watching: *Love Actually*. In this film, the love shared between a man and a boy is such a healthy portrayal that parents everywhere may benefit from watching. Both the stepson and stepfather are struggling with the loss of the stepson's biological mother and they help each other find and pursue new love. It is a bit of a fairy tale story; however, the dynamics of the relationship are worth observing.

If your stepson lives with you and his mother, he may find it easier to speak with you about subjects like puberty, dating, shaving, and body odor. It may just seem more natural for him to talk with you, especially if he doesn't spend much time with his biological father. If he does see his biological father often, or live with him, he may save most of his concerns for his father. It may be helpful for him to have a second opinion, however, and you may be the man for the job. If this is true, try not to negate or put down any of the advice he gleaned from his father. Instead, add to the advice or contribute your own advice while appreciating his father's advice as well.

E-QUESTION

My stepson is having a difficult time dealing with the fact that he has two stepfathers. I am in a relationship with his biological father, and my stepson is getting teased at school and by his other stepfather. What can I do?

You and your partner may wish to speak to school administrators and to the other biological parent and stepfather about your concerns. When speaking with the other biological parent and stepfather, emphasize that the teasing or statements of non-acceptance of your lifestyle only hurt your stepson. Most important, however, is to continue speaking to your stepson about how much you love him and support him.

Another stereotype you may wish to avoid is that you will become the disciplinarian simply because you are a male in the house. Instead of becoming just another person to discipline and manage your stepson, try and encourage your partner to take on a fair share of the discipline. You may find it beneficial to focus on building a relationship that is more focused on guiding, role modeling, and mentoring than discipline. If your partner struggles with discipline and expects you to take over, discuss with your partner your desire to build a loving relationship with your stepson first. A healthy, positive relationship may help with any behavioral issues more than constant discipline. Support your partner's discipline efforts, and hopefully your partner will support your efforts to build and nurture a relationship.

Stepmothers and Stepdaughters

Stepmother and stepdaughter relationships are perhaps the most frequently seen relationships in fairy tales and entertainment. The stepmothers are either ugly witches, or young, beautiful gold-diggers. Stepdaughters are portrayed as naïve and abused, often forgotten by their fathers once the stepmother comes into the picture. Although this could happen, there is a great deal you can do to avoid it. Your stepdaughter may be quite concerned that you are going to replace her as the woman in her father's life. She may also worry that his marrying you inevitably means you will have a child with him who may become more important. Make sure you do everything you can to support the relationship between your partner and your stepdaughter. There may be times when you feel pushed aside, but remember who the child is in the situation. Your stepdaughter may need extra reassurance that she is still loved and important in her father's eyes. It may be helpful for you to remind your partner of this as well, and encourage him to spend one-on-one-time with his daughter.

As your stepdaughter reaches puberty, you may be the one who has difficult discussions with her, or has to address uncomfortable issues. It is likely she will be more comfortable speaking with you than with her biological father. This is one situation where communicating with the biological mother is extremely important if she is available. Even if the two of you do not get along well, it may be easier for your stepdaughter if you tell her mother she got her period or needs a new bra, instead of telling her father to tell her mother. There are certain things her father may be too embarrassed to hear, and she might not be ready for him to hear these things. This might even help you develop a relationship with her biological mother.

You may have to mediate between your partner and your stepdaughter. As she gets older, he may be more and more uncomfortable with her and feel rather awkward. This is a time when he may need a great deal of support from you around how to talk to his adolescent daughter about relationships, curfew, makeup, and other difficult topics.

If you have been involved in your stepdaughter's life since she was young, you might find that she will start to pull away from and fight with you as she may with her biological mother when she reaches adolescence. This is a natural and difficult time for your stepdaughter, her biological mother, and potentially you. The closer she is to you beforehand, the more likely she may be to treat you like her biological mother and fight with you every step of the way. You could look at her actions as positive, as most adolescents don't do this with people they are not very close to, but you will likely find it rather trying to deal with it all. Remember her hormones are out of control, her body has taken on a life of its own, she may have skin issues to deal with, and boyfriends or girlfriends are starting to be a central focus in her life. This is no fun for her, and if she feels like she can take out all her anger on you, she just might do so. Try to be a little lenient and extra patient during this period. She will need some extra space and extra love all at the same time.

You may also find that your stepdaughter is having a difficult time with her biological mother and turns to you for additional support. This is a great time to bond with her; however, be sure you do not do so by undermining her mother or the relationship she has with her mother. If she is constantly coming to you with complaints about her mother, listen, but when you respond, do so diplomatically. Telling her that her mother is a lunatic is only going to hurt her mother, and the relationship you have with her mother and with your stepdaughter. Focus on guiding her to see that she is having a difficult time with her mother, but that her mother still loves her and is only trying to protect her and guide her in the right direction. If you can be as supportive as possible to your stepdaughter, while also sticking up for her biological mother and being considerate of their relationship, you will help her get through this time with as little angst as possible.

Stepmothers and Stepsons

Unfortunately this is a relationship that is rarely portrayed in movies or television yet it can be a great relationship and is a rather common relationship. Stepmothers and stepsons rarely have to deal with too much awkwardness, as the biological parent will usually deal with any uncomfortable topics such as puberty. As the stepmother, you can usually be the buffer between your partner and your stepson, or between the other biological parent and your stepson. As always, be sure to listen to your stepson, but do not undermine or make negative comments about either one of his biological parents or a stepparent. Instead, listen to his concerns, and offer suggestions as to how he can best manage talking to his parents about difficult issues.

Building a relationship with your stepson might actually be easier than building a relationship with a stepdaughter. It is less likely your stepson will feel competition with you when it comes to his biological parents, and you are also not dealing with puberty the way you have to with a stepdaughter. The role you can take on may be more of an older sister role, where you can help him with relationships, make sure he is polite and respectful to any dates and their parents, and keep him up to date on events that may be important for his biological parents. Reminding him that he needs to buy his mother and grandmothers cards on Mother's Day, helping him pick out cards for your partner on a birthday, and helping with homework, are all ways you can help him become a responsible young man, while also using that time to strengthen your relationship.

Offering your stepchild advice is helpful as is helping him navigate his parents' moods. Suggesting he doesn't ask his father permission to take the car as soon as his father walks in from work is a good idea, but teaching him how to manipulate a parent is not. Be careful not to instruct him in manipulating any parental figure by playing on any weaknesses. Teaching him how to be considerate and thoughtful is appropriate and should help him in most situations.

It is a wise idea to enforce appropriate boundaries if you are younger than or close in age to your stepson. Don't suggest you all go party together, show off your figure, or encourage relationships between your friends and your stepson and his friends. You are still a parental figure regardless of your age, and trying to be seen as "hot" by your stepson is not appropriate. You should hope that he sees you as a respectable adult that he can talk to and trust as a parental figure. Build a relationship of mutual respect that the two of you can have for a lifetime.

Stepsiblings

Stepsibling relationships can be close or virtually nonexistent. Depending on if the stepsiblings live together, their age, and their relationships with their parents, their relationships with one another may flourish or dissolve.

The great thing about stepsiblings, however, is they are not forced to be together forever, but instead can choose to have a relationship. This may actually help them build a stronger relationship. Also helpful is that they came from similar situations, and can offer each other advice on how to handle these situations. If you have children, and your children are angry with you, but your stepchildren adore you, your stepchildren may actually help your children see some good in you at times when they are struggling. It is important to nurture and encourage the relationship between stepsiblings, but to avoid forcing them to be friends. Their relationship needs to evolve on its own.

When stepsiblings are fighting, they can be pretty ruthless, as can most siblings. Your biological child may tell your stepchild you will always love her more since you are her real mom. Your stepchild may use the same tactics on your biological child when it comes to your partner. This is normal, but it should be addressed. Discussing with your children and stepchildren that you and your partner love them all no matter who they are biologically related to may help. Also important to address if it comes up is the difference children may feel when some live with you and some live with another biological parent. There may be some competition or concern that you like your stepchildren more since they live with you and your biological children do not. This may happen with your stepchildren and your partner as well. Try and maintain an equal field and their fighting may not be quite as nasty. Fighting will happen, however, and it is a normal occurrence.

Make events fun, but discourage any competition that may result in fighting. If your children and your stepchildren can handle healthy rivalry, it is okay to keep score or hand out prizes, but if they are still dealing with some heavy emotions, keep things light-hearted without focusing on a winner.

To encourage bonding, you could plan your own stepsibling day, and have all of the children suggest activities to take place on that day. Maybe you can have fun with the rivalries and have your children versus your partner's children for some events, girls versus boys for others, and then joint events where you mix the families. Make sure to include at least one event for each child where he or she will excel. For example, potato sack racing may be a strength for your daughter, while name that tune may be a strength for your stepson—include both. Let the children decide what the food will be and if gifts will be exchanged. Be creative and suggest they make gifts for each other. If there are quite a few stepsiblings, suggest they use a grab system. You may want to open the day up to the other biological parents, stepparents, and any stepsiblings who are not related to you or your partner. Make it a day all about them, and there is definitely going to be some bonding!

CHAPTER 18

Tough Decisions

Tough decisions need to be made in every family. As a stepparent you may be on the sidelines for many if not all of these decisions, but you may provide important input that could be helpful in decision making. Finding ways to share your insight without offending anyone may be difficult, but you may have insight into your stepchild that her biological parents do not.

Education

You may find that if your stepchild gets sick at school and your partner and the other biological parent are unreachable, you may be the next person on the emergency contact list. Be sure to find out if you are on the emergency contact sheet. If you aren't, you might suggest that you be added to the list if that is agreeable to everyone. Your partner or the other biological parent may have already put you on the contact sheet without informing you. This may be fine with you; however, plans should be made in advance in case you are called in an emergency. It is best to discuss such matters ahead of time so there is a plan in place before people are emotionally distraught under the stress of an emergency or frantically trying to contact each other. Would the biological parents want you to take the child to the doctor? If so, you will probably need signed permissions in order to speak to your stepchild's doctor. Do they want to provide you with those? If your stepchild is in big trouble, defer any decision making until the biological parents can be reached.

E-QUESTION

Who should go to open house at my stepson's school?
You should check this out with your partner and your stepchild. He may be going, the other biological parent may be going, and they may both be fine with you going. If you are interested in going or if your stepchild would like you to go, you may certainly voice that to your partner and see if he thinks it would be appropriate for you to attend. Your stepchild might really want you to be there, especially if you are involved in helping with homework and keeping tabs on your stepchild during the day.

You should inform your partner and the other biological parent of anything that is mailed to your house by the school, any phone calls, or any other type of communication received from the school.

When it comes to getting in trouble, getting bad grades, cheating, or any other negative educational-related situation, you should not keep any of these a secret from your partner or the other biological parent. Lying or keeping information from the biological parents is not fair and will only make you an unsafe person for your stepchild. This kind of behavior will also make your stepchild feel as though you are not a safe adult, as you do not set appropriate boundaries and are not honest with people.

Physical Health

You may not have the opportunity to voice an opinion about health care, but you should keep up with your stepchild's health. If the other biological parent does not feel this information is your business, suggest to your partner that they discuss the fact that you are a caretaker of their child, and knowing her health concerns will make you a more responsible caretaker. In some instances, such as a change in prescriptions, the information may be necessary for you to know.

FACT

The most frequently recommended vaccines, as reported by *www .kidshealth.org/parent/general/body/vaccine.html,* include hepatitis B, Pneumococcal conjugate vaccine, DTaP (diptheria, tetanus, acellular pertussis), Hib (meningitis), IPV (polio), Influenza, MMR (measles, mumps, and rubella), Varicella (chicken pox), MCV4 (bacterial meningitis), and Hepatitis A.

Physical health is also an arena where you may or may not be listed as an emergency contact. If you are, be sure that the doctor's office and dental office have any paperwork they need to release information. Most health-care facilities cannot release information to a noncustodial parent without written permission from a custodial parent. This could pose a problem if you are the emergency contact for school, but not for the doctor's office. In this case, you may pick your stepchild up from school when she is sick, only to discover at the doctor's office that you need parental permission to obtain treatment for her. If you are the emergency contact for one, you should probably be the emergency contact for the other. The reason our health-care rights are so protected is because of the Health Insurance Portability and Accountability Act (HIPAA). This is a federal rule that protects our rights to privacy when it comes to health care and health records. More information can be found at *www.hhs.gov/ocr/hipaa*.

When does your stepchild need to go to the doctor? This varies based on overall health and age. Most children see a doctor for well visits (a checkup), immunizations, and illness. If you have never had children, it is a good idea to get a list of symptoms or things to look out for with your stepchild that indicates she is getting sick. Also, you should stay aware of any quirky symptoms she might have that do not indicate illness. If you are worried about when you should take your stepchild to the doctor, call one of the biological parents and find out how she would handle the situation.

Mental Health

Mental health is often a rather touchy subject, even in the most functional of families. It is still difficult for many people to see mental health as a health issue and not something to be ashamed of as if it is the person's own doing. As a stepparent, you may find you are far enough removed from your stepchild that you are able to see his mental-health issues through a clearer lens. As an adult who may see the needs of your stepchild, it is important that you advocate for him while also respecting the feelings and positions of his biological parents.

According to *www.teendepression.org*, about 20 percent of teenagers will experience depression before they reach adulthood; 70 percent will suffer one more bout of depression prior to reaching adulthood.

One of the most important things you can do is remove any shame from the idea of mental illness. Even if your stepchild does not have any signs or symptoms of mental illness, taking stigma away from mental illness may help him accept others and any potential issues he may encounter later in life. Similar to talking about sex and drugs, the more open and honest you are about mental disorders, the more comfortable your stepchild may feel about speaking to you about any concerns. If you speak about mental illness without judgment, your stepchild may understand that you won't judge him or any of his friends who may be struggling.

Your stepchild may ask about mental illness if someone in his family or circle of friends is suffering from it or he is experiencing signs or symptoms. If he is experiencing symptoms or someone like a teacher, mentor, coach, or camp counselor has spoken to you, your partner, or the other biological parent about changes they have noticed, it is important to speak with him and support his biological parents in taking him to be seen by his primary care physician. One major obstacle with mental illness is the denial that comes along with it. Your partner may not want to accept that his child may have a mental illness. You may find that his other biological parent is also in denial. If you can encourage one or both of them to at least bring their child to see his regular doctor, you can let the doctor do the talking, and hopefully he will convince them to seek further help for your stepchild.

Signs That Your Teen May Be Depressed

- Sadness or hopelessness
- Anger or irritability
- Withdrawing or isolating from friends and family
- Loss of interest in previously enjoyable activities
- Change in appetite or sleep
- Weight gain or weight loss
- Difficulty concentrating
- Thoughts of suicide
- Feelings of guilt
- Crying spells or tearfulness

Don't do anything behind the biological parents' backs or try to force them to accept that their child may have a mental illness. Instead, encourage them to have the child screened by a mental-health professional just to make sure he is okay. It may be a sensitive situation for you to push, and most parents find it hard to accept a diagnosis of a mental illness. If they have met with a doctor and the doctor has expressed concern, support both of them in accepting their child may have a mental illness and that most mental disorders are treatable. Parents often blame themselves and question what they could have done differently to protect their child from mental illness. If they can instead focus on how to best help and support their child, they may feel more empowered than they would if they dwell on the past.

If your stepchild is diagnosed with a major mental illness such as bipolar disorder, major depressive disorder, schizophrenia, etc. it would be helpful if all parental figures in his life can come together on how to best support him and each other. Keeping everyone informed about mood changes your stepchild may be experiencing, if there are changes in medication, if a therapist is leaving, and if a second opinion is being considered. Your stepchild's therapist may have suggestions on how to best cope with his mental illness and they may include changing your routine in order to best accommodate his needs. If your stepson struggles with changes in routine, the therapist may recommend that he stay with one parent all week and only visit the other on the weekends in order not to disrupt his school schedule. Some suggestions may not work, but you will not know unless you try them.

Deaths in the Family

Death is generally a difficult experience for everyone, regardless of the age of the person left behind, age of the deceased, or relationship with the deceased. As a stepparent, your primary role will be supporting those who have been most impacted by the death—especially if it is your stepchild.

E-QUESTION

Should I go to the wake or funeral if it is someone from his other biological parent's side or his other stepparent's side?
If you have an amicable relationship, you might consider going to show your respect and support for the family. However, it might be a good idea to first ask your partner and the other biological parent if they are comfortable with you attending. If not, you could send a simple sympathy card or flowers as a gesture of support.

Your stepchild may have a huge family, as he may have the opportunity to be a part of your extended family, your partner's, his other biological parent's, and another stepparent's. This may be wonderful, but he also may deal with more loss than usual as people grow older. It may seem strange for you to help support him through the loss of potentially eight grandparents, four parents, numerous aunts and uncles, etc. Where this may seem particularly awkward for you is when your stepchild loses someone from his other biological parent's side that you do not know or did not realize he loved. You may never have met this person, but your stepchild may be devastated by the loss. To help you support him, think of loss as loss. Don't generalize it for him, but try to imagine how you would feel if you lost someone that you considered close to you.

When stepchildren have lost a biological parent to death they may have a hard time bonding with a stepparent. These children may feel accepting a stepparent makes them somehow disloyal to their deceased parent. Stepparents who encourage kids to remember and honor the memory of their lost parent show the child they are not trying to take that parent's place. This can help children accept a stepparent without feeling guilty.

Empathy is an important trait to develop when supporting someone who has just lost a loved one. Many times, people do not necessarily want to hear how you dealt with death, how you know "exactly how they feel," or that "it is not that bad, people die every day." No matter who the person is or what you perceive your stepchild's relationship to be with that person, your stepchild may actually feel the opposite of what you would expect. Listen to your stepchild before telling him you know how he feels. Do not belittle his loss by reminding him that loss is a part of life. Avoid recounting stories of your own losses instead of being attuned to his needs. Expressing your concern with phrases such as, "It sounds like you felt really close to your uncle. I am really sorry you are going through this, but I hope you know I am here to support you—if you want to cry or to be distracted by a movie, I am here."

If you do feel like telling your stepchild about a loss you encountered and how you handled your feelings or coped with the loss that is fine, as long as you don't compare your stepchild's loss to your own. Everyone deals with loss differently, as relationships are different. Support your stepchild, be available to him when he is in need, and be sure to recognize if he is having serious difficulty dealing with the loss. If he does appear to be struggling with unresolved grief, consider suggesting counseling to your partner or the other biological parent.

In times of loss, you may find your stepchild wants to stay home more often or not go on visitation. This is normal for a little while, and although keeping his routine as predictable as possible is generally wise, allowing flexibility is necessary at times. If he lost someone on his other biological parent's side, he may wish to spend more time there for now. If the loss impacted your family, he may wish to stay with you until everything is back to normal.

There will come a time when your stepchild loses a parent. If he loses his other biological parent, be supportive and help in any way you can, even if you didn't like his parent. Remind yourself that you are a stepparent and won't replace that parent, even after that parent's death. Encourage your partner to be open to maintaining contact between your stepchild and his other stepparent if he has one. Living arrangements may shift, as may visitation. Consult an attorney about any changes in custody. If your partner passes away, hopefully the other biological parent will be as sensitive and opt to help maintain a relationship between you and your stepchild.

Moving

Moving often uproots children from friends, school, sports teams, extracurricular activities, family, and more. Being taken away from what they see as their world can be extremely difficult to explain, and children often blame the parent who is the reason for the move. Many families do move, however, and it can be done without completely traumatizing your stepchild or making her hate you forever. Be sure to consult an attorney to find out if there are impediments to moving.

If your stepchild lives with you and your partner, moving may affect her more than it would if she simply visited from time to time. Either way, your stepchild will need to adjust to a new situation. One of the best ways to avoid any surprises is to keep the lines of communication open with your stepchild and the other biological parent. You may wish to take your stepchild with you when you look for houses to get her opinion. If she loves the local swimming club, perhaps finding a home near the swimming club will help her feel included in the decision. Coming up with a list of activities or places that might interest your stepchild may help her feel excited about the move.

If you cannot move to the place of your dreams due to your stepchild, be sure not to resent your stepchild; it is not her fault. Her other biological parent may be constrained with respect to moving as well.

If you are definitely moving, give your stepchild time to say goodbye to your current home. Even if you are moving from an apartment on one side of town to a house on the other side, it is nice to say goodbye to your old home. It is funny how attached people become to their homes. If your stepchild is having a hard time saying goodbye to your current home, find something she can take with her to your new home. Maybe the doorknob from her room can be removed and placed in the door in your new home? This way she can physically keep a piece of the old home, and may feel comforted. Just be sure to replace the doorknob for the incoming homeowners!

Breaking Up

Unfortunately, marriages do not always last. You may be very aware of this, as you may already be divorced and your partner may be as well. If stepchildren are involved, however, the breaking up affects them as well. Although you are breaking up with your partner you are not breaking up with your stepchild, and this needs to remain clear—even if you will no longer be able to see your stepchild.

In an article published in *The New York Times*, researchers Frank F. Furstenberg Jr. and Andrew J. Cherlin estimate that, "15 percent of all children in divorced families will see the parent they live with remarry and redivorce before they reach age eighteen. And that figure is a conservative estimate, they say, because it does not include couples who live together instead of remarry."

If you and your partner have decided to end your relationship, be sure you know that you are definitely ending the relationship before informing your stepchildren. Going back and forth between divorcing and staying together may confuse them more and increase any anxiety they may feel. Once you have decided that you are breaking up, tell your stepchildren in an environment where they feel supported and can react however they need to at the time. Let them be angry and let them be sad—these are normal reactions. They may also shut down or act as if they don't care. This is normal too, but it can be addressed by talking about how they may have feelings in the future and that you and your partner will both be there for them if they need to express these feelings.

Your stepchildren may have experienced a divorce before and be afraid that another divorce indicates that they are the problem. Confirm that this is not the case, but that the adults in the relationship have reached a point where they can no longer have a marital relationship. Try to keep their feelings at the forefront when you and your partner are going through your divorce.

If your partner agrees that staying in touch with your stepchildren is appropriate, you should do so, and try to maintain as consistent a schedule as possible. If you are going to commit to keeping a relationship, commit to the time and energy it may take. The worst thing you can do is promise your stepchildren you will stay in touch and then not follow through. If you know that a relationship with them is not feasible, do not promise them what you cannot give. For more on the subject of divorce, see Chapter 21.

CHAPTER 19

Your Extended Family and Your Stepchild

It can be strange enough adding a spouse to a family. What should your partner call your parents now that you are married? How should he address your aunts and uncles? Adding a stepchild can bring up similar questions. Who is your stepchild in the greater family picture? Does he have a specific place? Is he welcome? The addition of your stepchild can be quite fun if everyone knows what is expected of them, and how to best include your stepchild in the family.

Where Do They All Fit?

Your stepchild is not biologically related to your family. Even though you are a stepmother, that doesn't necessarily mean that your parents are going to take on your stepchild as their grandchild. Also, your extended family (aunts, uncles, cousins, etc.) might not see your stepchild as a relative—not because they don't care, but because his not being part of the family at birth often makes it difficult for people to remember to include him. They didn't experience a baby shower, a birth announcement, or any other ritual that occurs around the addition of a new child to the family. Even with adopted children, there is often some type of ceremony celebrating the child as a part of the family.

You have the potential to change this for your stepchild. The more you include your stepchild the more your family will think of him as part of the family unit. Once they recognize he is an extension of you, hopefully it will become second nature to include him in family events. Your family also might not know if they are supposed to invite him to certain events. Would he want to go to the family picnic that everyone complains about? Probably not—but it's great to let him have the option of going.

Even if you only have infrequent visitation with your stepchild, you should talk him up to your family. Let them know when he gets a great report card. If you are responding to parties, continue to mention that he might want to come if he is visiting during the next one. If they live out of town, send pictures of your stepchild. Fill your family in on what is going on in his life and this might help them feel a connection with him, or at least keep him present in their minds.

If there is an event to which you and your partner are invited by your side of the family and your stepchild isn't included, you can respond in the following ways: If your stepchild is not available to go, you could say, "Bob and I are really excited about coming to the party, but my stepson won't be coming this time. He is looking forward to coming to the next family get-together, and I am excited for him to get to know everyone." If your stepchild is available to go to the party, a not too pushy response, but one that gets your message across, might sound something like this: "Bob and I are really excited about coming to the party; would it be okay if we bring my stepson along? We are looking forward to him meeting everyone and feeling like part of the family." In most cases, this should work. If the party is an adult-only party, you need to be respectful of that. Your stepson probably wouldn't enjoy it anyway!

What happens if your extended family is posing for a family picture? Where does your stepchild fit in? He should fit in with you and your partner. Remember, marrying your partner included taking your stepchild on, and he is now a part of your family. If there is a family picture, he should be included just as a biological child of yours would be included. Leaving him out would symbolize that he is not truly a part of your family when this is not what you are trying to achieve. Your stepchild is part of your nuclear family, and thus a part of your extended family, just as much as you are. It might take some time for everyone to come around, but over time they should do so.

How to Introduce Them

Hopefully, your immediate family has met your stepchild at least once or twice. If you are married to your partner, extended family might have met her at the wedding or any prewedding parties. If not, natural opportunities to meet your family might arise. However, if you are eager for everyone to meet sooner, you can create a comfortable situation where everyone can interact. Having a family party such as a simple cookout or a celebration around a holiday could provide great opportunities. Hosting a party that is specifically for everyone to meet your stepchild might overwhelm her. If you decide to have a general party, make sure that a couple of people who know her well can attend. This should help her feel more comfortable and eliminate any worries she might have about not having anyone with whom to talk. Introducing her to a few people at a time at various events is another approach that can take the awkwardness out of the first meeting.

If you have family members who are her age, it might be nice to set up play dates with them so your stepchild can get to know her peers. These relatives could potentially show her around your town, introduce her to other kids her age, and make her feel more at home in the community as well as in your home. If your stepchild lives with you, relatives who live in the area can help her find her way around school, teach her the social ropes, and keep the boredom at family parties to a minimum. If your stepchild does not live with you, family members her age are still important people she should get to know. If she gets along well with them, she might look forward to coming over if they are going to be in the area. This will give her social interactions with someone other than you and your partner when she is visiting.

Introducing her to family her age is one thing; forcing a friendship between them is another. Make sure you let them decide for themselves if they want to be buddies. They might not, and that is fine; just let it be. However, they will have to tolerate each other, as they are now family!

The comfort of your stepchild is what's most important when introducing her to your extended family. Introduce her to those you are most comfortable with first. If you have an aunt who has always been special to you, tell your stepchild about her before you introduce them. Knowing your aunt is special in your life might peak your stepchild's interest and make her excited about the meeting. Also, if you are comfortable with certain relatives, that will come across in your body language and anything you say about them prior to your stepchild meeting them.

Just as your comfort level comes across, so will any anxiety you may feel. If there are certain family members you dislike, delay introducing them to your stepchild until you absolutely must. Try to introduce them at a busy party or function where there will be plenty of other people or activities to keep your stepchild from being stuck with that family member. Don't frighten her about meeting family members; let her form her own opinions. People react quite differently to different people; she might find the uncle who annoys you hilarious.

What Is Expected of Your Extended Family?

This could be a concern for all of your family members. How are they supposed to treat your stepchild? Should they prepare gifts for your stepchildren for the holidays? What if your grandfather gives all of his great-grandchildren a car for graduation? Does this hold true for your stepchild as well? Will they be babysitting your stepchild? Will he be over every weekend? Can they reprimand him if he misbehaves? At first, it will probably be awkward, and they won't have any idea what to do with him; and he might not have any idea how to interact with them. Your stepchild's age and the relationships he has with his biological family will both play a role in the way he interacts with your extended family.

FACT

According to the State Department of the United States, the extended family is defined as a family that includes three or more generations. Normally, that would include grandparents, their sons or daughters, and their children, as opposed to a nuclear family, which is only a married couple and their offspring. Families often have their own interpretation of extended family and include very distant relatives and ancestors.

If your stepchild is quite close to his biological family and your extended family is more of a secondary family with whom he doesn't regularly interact, they will not be as involved in his life. Any expectations of your stepchild having a relationship with them will be minimal. However, if your stepchild does not have frequent or consistent contact with his biological family, your family might become his primary extended family. Either way, your extended family is likely to take their cues from you. If there is a holiday party and your stepchild is coming with gifts for everyone, let your family know this ahead of time. It isn't rude, but actually helpful for your family to know that you are expecting them to take him in as one of their own. For a stepchild who is not around frequently and mostly engages with his own family, gestures like sending cards for certain occasions and inviting him to events might be all that you can expect of your family.

The age at which your stepchild becomes a part of your family will also impact how involved he is with the family. A child who is young will most likely see family more, as he is forced to go where the adults in his life go for the time being. As children age, they become more independent and don't necessarily need to go to Aunt Betty's birthday party. An older child or teenager might not have much interaction with your extended family, and it is not something that needs to be forced upon either party. Regardless of age, a child who has experienced multiple marriages and divorces by either parent is not likely to be quick to bond with your extended family. He might think it is pointless to engage with any family members, as he might see them as temporary. A child who has this type of experience should be given plenty of time to feel comfortable forming relationships with family members. It might take years, but it is important that you do not push these relationships. Forcing him to hurry up and create a bond will create a sense of urgency that is unnecessary if you are planning on staying with your partner forever.

For the comfort of everyone, be clear with your extended family on what your expectations are and have patience, as this might be a new type of relationship for them. Encourage your family to treat your stepchild as they would any other child, keeping in mind that special treatment can also make him feel out of place.

Helping Your Stepchild Find an Identity in Your Family

Your stepchild might feel very out of place in your family. He is the outsider, so feeling like one wouldn't be surprising. He might also have had life experiences that have made him self-conscious. As the child whose father died, whose mother deserted him, or who was taken away from the other biological parent due to abuse, he might feel labeled and judged. Even if he is coming from the best of circumstances, he is still "different" when it comes to your extended family. If there are other stepchildren within your extended family he will not be alone, but it will still take time for him to figure out who he is within your family.

Instead of focusing on the fact that he is the stepchild, try to focus on his other attributes. Perhaps he is a great trivia player and your family plays trivia at every get-together; let him demonstrate his talent. If you know your great-uncle is a baseball fan and your stepson is a great pitcher, introduce them and inform them of their common interest. The more comfortably he can blend in with your extended family the less obvious it will be to everyone that he is a bit of an outsider, and hopefully they will forget that he hasn't been there forever.

E-QUESTION

I have been married to my partner for over a year, but it is still painfully awkward for my stepdaughter when she visits; it is clear she feels like the outsider in the family. What can I do?
Remain patient. Bonds are not formed overnight, and although a year might seem like a long time, if she is only visiting occasionally what is the cumulative amount of time she has been with you? It probably isn't as long as it seems. Also, talk to her! Why does she feel uncomfortable? Is there something you could do to make her feel more comfortable?

Another way of helping him find his identity is by letting him find where he best fits in. You can encourage this by introducing him to family members his age and family members with common interests; but in the end, he will determine where he feels most comfortable. The cousin who is his age and loves the same author may not wind up being his friend. Instead, he might ally himself with the great-uncle who makes fabulous cakes. Help as much as you can by creating a comfortable setting, but it is the time he has on his own with your extended family that will determine his identity.

Holidays and Celebrations

Holidays and celebrations might be awkward for your stepchild and your extended family. People have family rituals that are often set and it can be difficult to make room for new people to join. Your stepchild might also find that she misses celebrations she had with her family prior to your involvement in her family, and she might resent the fact that she is spending the holidays with your extended family and not her own. In order to make holidays and celebrations more welcoming for your stepchild, find out if there are any rituals from the holidays she has experienced prior to becoming part of your family that you can incorporate into your family celebration. You could also find out her favorite holiday food and make sure it is available. Incorporating pieces of her holidays into your family celebrations can benefit both your stepchild and your family. They may find the new ritual fun, and it will give everyone a positive topic about which to speak with your stepchild.

According to the website *www.successfulstepfamilies.com/view/20*, "African-American stepfamilies may adjust to stepfamily living more easily than White or Hispanic families. In general, family boundaries in African-American families are less rigid and more fluid than those of Whites. Throughout US history, black families have included *fictive kin,* i.e., people with no biological or legal tie to the family who are nevertheless considered family members. Given this cultural history, welcoming and bonding with new stepfamily members may be less intrusive and easier than in White families."

Similar to laying out how your extended family should act in general around your stepchild and how your stepchild should act around them, laying out what to expect from one another during holidays or other celebrations can be quite helpful. For example, if your stepchild follows a different religion than your extended family, you may have to educate your family on her beliefs and her on your family's beliefs. This can be an interesting lesson for both, as long as you do so with respect. They might decide they would like to ask each other questions about their beliefs, which might help them bond and get to know each other better. It might help them open up with their own beliefs and become more accepting of others in general.

For celebrations your extended family is planning, make sure you let them know any necessary information about your stepchild. If, for example, she is a vegetarian, informing them of this while also offering to bring a meatless dish for her would be a good idea. This way, your family is aware that she does not eat meat, but is not burdened by needing to change their menu. As time goes on, they will hopefully get used to her eating habits and prepare a meatless dish as well as a regular dish for celebrations. If your stepchild has any particularities, it is also important to share these with your extended family so they are prepared to be as welcoming as possible.

What to Do if They Are Not Welcoming

If your family is not welcoming of your stepchild then they need a reality check. If you have done something horrendous to your family or if they do not approve of your marriage to your partner, it is not your stepchild's fault. No matter how "bad" a parent or stepparent may be, it is not fair for people to impose their anger or dislike for the adult onto the child. Without your stepchild present, meet with those family members who are not welcoming and find out what it is that is keeping them from embracing your stepchild as part of the family. If they have issues with you or your partner, ask them to keep it that way and leave your stepchild alone, as he is innocent.

If your family continues to give your stepchild the cold shoulder, there is no reason to subject him to their rude behavior. It is not fair to force him to be around them if they are only going to act mean. It is unlikely they will change if you force them into situations with your stepchild.

After speaking with your family they may or may not tell you what is really going on and why they are not more open to your stepchild. If you have brought multiple children into the family only to divorce later on, your family might be worried and not want to develop another relationship with a child they see as being a temporary family member. Even if this is the case, they should bring this up with you and not your stepchild. Putting him in the middle is still not fair, as he is an innocent party. If your family is not willing to accept him because they do not approve of your partner, you might find it is best to keep your distance from them until they are ready to accept your partner with all that he brings to the relationship—including your stepchild. Put the ball in their court, and offer to stay away from family functions until they are ready to accept you and your entire family.

With time, hopefully your family will tire of being standoffish to your stepchild and accept him. It is often difficult for people to accept others into their family if they are not sure of the outcome—which, unfortunately, no one knows. You cannot guarantee that your partner will suddenly endear himself to them or that you will stay married to him forever. What you can remind them is that there is a child in the family who should be judged for who he is and not for his position as stepchild or his relation to your partner. Hopefully, they will recognize this and welcome your stepchild.

CHAPTER 20

Unforeseen Problems

Even the best marriages and relationships will encounter unforeseen problems. No matter what kind of preparation you do beforehand, such as pre-marriage counseling, situations are going to arise that you could not have planned for and may never even have considered. When there is a stepchild in the mix, you now have another person and her family impacting your marriage. More people often mean more opportunity for obstacles to arise.

Managing Frustration

Dealing with a spouse, stepchild, and biological children on top of life in general can be frustrating even with the best spouse, children, and circumstances. You are bound to get frustrated at some point. Perhaps the best protection against frustration is admitting you are feeling this emotion and knowing how to manage it.

First, it is important to learn to recognize the signs that indicate you are frustrated. Are you irritable? Losing patience more easily? Grumpy? Stressed? Do you find you are aggravated by the thought of spending time with your stepchild, spouse, or others? Are you annoyed by things that did not previously annoy you? If you notice any of these things occurring, chances are you are feeling frustrated.

Before addressing any annoying behaviors, make sure you are calm and not aggravated. Take your time and approach people with kindness and patience—not with annoyance and anger. Many people don't realize when they are frustrating others, and might get defensive if they are not approached in a reasonable manner. Point out your concerns in a matter-of-fact way; try not to hurt anyone's feelings.

The second task is to figure out what it is that is frustrating you. If you seem to be frustrated primarily with a certain person or certain habits that a person exhibits, think about why it is bothering you now. Have your spouse and stepchild made a habit of coming home late? Are their late arrivals keeping you from having time you need or participating in something you enjoy? If there is one person who is getting on your nerves, how is his behavior affecting your life? Does your partner continuously forget to empty the dishwasher, making it difficult to organize the kitchen? Does having to organize it yourself then cut into the time you have for yourself? Once you figure out the source of your frustration and how it is affecting your life, it will be easier to address it.

Now that you know the source of your frustration, you will need to address it. If it is your partner, explain that when you are frustrated with him you struggle to be the stepparent you know you can be. If it is your stepchild who is exhibiting behaviors that frustrate you, you might want to talk to your partner first—especially if your stepchild is quite young. Is your stepchild continuing to exhibit these behaviors because you and your partner are not practicing consistent discipline? Or is your stepchild exhibiting a problem behavior that might need extra attention?

Once these concerns are addressed you might feel a little better. However, you might still experience frustration or annoyance from time to time. Dealing with these emotions can be eased if you practice self-care, take time for yourself, participate in hobbies or activities that you enjoy, and speak up about frustration instead of letting it fester. Not addressing frustration sets the stage for resentment and anger. It is up to you to recognize your feelings, express them, and do something about them. If you don't, how are those around you supposed to know that you are frustrated? Not addressing a situation that is frustrating you will only make situations more stressful. Being open and honest about your feelings will set a positive example for your stepchild and help in future communications. Just remember, if you express your frustrations others might express their frustrations with you. You need to be fair and hear them out!

Dealing with Skewed Stepparent Expectations

It is not rare for people to have varying expectations of you depending on your role, their role, and how they intertwine. You might be surprised to find that people expect more (and in some instances, less) from you in the role of stepparent than you had planned. Your partner, the other biological parent, your stepchild, your partner's parents, and others might have expectations of you that differ dramatically from your own. Depending on the circumstances of your stepchild's life, some people might expect you to replace the other biological parent, take over responsibilities of child care, contribute monetarily, and even change your goals. On the other hand, others might expect you to fade into the background and be available only when there is no one else. Such expectations can create tension and resentment.

Expectations from Others

If the other biological parent has passed away or is no longer in touch with your stepchild, you might find that people are excited about you taking over that missing position in your stepchild's life. They might look at you and see the person who can fill the void of home-cooked family meals, playing catch in the yard, and providing financial security. Instead of developing your own relationship with your stepchild, others might predetermine the role for you, and place every expectation they had for the other biological parent on you. This is not usually done with malice, but often out of fear and concern for your stepchild and excitement that there is someone to replace what is missing. When a parental figure is missing somehow in a child's life, other family members and friends might become concerned that your step-child will suffer outrageously due to the loss of a parent. While it is great that your stepchild has caring and concerned folks around him, it is important that you assert yourself as someone separate from the other biological parent, and an adult with your own role that will be determined by you and your stepchild.

E-QUESTION

My mother-in-law is fixated on my taking over for my stepson's biological mother. She comments on how I should make family dinners, iron his clothes, and get to know the other mothers in the neighborhood. This isn't my idea of being a stepmom; what should I do?
You could talk to your mother-in-law about how you define stepmom and what your own expectations are. Explain that you see yourself as being a positive influence in your stepchild's life, but that it doesn't necessarily mean cooking, ironing, and mother's groups. Focus on telling her the positive things you expect of yourself as a stepparent. If this doesn't work, you might need some extra support or backup from your partner.

Just as others outside your immediate family might put expectations on you, so might your partner and stepchild. They might have been missing the other biological partner and see you as a replacement. Remind them that you want to respect the other biological parent's position in the family, and would like to create your own position—one that might including ironing, playing catch, and cooking or that might bring a whole new gamut of fun and appropriate activities and opportunities for bonding.

The Other Biological Parent's Expectations

Surprisingly, the other biological parent might have her own expectations of how you should act as a stepparent. If she is actively involved in your stepchild's life, she might see you as central in your partner's life but not necessarily a part of her child's life. If you can talk to her about your stepchild whenever the opportunity arises and ask if there are ways to be more involved or to help out, over time she might start to recognize that you are willing to take on a relationship with her child and see you as more of an integral part of her child's life.

On the other hand, you might encounter a biological parent who expects you to take on all the responsibility for her child, as well as for any other children she has. If she is asking you to do all the parenting, no longer following through on her own duties, or asking you to take care of her other biological children as well, this is not your responsibility unless you want it to be. To manage this, try talking to her about how you see yourself in your stepchild's life and also how you do not find these other expectations appropriate. Do your best to talk up the expectations you have for yourself. You might learn from the expectations of others and even implement some of them, but try not to let these expectations overwhelm you or change an already caring and wonderful relationship.

When a Biological Parent Is Ill

There may be a time when either your partner or the other biological parent becomes ill. Your primary job (in addition to the role of caregiver) if this happens will be to support your stepchild in any way you can. This might mean mending a negative relationship with the other biological parent, encouraging your partner to be more flexible with visitation, or taking on greater responsibility for your stepchild.

If it is your partner who falls ill, it is important to support your stepchild and take care of yourself as well. You might find that you need some time to yourself. In order to accomplish this, you could ask other family members or the other biological parent to take on more visitations or change days of visitation. You might need the other biological parent more than ever right now, so it is time to mend or push aside any animosity. It is also important that you keep an open dialogue with the other biological parent. He needs to know what is going on, as this will not only affect him, but also his child. If the illness is grave, the other biological parent might find himself more emotional or sadder than he expected. Remember, he did have a relationship with your partner at some point, and old feelings, regrets, or just plain old confusion may emerge. In spite of your own pain, try to keep in mind that he might be hurting, too, and now is not the time to argue or fight with him. For your stepchild's sake, it is necessary that his other biological parent knows about the illness and how best to support and talk to his child. If your partner is dying, it might be the other biological parent who has the conversation with your stepchild. You also might decide to have this discussion together. This is a time when you need to unite or at least be cordial in order to help your stepchild cope.

Hospitals often have support groups for families and children. Usually there is a social worker on staff that can help connect you, your stepchild, or your partner to mental health services. Take advantage of these services and get everyone the support they need.

If it is the other biological parent who falls ill, you might need to take on more responsibility as far as parental duties. Driving your stepchild places, making lunches, going to school meetings, and other such jobs might fall on you. This is about the best care for your stepchild, and being a kind person in general. Even if you think the other person is atrocious, now is not the time to punish or get back at him. What is important is that your stepchild feels supported and loved and any anger or negativity be kept to a minimum. Your partner might also have a stronger reaction than expected and might feel the need for time with the other biological parent. Let her have this time, as it will help her deal with her emotions.

If the illness progresses, it is important that you and your partner consult an attorney. If the other biological parent is dying, you might be taking on custody of your stepchildren. If the other biological parent is married as well, you will need to figure out how the other stepparent will remain a part of your stepchild's life. If it is your partner who is dying, it is also important to seek advice from an attorney. If your partner had custody of your stepchild, this could now mean that the other biological parent will take over custody and change your involvement in your stepchild's life. If the other biological parent already had custody, she might not think about continuing visitation to your house since your partner is no longer living. It is important to find out your rights and fight for the best scenario for your stepchild.

When a Biological Parent Dies

Death can take quite a toll on children and spouses. The death of a parent is one of the most stressful events one can experience, as is the death of a spouse. Similar to dealing with the illness of a biological parent, you might have to put any negative feelings you have for the other biological parent aside in order to best support your stepchild. Hopefully, everyone in the family will see that your relationship with your stepchild is necessary and any animosity they hold toward you can be set aside as well. Regardless of which parent passes away, you will probably take a central role in supporting your stepchild.

A study published in the *Journal of Youth and Adolescence* found that a child's perception of the surviving parent's level of openness in parental communication was found to be related to lower levels of depressive symptoms and anxiety in bereaved children. Encourage your partner or the other biological parent to speak openly with your stepchild and give her opportunities to talk and ask questions.

If your partner passes away, it is important that you not only find the support you need, but also that you make sure your stepchild receives support from family or professionals if necessary. In the event of a death following a long-term illness, you might have secured support ahead of time. If this is a sudden death, finding support in your family will come first; however, it is important that you find professional support as well as support from neighbors, friends, and family. Your primary care physician, your stepchild's pediatrician, school guidance counselors, school administrators, hospital social workers, and your local emergency room should all have services you can obtain quickly. Do not try and take all the stress and grief by yourself. Take help when offered, even if it is from the other biological parent with whom you do not always get along. This is a time when you need to take care of yourself in order to best take care of your stepchild.

FACT

Legally stepparents do not have automatic rights to their stepchildren. Therefore if your spouse were to die you may lose touch with your stepchildren unless the other biological parent chooses to keep in touch. This can be very traumatic for children who will essentially have lost their parent and stepparent all at one time. You may want to approach the other parent and suggest that you don't want to be intrusive but do want to be available to your stepchild.

If the other biological parent passes away, you should put the needs of your stepchild first. Your partner might be distraught and unable to tend to your stepchild as usual. Try to step in and take care of even the smallest items, such as picking up dry cleaning for the memorial ceremonies, ordering flowers, and informing school officials. Do not be consumed by your partner's sadness or let jealousy rear its ugly head—focus on the emotional needs of your partner and stepchild. If you notice your stepchild is quite distressed, suggest to your partner that professional help might be necessary. Your partner might feel too overwhelmed to look for services, so consider compiling a list of potential services that your partner can easily reference.

In the case of a death after a long-term illness, there will have been more opportunity to draw up appropriate legal documentation and make plans for your stepchild's care. Hopefully, this was done prior to the passing on of the biological parent. If not, you will need to seek legal advice relatively soon to avoid confusion or unsettled feelings on the part of your stepchild. In the event of the sudden death of either parent you might find added confusion, as there would not have been pressing reasons to plan for your stepchild's custody, living arrangements, schooling, etc. Since you never do know what the world holds, it is a great idea to write up specific plans and consult an attorney prior to any unforeseen illness or death. Taking precautions will only help everyone manage a sudden death or illness with more stability and less opportunity for disagreements.

When Your Stepchild Is in Trouble

Kids can get into mischief and make innocent mistakes, but as they get older simple mischief might turn into trouble in school or even trouble with the law. Serious trouble can stem from years of behavioral issues or from a one-time bad decision. Either way, it can impact your stepchild's entire future and disrupt the whole family. Unfortunately, when kids get in trouble people often point fingers at the parents, and if the parents are not together or do not get along, such events provide a great opportunity for them to point fingers at one another. You could even find the fingers get pointed at you for being a bad influence, too lenient, or the cause of all that is wrong with your stepchild. If you can keep an even head through this and not take the anger of either parent personally, you are likely to fare better through any turmoil.

When children misbehave, others can judge parents rather harshly and it can set the stage for parents to become quite defensive. No one wants to be blamed for his child robbing stores, cutting school, or smoking marijuana. It is much easier to blame it on another party. The fear that a parent has somehow made their child "bad" can be significant. And if a parent admits that he has neglected his child, wrongly influenced her, or somehow caused her behavior, what does that say about his parenting skills? These are real fears, and fears that many parents do not know how to handle.

One of the best ways to face the fact that a child is in trouble is to accept the news and then figure out how to tackle the issue. If the trouble has been serious enough to require court involvement, there will likely be a prescription of sorts through the court system as far as what is expected of your stepchild and the family in order to rehabilitate your stepchild. It is a good idea to consult an attorney if your stepchild is in court for even a minor offense. If your stepchild is not in legal trouble yet, exploring why she is getting in trouble is a first step to avoiding future issues. Is she unsupervised at home? Tired of her biological parents bad mouthing one another? Rebelling against you? Whatever the reason, it is helpful to know. Once you know, you can work on helping her express her anger in a healthier way.

Often kids do not know why they are misbehaving and don't necessarily like that they are getting in trouble or feeling angry. They can usually tell you they are angry (which was probably pretty obvious anyway!), but they don't always know why, and need help figuring it out. Talking to a therapist or counselor can be quite useful for your stepchild, and she might find a neutral party easier to speak with than you or her biological parents.

As you are not a biological parent, you might be able to see the situation through a less emotionally clouded lens than the biological parents. This does not mean that you are the expert or that you should make the decisions, but you might be able to lend a different perspective to your partner and the other biological parent. Pointing out what your stepchild might be angry about can be very helpful, but it must be done in a nonjudgmental way that does not point fingers at either biological parent. Noticing that your stepchild has seemed frustrated on days that her mother works late and that maybe she really misses time with her mom is a way you might be able to successfully point out your observation. If you exclaim that your stepchild is obviously angry because her mother is never around, you aren't going to be very helpful. Try to be kind to everyone involved, as trouble can be quite stressful. Approach the issue as a cry for help from your stepchild and figure out what she needs and how you and her parents can best support her and listen to her needs.

CHAPTER 21

In the Event of Divorce

Divorce is difficult for everyone, but it can really disrupt a child who has already experienced the divorce
or breakup of his biological parents. Unfortunately,
your stepchild might assume that your breakup with
your partner is going to be just like the previous
breakup—whether good or bad. Try to learn from
past experiences and implement any positive strategies you have learned about supporting your stepchild through difficult situations. Your role and your
stepchild's tolerance for the breakup will depend on
many factors.

Divorce Doesn't Necessarily Mean You're No Longer a Stepparent

Although your stepchild came with your partner, that doesn't necessarily mean that when you cut ties with your partner you also cut ties with your stepchild. You might have developed a very strong relationship with your stepchild, and dissolving it because of what happened between you and your partner is not always necessary. If the breakup is amicable, continuing a relationship with your stepchild will probably be easier than if the breakup is charged with negativity.

Regardless of how you break up, it is important that your stepchild recognizes that the breakup is an adult matter and not because of her or something she could have prevented. In order to reinforce this point, it is important for you and your partner to speak with her about any questions, concerns, or feelings she may be experiencing. Emphasize that the breakup does not in any way make your relationship with her any less special. What you have with your stepchild should be left somewhat sacred and untarnished by any arguing or disagreeing that goes on between you and your partner. If your partner cheated or did something else you see as unforgivable, do not take it out on your stepchild. She is a separate person from her parents, and what they have done is not a reflection of her.

FACT

A study found on *www.CNN.com* points out that children who experience multiple divorces and remarriages of parents are more likely to divorce and experience multiple failed marriages.

Depending on the length of time you have been with your partner, you might be the only maternal or paternal figure your stepchild had growing up. You may have gone through major milestones with your stepchild—such as puberty, prom, and driving lessons. These are huge parts of a child's life, and even if you don't think you had an impact, you probably did. Even in a scenario where your stepchild didn't live with you and you only knew her for a short time, she might feel as though you were a very important part of her life. It is important for both you and your partner to understand what your stepchild needs from you after the split. For the sake of her feelings and emotional health, you and your partner will need to figure out how to best continue a relationship between you and your stepchild in the future. As always, putting your stepchild's needs first is of the utmost importance and might help you and your partner remain civil.

What's the Best Role for You?

As mentioned above, your stepchild's needs dictate a great deal of what your role will be. He might feel the need to have you continue to attend all of his baseball games or help him with his homework once a week. He might also decide that seeing you occasionally is fine, but communicating via e-mail is enough for day-to-day interaction. As long as your stepchild's needs are at the forefront of your and your partner's concerns, you should be able to craft a relationship that is livable for both of you as well.

If your breakup is amicable, you can allow your stepchild to voice what he would like as a relationship and then work on the logistics. If the breakup is difficult, you and your partner might have to step in and set ground rules. For instance, your partner might not want to see you, and can only tolerate a quick exchange to drop your stepchild off with you. Also, your partner might only want you to see your stepchild at large functions so he is not stuck in situations where the two of you have to do too much communicating.

If your partner is greatly hurt by something you did that caused the breakup, he might not want you around his child at all. Your actions might have hurt your stepchild as well, and your partner might want to protect him from any further pain. If this is so, you need to respect your partner's wishes and your stepchild's emotional state.

When your breakup is one that occurs after a long relationship, you might find that you and your stepchild wish to stay close. You can take on a mentoring role and continue to connect with him as he grows up. If your stepchild does not feel the need to continue a relationship, you might just want to check in from time to time via your partner, asking how his year has gone or if he needs anything where you can be of assistance. Giving your stepchild your contact information if that is okay with your partner is also a possibility. If he is old enough, he might feel comfortable reaching out to you himself. Sending gifts for events is appropriate if your partner agrees, and you might find you are invited to major milestone celebrations.

If you would like to continue visiting your stepchild, have some sort of custodial agreement, or continue to support them in some way, you should consult an attorney whether or not you and your partner agree on a way for you to continue your relationship with your stepchild.

Whatever role you take on, make sure you do not, under any circumstances, try to find out information about your partner or badmouth your partner to your stepchild. There is no reason for your stepchild to be involved in your drama with his parent, and pulling him into it will only disrupt any relationship you had with your partner to a greater degree.

The Age of Your Stepchild Affects His Coping

Age and the number of broken relationships your stepchild has experienced will affect his ability to cope with your divorce. A baby or toddler might not remember a breakup unless you have been the primary caretaker throughout the child's life. Children three years of age and older, however, will most likely remember a breakup or at least the stress related to the event. Although your breakup will cause some emotional upheaval regardless of your stepchild's age or past experiences, there are certain things that may hinder or help him cope depending on his age.

For children under four years of age, the parting might be more traumatic for you. It will become quite traumatic for any child if you cry excessively or argue with your partner in front of your stepchild.

How It Affects Children Four to Ten Years Old

Children from four to about ten years of age will probably have a lot of questions that they may or may not ask. There is often confusion for children experiencing a divorce between adults involved in their lives and fear about what it means for them and their relationship with you and their biological parent. Talk to your stepson and find out if he has any questions. Does he understand that you will still love him even if you don't stay married to his parent? Does he know that this isn't his fault and sometimes adults need time apart? These are questions he might have, but be too afraid to ask. Addressing them up front will let him know that you are open to discussing this and that you do want to hear his concerns. Children in this age group might also feel very unsettled if this is a pattern for their biological parent. Talking to them regarding fears about losing multiple parental figures is also important.

Shield any child from emotional situations when you do not feel that you have control. It is appropriate for you to show emotions like sadness, frustration, or even anger, but it must be done in a controlled way, where no one feels unsafe or overwhelmed.

How It Affects Preteens and Teens

Preteens and teens tend to be savvy about relationships and might have already picked up on the fact that you are breaking up. You might start discussions with a teenager a bit earlier than you would with a child, and also have more candid discussions. There is still no need to tell a teen the nitty-gritty of the relationship, but he will understand more than a younger child. Adolescents will probably have questions similar to those of their younger counterparts, but they might be able to ask them more comfortably. Also, at this age teenagers tend to confide in each other, school personnel, and other trustworthy adults. If your stepchild is finding comfort in speaking with his school counselor, be happy that he has found someone to talk to about the situation.

Any time a pattern of multiple relationships and breakups occurs, kids involved are at risk of becoming hardened to relationships and rather disenchanted. This tends to be more obvious with teenagers and those who are older than teens. They might have assumed you were going to leave the day they met you, so it doesn't appear to have much of an impact on them. They also might be angry that this is happening again, and not want to maintain a relationship with you after the split. You can't force a relationship on your stepchildren—especially teenagers. But, you can continue to reach out in a nonthreatening way, just to let them know you are still there. E-mail, text messaging, letters, or cards are ways of connecting that your stepchild will not have to respond to if he doesn't feel ready. You are still letting him know that you are there for him, but not forcing him to respond or communicate with you.

How It Affects Adult Stepchildren

Older teenagers and adults are really at a point where they can determine how they would like their relationship with you to continue and are often more vocal about space they need or what they need to best deal with the split. With age comes emotional knowledge, but don't forget that they still might be hurting. Your thirty-year-old stepson might be very upset and quite worried that your relationship with him will disappear now that the marriage is over. No matter what your stepchild's age, be open and honest, give him the space he needs, and continue to follow through on any promises you made.

Your Ex Is Already in Another Relationship

If your partner was in another relationship prior to your divorce or is in one immediately following your divorce, it might be more difficult to interact with him or your stepchild. Remember that your stepchild is not a reflection of him. Also, it is not fair to put your stepchild in the middle of you and your partner. Do not ask him about your partner's new relationship, if he is in a new relationship, if he goes out on dates, or any similar questions. If this will be difficult for you, you may have to minimize your time with your stepchild until you can act appropriately.

If you decide to cut down on time with your stepchild, do not blame it on your former partner's new relationship or his new partner. Blaming your inability to spend time with your stepchild on the new relationship might tarnish your stepchild's opinion of his parent's new partner. Although you might secretly wish that the relationship wouldn't last, think of how disruptive another breakup might be for your stepchild. This is where you need to keep your focus—on your stepchild, and what is best for him. Be sure your stepchild does not think he has caused you to spend less time with him. You can make up an excuse that is totally unrelated or be honest and tell him you are in a bit of a funk right now and need some alone time to be the supportive person you want to be for him.

E-QUESTION

Can you be angry, hurt, jealous, annoyed, or totally against this new relationship?
Absolutely, but don't show it to your stepchild. If you have a major issue with the new relationship you can bring it up to your former partner, but don't put your stepchild in the middle. If you need to express your feelings, do so with friends, family, or a counselor.

If your partner becomes serious with his new partner, your time with your stepchild might decrease. There might be more family activities that now take the place of time you once had together. Instead of being jealous or angry, encourage your stepchild to take part in his new family situation. As the relationship becomes more serious, it is possible your partner will remarry. Be supportive in front of your stepchild, and do not speak negatively about your partner's decisions. It might be tough, but it will show your stepchild that your relationship with him is central in your mind and what happens between you and your former partner will not intervene.

Moving On

Eventually, the time might come for you to move on as well. You might move on before or after your partner. Whatever the case, this could affect your stepchild more than you expect. With many children, the fantasy that their parents will reunite is quite common. Your stepchild might impose this fantasy on you and her biological parent as well. Depending on the age of your stepchild, she might not have known life without you and she might have difficulty seeing you start dating someone else. Once you are dating someone new, the fantasy of reconciliation will be clouded and the reality of the situation will be apparent. This could cause her to become quite angry or hurt. She might not want to see you for a while and she may need some space. Allowing her space and talking openly and honestly with her might help avoid a negative reaction or hurt feelings.

Similar to how you were first introduced to your stepchild, you should also think through introducing her to anyone you are dating:

- Is this a person she needs to meet?
- Is this new love interest someone who is ready to meet her?
- Is your stepchild ready to see you dating someone other than her biological parent?
- Is her biological parent okay with her meeting your new love interest?

Be very considerate and quite cautious when it comes to introducing your stepchild to anyone new. If this is someone you do not expect to be with for a long time, there is no need for her to meet him. If he is going to be around or you are planning on marrying him or moving in with him, then you should consider introducing them and letting them get to know one another.

If your former partner is not yet dating or seems to be a bit jealous of your relationship, it is possible he will encourage your stepchild to find out some facts about the people you are dating. Do not take out your anger on her; instead, explain that it is not something she needs to worry about at this time because any potential dates will not affect your relationship with her. You can also explain that when you do find someone worthy of meeting her you will introduce her when the moment is right. The person you can speak with about not putting your stepchild in the middle is your former partner. Hopefully, he will be mature and understanding and not attempt to withhold visits with your stepchild or distort her image of you or anyone you might be dating. Remember to handle adult issues with adults and leave children out of it!

Maintaining Relationships after the Fact

After you and your former partner have been apart for a substantial amount of time, you can still keep in touch with your stepchild. The relationship doesn't need to fade with time, although it might. You might be remarried with a family, and your former partner might be as well. Sometimes relationships do become distant, and this is normal. It would be a nice idea, however, to maintain contact somehow, even if it seems minimal. Sending holiday cards, birthday cards, care packages in college, and e-mails every couple of weeks are nice ways of letting your stepchild know he is still in your thoughts even if you don't see him often. Inviting him to events that you have might be appropriate as long as the relationship with you and your former partner is solid. Attending events that your stepchild invites you to is also important. If he invites you to an event it means he would like you there and values your attendance. If you cannot follow through, call and offer to celebrate by going to dinner or spending time with him.

Keeping your stepchild as important in your life as he was prior to the divorce might be difficult, but it is important that your stepchild continues to feel as though your relationship with one another did not suffer because of your relationship with your former partner.

Allow Stepsiblings to Stay in Touch

If you had other children who would be your stepchild's stepsiblings, let them create their own ways of staying in touch and maintaining a relationship. They might have become quite close, and they might become closer because of the commonality they now share with the breakup of the marriage. Even if you do not get along well with your former partner, protect the relationship between your children. Losing a parental figure is enough; there is no need for your child or stepchild to lose another relationship. Encourage them to stay in touch and do your best to support their friendship.

Maintaining relationships between you and your stepchild, your family and your stepchild, and any siblings and your stepchild will be more difficult when they are younger. As they grow up, they will be able to figure out where they best fit into each other's lives. You might become a mentor to your stepchild who helps him apply to colleges. Your son might be his basketball teammate and eventually a roommate after college. The options are endless—be sure to allow time for these relationships to grow past any hurt that occurred in the breakup.

Resources

Adopting.org

This website provides general adoption information as well as links for adoption resources for specific states. There are articles and discussion boards dedicated to stepparent adoption.

www.adopting.org

American Academy of Child and Adolescent Psychiatry

This website has sections for families and parents as well as for doctors and mental-health professionals. They offer great resources on child and adolescent mental health, a searchable database to find a psychiatrist, and general information about divorce and stepfamilies.

www.aacap.org

Bonus Families

This website refers to stepfamilies as bonus families. It contains articles and discussions about topics such as ex-etiquette, co-parenting, divorce, bonus teens, and support groups. It is a positive website that is quite helpful for everyday questions that might arise.

www.bonusfamilies.com/index.php

Break the Cycle

This website provides information for survivors and supporters of survivors of childhood trauma. It also contains a large and informative section on stepfamilies, divorce, and helping children through the trauma of divorce.

http://sfhelp.org

California Department of Child Support Services

This website has tons of information on child support in California.

www.childsup.cahwnet.gov

Family Education

This website offers resources on child health, child development, nutrition for kids and teens, fitness for the whole family, and child safety as well as information on social and emotional issues, child discipline, communicating with your kids, teaching good behavior, and building your child's self-esteem.

http://life.familyeducation.com

familyresource.com

A website that provides general family information and resources. It provides many articles on divorce and separation and how to talk to children about tough issues.

www.familyresource.com

I Do Take Two

A website dedicated to etiquette and issues surrounding second marriages. It addresses how to best incorporate children from either party into the wedding ceremony and life following the second marriage.

www.idotaketwo.com

Kiwi Families

This is a New Zealand website that has great information and articles about stepfamilies and parenting in general. They provide a few different experts on medical and parenting issues who respond to questions.

www.kiwifamilies.co.nz

National Conference of State Legislatures

This website has a great deal of information about legislature and government issues; it has interesting links, statistics, and information such as state guidelines regarding child support.

www.ncsl.org/index.htm

National Stepfamily Resource Center

A very informative website providing resources and articles for stepfamilies. It also provides links for professionals to find training on how to work with stepfamilies.

www.stepfamilies.info/index.php

The Parent Report

This website contains many resources for parents on behavior, limit setting, family life, and more. There are articles and tips on stepfamilies as well as community forums and a radio show on parenting topics.

www.theparentreport.com

Parents. The Anti-drug

This is a fantastic website for any adult who interacts with kids. It has tips on preventing drug use and abuse, great resources to find help for someone who is using drugs, and a useful newsletter you can subscribe to. It also provides health information for teens and packets for community groups to distribute about teen substance use and abuse and how to address it.

www.theantidrug.com

PBS Parents

A website affiliated with PBS. It contains many helpful parenting tips, such as how to consistently discipline children, benefits of talking with your children, and a newsletter you can receive by e-mail.

www.pbs.org/parents

The Stepfamily Life

A website focused around a blog by a current stepmom. It includes tips and articles about stepfamilies.

www.thestepfamilylife.com

Stepfamily Network

A website primarily for message boards and chatting with other stepparents and stepchildren about issues and experiences.

www.stepfamily.net

Successful Stepfamilies

This is a Christian website that has great statistics and research. Also, there are some interesting and helpful tips on parenting and stepparenting.

www.successfulstepfamilies.com

Index

THE EVERYTHING SERIES!

BUSINESS & PERSONAL FINANCE

Everything® Accounting Book
Everything® Budgeting Book, 2nd Ed.
Everything® Business Planning Book
Everything® Coaching and Mentoring Book, 2nd Ed.
Everything® Fundraising Book
Everything® Get Out of Debt Book
Everything® Grant Writing Book, 2nd Ed.
Everything® Guide to Buying Foreclosures
Everything® Guide to Fundraising, $15.95
Everything® Guide to Mortgages
Everything® Guide to Personal Finance for Single Mothers
Everything® Home-Based Business Book, 2nd Ed.
Everything® Homebuying Book, 3rd Ed., $15.95
Everything® Homeselling Book, 2nd Ed.
Everything® Human Resource Management Book
Everything® Improve Your Credit Book
Everything® Investing Book, 2nd Ed.
Everything® Landlording Book
Everything® Leadership Book, 2nd Ed.
Everything® Managing People Book, 2nd Ed.
Everything® Negotiating Book
Everything® Online Auctions Book
Everything® Online Business Book
Everything® Personal Finance Book
Everything® Personal Finance in Your 20s & 30s Book, 2nd Ed.
Everything® Personal Finance in Your 40s & 50s Book, $15.95
Everything® Project Management Book, 2nd Ed.
Everything® Real Estate Investing Book
Everything® Retirement Planning Book
Everything® Robert's Rules Book, $7.95
Everything® Selling Book
Everything® Start Your Own Business Book, 2nd Ed.
Everything® Wills & Estate Planning Book

COOKING

Everything® Barbecue Cookbook
Everything® Bartender's Book, 2nd Ed., $9.95
Everything® Calorie Counting Cookbook
Everything® Cheese Book
Everything® Chinese Cookbook
Everything® Classic Recipes Book
Everything® Cocktail Parties & Drinks Book
Everything® College Cookbook
Everything® Cooking for Baby and Toddler Book
Everything® Diabetes Cookbook
Everything® Easy Gourmet Cookbook
Everything® Fondue Cookbook
Everything® Food Allergy Cookbook, $15.95
Everything® Fondue Party Book
Everything® Gluten-Free Cookbook
Everything® Glycemic Index Cookbook
Everything® Grilling Cookbook
Everything® Healthy Cooking for Parties Book, $15.95
Everything® Holiday Cookbook
Everything® Indian Cookbook
Everything® Lactose-Free Cookbook
Everything® Low-Cholesterol Cookbook

Everything® Low-Fat High-Flavor Cookbook, 2nd Ed., $15.95
Everything® Low-Salt Cookbook
Everything® Meals for a Month Cookbook
Everything® Meals on a Budget Cookbook
Everything® Mediterranean Cookbook
Everything® Mexican Cookbook
Everything® No Trans Fat Cookbook
Everything® One-Pot Cookbook, 2nd Ed., $15.95
Everything® Organic Cooking for Baby & Toddler Book, $15.95
Everything® Pizza Cookbook
Everything® Quick Meals Cookbook, 2nd Ed., $15.95
Everything® Slow Cooker Cookbook
Everything® Slow Cooking for a Crowd Cookbook
Everything® Soup Cookbook
Everything® Stir-Fry Cookbook
Everything® Sugar-Free Cookbook
Everything® Tapas and Small Plates Cookbook
Everything® Tex-Mex Cookbook
Everything® Thai Cookbook
Everything® Vegetarian Cookbook
Everything® Whole-Grain, High-Fiber Cookbook
Everything® Wild Game Cookbook
Everything® Wine Book, 2nd Ed.

GAMES

Everything® 15-Minute Sudoku Book, $9.95
Everything® 30-Minute Sudoku Book, $9.95
Everything® Bible Crosswords Book, $9.95
Everything® Blackjack Strategy Book
Everything® Brain Strain Book, $9.95
Everything® Bridge Book
Everything® Card Games Book
Everything® Card Tricks Book, $9.95
Everything® Casino Gambling Book, 2nd Ed.
Everything® Chess Basics Book
Everything® Christmas Crosswords Book, $9.95
Everything® Craps Strategy Book
Everything® Crossword and Puzzle Book
Everything® Crosswords and Puzzles for Quote Lovers Book, $9.95
Everything® Crossword Challenge Book
Everything® Crosswords for the Beach Book, $9.95
Everything® Cryptic Crosswords Book, $9.95
Everything® Cryptograms Book, $9.95
Everything® Easy Crosswords Book
Everything® Easy Kakuro Book, $9.95
Everything® Easy Large-Print Crosswords Book
Everything® Games Book, 2nd Ed.
Everything® Giant Book of Crosswords
Everything® Giant Sudoku Book, $9.95
Everything® Giant Word Search Book
Everything® Kakuro Challenge Book
Everything® Large-Print Crossword Challenge Book
Everything® Large-Print Crosswords Book
Everything® Large-Print Travel Crosswords Book
Everything® Lateral Thinking Puzzles Book, $9.95
Everything® Literary Crosswords Book, $9.95
Everything® Mazes Book
Everything® Memory Booster Puzzles Book, $9.95

Everything® Movie Crosswords Book, $9.95
Everything® Music Crosswords Book, $9.95
Everything® Online Poker Book
Everything® Pencil Puzzles Book, $9.95
Everything® Poker Strategy Book
Everything® Pool & Billiards Book
Everything® Puzzles for Commuters Book, $9.95
Everything® Puzzles for Dog Lovers Book, $9.95
Everything® Sports Crosswords Book, $9.95
Everything® Test Your IQ Book, $9.95
Everything® Texas Hold 'Em Book, $9.95
Everything® Travel Crosswords Book, $9.95
Everything® Travel Mazes Book, $9.95
Everything® Travel Word Search Book, $9.95
Everything® TV Crosswords Book, $9.95
Everything® Word Games Challenge Book
Everything® Word Scramble Book
Everything® Word Search Book

HEALTH

Everything® Alzheimer's Book
Everything® Diabetes Book
Everything® First Aid Book, $9.95
Everything® Green Living Book
Everything® Health Guide to Addiction and Recovery
Everything® Health Guide to Adult Bipolar Disorder
Everything® Health Guide to Arthritis
Everything® Health Guide to Controlling Anxiety
Everything® Health Guide to Depression
Everything® Health Guide to Diabetes, 2nd Ed.
Everything® Health Guide to Fibromyalgia
Everything® Health Guide to Menopause, 2nd Ed.
Everything® Health Guide to Migraines
Everything® Health Guide to Multiple Sclerosis
Everything® Health Guide to OCD
Everything® Health Guide to PMS
Everything® Health Guide to Postpartum Care
Everything® Health Guide to Thyroid Disease
Everything® Hypnosis Book
Everything® Low Cholesterol Book
Everything® Menopause Book
Everything® Nutrition Book
Everything® Reflexology Book
Everything® Stress Management Book
Everything® Superfoods Book, $15.95

HISTORY

Everything® American Government Book
Everything® American History Book, 2nd Ed.
Everything® American Revolution Book, $15.95
Everything® Civil War Book
Everything® Freemasons Book
Everything® Irish History & Heritage Book
Everything® World War II Book, 2nd Ed.

HOBBIES

Everything® Candlemaking Book
Everything® Cartooning Book
Everything® Coin Collecting Book
Everything® Digital Photography Book, 2nd Ed.

Everything® Drawing Book
Everything® Family Tree Book, 2nd Ed.
Everything® Guide to Online Genealogy, $15.95
Everything® Knitting Book
Everything® Knots Book
Everything® Photography Book
Everything® Quilting Book
Everything® Sewing Book
Everything® Soapmaking Book, 2nd Ed.
Everything® Woodworking Book

HOME IMPROVEMENT

Everything® Feng Shui Book
Everything® Feng Shui Decluttering Book, $9.95
Everything® Fix-It Book
Everything® Green Living Book
Everything® Home Decorating Book
Everything® Home Storage Solutions Book
Everything® Homebuilding Book
Everything® Organize Your Home Book, 2nd Ed.

KIDS' BOOKS

All titles are $7.95
Everything® Fairy Tales Book, $14.95
Everything® Kids' Animal Puzzle & Activity Book
Everything® Kids' Astronomy Book
Everything® Kids' Baseball Book, 5th Ed.
Everything® Kids' Bible Trivia Book
Everything® Kids' Bugs Book
Everything® Kids' Cars and Trucks Puzzle and Activity Book
Everything® Kids' Christmas Puzzle & Activity Book
Everything® Kids' Connect the Dots
    Puzzle and Activity Book
Everything® Kids' Cookbook, 2nd Ed.
Everything® Kids' Crazy Puzzles Book
Everything® Kids' Dinosaurs Book
Everything® Kids' Dragons Puzzle and Activity Book
Everything® Kids' Environment Book $7.95
Everything® Kids' Fairies Puzzle and Activity Book
Everything® Kids' First Spanish Puzzle and Activity Book
Everything® Kids' Football Book
Everything® Kids' Geography Book
Everything® Kids' Gross Cookbook
Everything® Kids' Gross Hidden Pictures Book
Everything® Kids' Gross Jokes Book
Everything® Kids' Gross Mazes Book
Everything® Kids' Gross Puzzle & Activity Book
Everything® Kids' Halloween Puzzle & Activity Book
Everything® Kids' Hanukkah Puzzle and Activity Book
Everything® Kids' Hidden Pictures Book
Everything® Kids' Horses Book
Everything® Kids' Joke Book
Everything® Kids' Knock Knock Book
Everything® Kids' Learning French Book
Everything® Kids' Learning Spanish Book
Everything® Kids' Magical Science Experiments Book
Everything® Kids' Math Puzzles Book
Everything® Kids' Mazes Book
Everything® Kids' Money Book, 2nd Ed.
**Everything® Kids' Mummies, Pharaoh's, and Pyramids
    Puzzle and Activity Book**
Everything® Kids' Nature Book
Everything® Kids' Pirates Puzzle and Activity Book
Everything® Kids' Presidents Book
Everything® Kids' Princess Puzzle and Activity Book
Everything® Kids' Puzzle Book

Everything® Kids' Racecars Puzzle and Activity Book
Everything® Kids' Riddles & Brain Teasers Book
Everything® Kids' Science Experiments Book
Everything® Kids' Sharks Book
Everything® Kids' Soccer Book
Everything® Kids' Spelling Book
Everything® Kids' Spies Puzzle and Activity Book
Everything® Kids' States Book
Everything® Kids' Travel Activity Book
Everything® Kids' Word Search Puzzle and Activity Book

LANGUAGE

Everything® Conversational Japanese Book with CD, $19.95
Everything® French Grammar Book
Everything® French Phrase Book, $9.95
Everything® French Verb Book, $9.95
Everything® German Phrase Book, $9.95
Everything® German Practice Book with CD, $19.95
Everything® Inglés Book
Everything® Intermediate Spanish Book with CD, $19.95
Everything® Italian Phrase Book, $9.95
Everything® Italian Practice Book with CD, $19.95
Everything® Learning Brazilian Portuguese Book with CD, $19.95
Everything® Learning French Book with CD, 2nd Ed., $19.95
Everything® Learning German Book
Everything® Learning Italian Book
Everything® Learning Latin Book
Everything® Learning Russian Book with CD, $19.95
Everything® Learning Spanish Book
Everything® Learning Spanish Book with CD, 2nd Ed., $19.95
Everything® Russian Practice Book with CD, $19.95
Everything® Sign Language Book, $15.95
Everything® Spanish Grammar Book
Everything® Spanish Phrase Book, $9.95
Everything® Spanish Practice Book with CD, $19.95
Everything® Spanish Verb Book, $9.95
Everything® Speaking Mandarin Chinese Book with CD, $19.95

MUSIC

Everything® Bass Guitar Book with CD, $19.95
Everything® Drums Book with CD, $19.95
Everything® Guitar Book with CD, 2nd Ed., $19.95
Everything® Guitar Chords Book with CD, $19.95
Everything® Guitar Scales Book with CD, $19.95
Everything® Harmonica Book with CD, $15.95
Everything® Home Recording Book
Everything® Music Theory Book with CD, $19.95
Everything® Reading Music Book with CD, $19.95
Everything® Rock & Blues Guitar Book with CD, $19.95
Everything® Rock & Blues Piano Book with CD, $19.95
Everything® Rock Drums Book with CD, $19.95
Everything® Singing Book with CD, $19.95
Everything® Songwriting Book

NEW AGE

Everything® Astrology Book, 2nd Ed.
Everything® Birthday Personology Book
Everything® Celtic Wisdom Book, $15.95
Everything® Dreams Book, 2nd Ed.
Everything® Law of Attraction Book, $15.95
Everything® Love Signs Book, $9.95
Everything® Love Spells Book, $9.95
Everything® Palmistry Book
Everything® Psychic Book
Everything® Reiki Book

Everything® Sex Signs Book, $9.95
Everything® Spells & Charms Book, 2nd Ed.
Everything® Tarot Book, 2nd Ed.
Everything® Toltec Wisdom Book
Everything® Wicca & Witchcraft Book, 2nd Ed.

PARENTING

Everything® Baby Names Book, 2nd Ed.
Everything® Baby Shower Book, 2nd Ed.
Everything® Baby Sign Language Book with DVD
Everything® Baby's First Year Book
Everything® Birthing Book
Everything® Breastfeeding Book
Everything® Father-to-Be Book
Everything® Father's First Year Book
Everything® Get Ready for Baby Book, 2nd Ed.
Everything® Get Your Baby to Sleep Book, $9.95
Everything® Getting Pregnant Book
Everything® Guide to Pregnancy Over 35
Everything® Guide to Raising a One-Year-Old
Everything® Guide to Raising a Two-Year-Old
Everything® Guide to Raising Adolescent Boys
Everything® Guide to Raising Adolescent Girls
Everything® Mother's First Year Book
Everything® Parent's Guide to Childhood Illnesses
Everything® Parent's Guide to Children and Divorce
Everything® Parent's Guide to Children with ADD/ADHD
Everything® Parent's Guide to Children with Asperger's
    Syndrome
Everything® Parent's Guide to Children with Anxiety
Everything® Parent's Guide to Children with Asthma
Everything® Parent's Guide to Children with Autism
Everything® Parent's Guide to Children with Bipolar Disorder
Everything® Parent's Guide to Children with Depression
Everything® Parent's Guide to Children with Dyslexia
Everything® Parent's Guide to Children with Juvenile Diabetes
Everything® Parent's Guide to Children with OCD
Everything® Parent's Guide to Positive Discipline
Everything® Parent's Guide to Raising Boys
Everything® Parent's Guide to Raising Girls
Everything® Parent's Guide to Raising Siblings
**Everything® Parent's Guide to Raising Your
    Adopted Child**
Everything® Parent's Guide to Sensory Integration Disorder
Everything® Parent's Guide to Tantrums
Everything® Parent's Guide to the Strong-Willed Child
Everything® Parenting a Teenager Book
Everything® Potty Training Book, $9.95
Everything® Pregnancy Book, 3rd Ed.
Everything® Pregnancy Fitness Book
Everything® Pregnancy Nutrition Book
Everything® Pregnancy Organizer, 2nd Ed., $16.95
Everything® Toddler Activities Book
Everything® Toddler Book
Everything® Tween Book
Everything® Twins, Triplets, and More Book

PETS

Everything® Aquarium Book
Everything® Boxer Book
Everything® Cat Book, 2nd Ed.
Everything® Chihuahua Book
Everything® Cooking for Dogs Book
Everything® Dachshund Book
Everything® Dog Book, 2nd Ed.
Everything® Dog Grooming Book

Everything® Dog Obedience Book
Everything® Dog Owner's Organizer, $16.95
Everything® Dog Training and Tricks Book
Everything® German Shepherd Book
Everything® Golden Retriever Book
Everything® Horse Book, 2nd Ed., $15.95
Everything® Horse Care Book
Everything® Horseback Riding Book
Everything® Labrador Retriever Book
Everything® Poodle Book
Everything® Pug Book
Everything® Puppy Book
Everything® Small Dogs Book
Everything® Tropical Fish Book
Everything® Yorkshire Terrier Book

REFERENCE

Everything® American Presidents Book
Everything® Blogging Book
Everything® Build Your Vocabulary Book, $9.95
Everything® Car Care Book
Everything® Classical Mythology Book
Everything® Da Vinci Book
Everything® Einstein Book
Everything® Enneagram Book
Everything® Etiquette Book, 2nd Ed.
Everything® Family Christmas Book, $15.95
Everything® Guide to C. S. Lewis & Narnia
Everything® Guide to Divorce, 2nd Ed., $15.95
Everything® Guide to Edgar Allan Poe
Everything® Guide to Understanding Philosophy
Everything® Inventions and Patents Book
Everything® Jacqueline Kennedy Onassis Book
Everything® John F. Kennedy Book
Everything® Mafia Book
Everything® Martin Luther King Jr. Book
Everything® Pirates Book
Everything® Private Investigation Book
Everything® Psychology Book
Everything® Public Speaking Book, $9.95
Everything® Shakespeare Book, 2nd Ed.

RELIGION

Everything® Angels Book
Everything® Bible Book
Everything® Bible Study Book with CD, $19.95
Everything® Buddhism Book
Everything® Catholicism Book
Everything® Christianity Book
Everything® Gnostic Gospels Book
Everything® Hinduism Book, $15.95
Everything® History of the Bible Book
Everything® Jesus Book
Everything® Jewish History & Heritage Book
Everything® Judaism Book
Everything® Kabbalah Book
Everything® Koran Book
Everything® Mary Book
Everything® Mary Magdalene Book
Everything® Prayer Book

Everything® Saints Book, 2nd Ed.
Everything® Torah Book
Everything® Understanding Islam Book
Everything® Women of the Bible Book
Everything® World's Religions Book

SCHOOL & CAREERS

Everything® Career Tests Book
Everything® College Major Test Book
Everything® College Survival Book, 2nd Ed.
Everything® Cover Letter Book, 2nd Ed.
Everything® Filmmaking Book
Everything® Get-a-Job Book, 2nd Ed.
Everything® Guide to Being a Paralegal
Everything® Guide to Being a Personal Trainer
Everything® Guide to Being a Real Estate Agent
Everything® Guide to Being a Sales Rep
Everything® Guide to Being an Event Planner
Everything® Guide to Careers in Health Care
Everything® Guide to Careers in Law Enforcement
Everything® Guide to Government Jobs
Everything® Guide to Starting and Running a Catering
    Business
Everything® Guide to Starting and Running a Restaurant
**Everything® Guide to Starting and Running
    a Retail Store**
Everything® Job Interview Book, 2nd Ed.
Everything® New Nurse Book
Everything® New Teacher Book
Everything® Paying for College Book
Everything® Practice Interview Book
Everything® Resume Book, 3rd Ed.
Everything® Study Book

SELF-HELP

Everything® Body Language Book
Everything® Dating Book, 2nd Ed.
Everything® Great Sex Book
**Everything® Guide to Caring for Aging Parents,
    $15.95**
Everything® Self-Esteem Book
Everything® Self-Hypnosis Book, $9.95
Everything® Tantric Sex Book

SPORTS & FITNESS

Everything® Easy Fitness Book
Everything® Fishing Book
Everything® Guide to Weight Training, $15.95
Everything® Krav Maga for Fitness Book
Everything® Running Book, 2nd Ed.
Everything® Triathlon Training Book, $15.95

TRAVEL

Everything® Family Guide to Coastal Florida
Everything® Family Guide to Cruise Vacations
Everything® Family Guide to Hawaii
Everything® Family Guide to Las Vegas, 2nd Ed.
Everything® Family Guide to Mexico
Everything® Family Guide to New England, 2nd Ed.

Everything® Family Guide to New York City, 3rd Ed.
**Everything® Family Guide to Northern California
    and Lake Tahoe**
Everything® Family Guide to RV Travel & Campgrounds
Everything® Family Guide to the Caribbean
Everything® Family Guide to the Disneyland® Resort, California
    Adventure®, Universal Studios®, and the Anaheim
    Area, 2nd Ed.
Everything® Family Guide to the Walt Disney World Resort®,
    Universal Studios®, and Greater Orlando, 5th Ed.
Everything® Family Guide to Timeshares
Everything® Family Guide to Washington D.C., 2nd Ed.

WEDDINGS

Everything® Bachelorette Party Book, $9.95
Everything® Bridesmaid Book, $9.95
Everything® Destination Wedding Book
Everything® Father of the Bride Book, $9.95
Everything® Green Wedding Book, $15.95
Everything® Groom Book, $9.95
Everything® Jewish Wedding Book, 2nd Ed., $15.95
Everything® Mother of the Bride Book, $9.95
Everything® Outdoor Wedding Book
Everything® Wedding Book, 3rd Ed.
Everything® Wedding Checklist, $9.95
Everything® Wedding Etiquette Book, $9.95
Everything® Wedding Organizer, 2nd Ed., $16.95
Everything® Wedding Shower Book, $9.95
Everything® Wedding Vows Book, 3rd Ed., $9.95
Everything® Wedding Workout Book
Everything® Weddings on a Budget Book, 2nd Ed., $9.95

WRITING

Everything® Creative Writing Book
Everything® Get Published Book, 2nd Ed.
Everything® Grammar and Style Book, 2nd Ed.
Everything® Guide to Magazine Writing
Everything® Guide to Writing a Book Proposal
Everything® Guide to Writing a Novel
Everything® Guide to Writing Children's Books
Everything® Guide to Writing Copy
Everything® Guide to Writing Graphic Novels
Everything® Guide to Writing Research Papers
Everything® Guide to Writing a Romance Novel, $15.95
Everything® Improve Your Writing Book, 2nd Ed.
Everything® Writing Poetry Book